Runners and Riders

RUNNERS AND RIDERS

---

*An anthology
of writing on racing*

Edited by
SEAN MAGEE

METHUEN · LONDON

First published in Great Britain by Methuen London
an imprint of Reed Consumer Books Ltd
Michelin House, 81 Fulham Road, London SW3 6RB
and Auckland, Melbourne, Singapore and Toronto

Copyright in this selection and introductions © 1993 Sean Magee
The author has asserted his moral rights

A CIP catalogue record for this book
is available from the British Library
ISBN 0 413 67830 X

Phototypeset by Intype, London
Printed and bound in Great Britain
by Clays Ltd, St Ives plc

Contents

Contents

3 'Lunatics, criminals, idiots, charmers, bastards and exceptionally nice people': *The humans* — 65

4 'He's going to win big, Herb!': *The race* — 119

Contents

Contents

Preface

Editing an anthology is an extremely pleasurable task, but there is a catch. However loosely you interpret the delivery date on the publisher's contract, there comes a time when you have to stop working on the text and let go, and it's odds on that soon after that traumatic moment you will discover a wonderful piece which really should have been included. But the edition has gone beyond recall, and in contrast with that optimistic prophecy of bus conductors, there won't be another one along in a minute.

That situation comes, as they say, with the territory. What also came with *Runners and Riders* was an immense amount of enjoyment, not only from discovering the variety of ways in which the multi-faceted activity of horse racing has been written about in all its various moods and by widely differing kinds of writer, but also from the encounter with books and authors whose appeal goes far beyond the racetrack.

Indeed, while the aim of a collection such as this is the simple one of sharing with fellow racing enthusiasts some entertaining and thought-provoking treatments of the sport, any success this anthology can claim will come only when its readers pursue some of the hares set running here. It would be invidious to single out particular favourites, but if there is one book represented in this collection which would make the shortlist for my desert island reading, it would have to be Guy Griffith and Michael Oakeshott's *A Guide to the Classics*, as well written and as wittily argued as any racing book I have ever read – and I have read a good few, including several previous anthologies of racing writing.

Among the best racing anthologies of recent years are *The Paddock Book*, edited by Robert Rodrigo (1967); *The Racing Man's Bedside Book*, edited by Dick Francis and John Welcome (1969); *Heard in the Paddock*, edited by Roderick Bloomfield (1970); *The Turf*, compiled by Alan Ross (1982); *The Faber Book of the Turf*, edited by John Hislop and David Swannell (1990); and *A Racing Companion*, edited by Lord Oaksey and Bob Rodney (1992). The two volumes of *Best Racing and Chasing Stories*, edited by Dick Francis and John Welcome (1964 and 1969) are also strongly recommended.

Since I have never taken the pious line that *Runners and Riders* should not contain material which has been included elsewhere, such collections have naturally furnished clues and suggestions. But the real pleasure of compiling the present anthology has been building it up from a variety of sources. There are pieces which have lived with me since childhood – John Hislop's account of the pre-Grand National changing room, for instance, or Peter O'Sulle-van's 'A Hundred Monkeys', a wonderful piece of whimsy which I first read when I was eleven and parts of which I have carried around in my head ever since.

There are pieces which were recommended by friends once they learned of this project: 'Have you included that bit in *Oscar and Lucinda*? . . . Isn't there something in Flann O'Brien?'

And there are pieces to which I have been drawn by references elsewhere. For example, I knew that John Steinbeck had written of a visit to the Kentucky Derby, but had never seen it until I came across an extract in *The Kentucky Derby Museum Cook Book* (which includes such delicacies as 'Ophelia's Derbytime One-Step Tomato Sandwiches' and several demon recipes for mint juleps). A tortuous succession of transatlantic phone calls and faxes ensued before the article was finally reeled in, thanks to the good offices of Beth Atkins at the Kentucky Derby Museum, Jerry Crouch at the University Press of Kentucky, Rich Hendel, Johanna Grimes, Brian Alderson and Sherry Laughlin.

Not every piece in this volume has required such a level of support, but many other people have earned my gratitude. Ann Mansbridge at Methuen commissioned the book and has maintained her serenity as it edges towards publication. Gillian Bromley acted as sounding board and helped prepare the text, while Sandra Sljivic at Faber gave invaluable advice on the vexed question of clearing permissions. Of those who suggested avenues to be investigated, I owe particular thanks to Finbarr Slattery, who proved wonderfully helpful with the Irish material. Chris Jones, Jamie Reid, John White, Gillian Forrester, Raymond Smith, Paul Ross, Gillian Peele and Alan Brooke also offered bright ideas which have borne fruit, while a variety of assistance was further provided by Richard Onslow, Rory Roper-Caldbeck, Phillip Jones, Tony Allan, Peter Dougherty, Lauren Clark, John Bodley, Robert Cooper, Ron Costley and Caroline Baldock. Mike Barfield helped immensely in digging out the racing passages in Beachcomber, and Nicholas Shrimpton brought his formidable academic skills to the matter of how racing was depicted by Victorian writers. Formal acknowledgement of permission to reproduce works is made elsewhere in this book, but on a more personal note I am particularly grateful to John B. Keane, John Oaksey, Peter O'Sullevan, Hugh McIlvanney, Brough Scott, Sue Montgomery, Bill Bryson, Matthew Engel, Alastair Down and Bill Nack for cheerfully agreeing for their work to be included.

Paul Zimmer, who has won more American poetry awards than he and I have killed shots of Calvados together (which is a good many), deserves a paragraph of thanks all to himself for accepting the challenge of writing a poem specifically for this book.

Despite that barrage of assistance, there have been the ones that got away. I never did manage to track down a copy of the 1859 pamphlet *Some Observations upon the Question 'Will Horse Racing Benefit Worthing?'* by the Reverend P. B. Power, and Bill Nack's wonderful *Sports Illustrated* elegy to Secretariat, published in 1990, came to my attention just too late to be included. Oh well, here's to the next edition!

S.M.

Sources and Acknowledgements

The following list gives in alphabetical order by author the sources of all the pieces in this book, with copyright details where appropriate. The editor and publishers are grateful to all the copyright-holders for permission to reproduce material under their control, and apologise for any errors or omissions. It has not proved possible to trace the copyright holder of every piece – though the editor is labouring to do so even as this book goes to press, and would be grateful to be notified of any corrections, which will be incorporated in reprints and future editions of this volume.

Dannie Abse, 'A Note Left on the Mantelpiece', from *Collected Poems* (Hutchinson, 1977). Reproduced by permission of Sheil Land Associates Ltd (copyright © Dannie Abse 1977).

Sherwood Anderson, 'The Man who Became a Woman', from *Horses and Men* (1924).

Sir John Astley, *Fifty Years of My Life* (1894).

Enid Bagnold, *National Velvet* (1935). Reproduced by permission of William Heinemann Ltd.

Simon Barnes, *Horsesweat and Tears* (1988). Reproduced by permission of William Heinemann Ltd (copyright © Simon Barnes, 1988).

'Beachcomber' [J. B. Morton], *Mr Thake and the Ladies* (1935); 'Buttercup' from *By the Way* (1932); 'The Horse' from *The Dancing Cabman* (1938). Reproduced by permission of the Peters Fraser & Dunlop Group Ltd.

Dominic Behan, 'Arkle' (1965). Reproduced by permission of Coda Music Ltd (© Coda Music Ltd, 1965. International copyright secured. All rights reserved).

Bell's Life in London, 21 May 1837.

Hilaire Belloc, 'Lord Hippo', from *Cautionary Tales* (1907). Reproduced by permission of Gerald Duckworth and Co.

Jeffrey Bernard, *Talking Horses* (1987). Reproduced by permission of Fourth Estate Ltd (copyright © Jeffrey Bernard, 1987).

Howard Brenton, *Epsom Downs* (1977). Reproduced by permission of Eyre Methuen (copyright © Howard Brenton, 1977).

Bill Bryson, 'The Sport of Gipsies and Kings', from *The Sunday Correspondent*, 10 June 1990. Reproduced by kind permission of the author.

Phil Bull, 'Nasrullah', from *Best Horses of 1943* (1944). Reproduced by kind permission of the Timeform Organisation.

A. S. Byatt, *Possession: A Romance* (1990). Reproduced by permission of Chatto and Windus Ltd.

Peter Carey, *Oscar and Lucinda* (1988). Reproduced by permission of Faber and Faber Ltd.

Les Carlyon, 'How it was in 1983, and still is . . .', in *Chasing a Dream* (Raceplay and Carlyon Press and Publications Pty Ltd, Melbourne, 1988). Originally published in *The Age*, 3 January 1983. Reproduced by permission.

The Derby Day, or, Won by a Neck – A Sporting Novel (1864) [anonymous].

Charles Dickens, 'The Dirty Derby', in *All the Year Round*, 13 June 1863.

Charles Dickens and W. H. Wills, 'Epsom', in *Household Words*, 7 June 1851.

Benjamin Disraeli, *Sybil* (1845). Published by Oxford University Press in the World's Classics series, 1981.

Alastair Down, 'Fulke Walwyn – One of the Last of the "Old" School', in the *Sporting Life Weekender*, 21 February 1991. Reproduced by kind permission of the author.

'The Druid' [Henry Hall Dixon], 'The Betting Ring', in *The Post and the Paddock* (1856).

The Economist, 10 April 1993.

Matthew Engel, 'An Officer, an Erk and a Horse Laugh', from *The Guardian*, 5 April 1993. Reproduced by permission of *The Guardian*.

John Evelyn, *The Diary of John Evelyn*, edited by E. S. De Beer (1955).

William Faulkner, 'Kentucky: May: Saturday – Three Days to the Afternoon', in *Sports Illustrated*, 16 May 1955. Reproduced by permission of the estate of William Faulkner.

Bernard Fergusson, 'The Higher Motive', from *Yet More Comic and Curious Verse*, edited by J. M. Cohen (1959). Originally published in *Punch*.

Dick Francis, *Dead Cert* (1962). Reproduced by permission of Michael Joseph Ltd (copyright © Dick Francis, 1962).

Percy French, 'Sweet Marie', in *Prose, Poems and Parodies* (1925).

Susan Gallier, *One of the Lads* (1988). Reproduced by permission of Stanley Paul Ltd.

Geoffrey Gilbey, 'The Stewards', in *Steeplechasing*, The Lonsdale Library volume XXXII (1954).

Adam Lindsay Gordon,'How We Beat the Favourite', from *Collected Poems* (1912).

Graham Greene, *Brighton Rock* (William Heinemann Ltd, 1938). Reproduced by permission of David Higham Associates Ltd (copyright © Verdant S.A., 1938).

Charles Greville, *The Greville Memoirs 1814–1860*, edited by Lytton Strachey and Roger Fulford (1938).

Guy Griffith and Michael Oakeshott, *A Guide to the Classics* (1936). Reproduced by permission of Faber and Faber Ltd.

Ernest Hemingway, *A Moveable Feast* (1964). Reproduced by permission of Jonathan Cape Ltd.

Ernest Hemingway, 'My Old Man', from *The First Forty-Nine Stories* (Jonathan Cape, 1939). Reproduced by permission of the estate of Ernest Hemingway.

John Hislop, *Steeplechasing* (Hutchinson, 1951). Reproduced by permission of J. A. Allen and Co. Ltd.

'The Intellectual Side of Horse Racing' [anonymous], from the *New Statesman*, 12 June 1920. Reproduced by kind permission of the *New Statesman*.

Henry James, *English Hours* (1877).

James Joyce, *Ulysses* (1922). Published by Penguin Books, 1969.

Patrick Kavanagh, 'Going Racing', in the *Irish Farmers' Journal*, 9 August 1958. Reproduced by kind permission of the *Irish Farmers' Journal*.

John B. Keane, 'A Genuine Tip', from *Love Bites and Other Stories* (The Mercier Press, 1991). Reproduced by kind permission of The Mercier Press and of the author.

Rudyard Kipling, 'The Broken-Link Handicap', in *Plain Tales from the Hills* (1888).

George Lambton, *Men and Horses I Have Known* (1924). First published by Thornton Butterworth Ltd. Reprinted by J. A. Allen and Co., 1963. Reproduced by permission of J. A. Allen and Co. Ltd.

Philip Larkin, 'At Grass', from *The Less Deceived* (1955). Reprinted by permission of The Marvell Press, England and Australia.

D. H. Lawrence, 'The Rocking-Horse Winner', in *The Tales of D. H. Lawrence* (1934).

Jack Leach, *Sods I Have Cut on the Turf* (Victor Gollancz, 1961).

Reprinted by J. A. Allen, 1973. Reproduced by permission of J. A. Allen and Co. Ltd.

Roger Longrigg, *Daughters of Mulberry* (1961). First published by Faber and Faber Ltd. Reproduced by permission of Curtis Brown Ltd.

R. C. Lyle, *Brown Jack* (George Putnam, 1934). Rights transferred to The Bodley Head.

Mrs Massey Lyon, *Etiquette* (Cassell, 1927).

John Masefield, 'Right Royal', from *Collected Poems* (Heinemann, 1923). Reproduced by permission of The Society of Authors as the literary representative of the estate of John Masefield.

Hugh McIlvanney, 'In Pursuit of a Punter's Paradise', from *The Sport of Kings*, the official brochure of the Festival of British Racing at Ascot, September 1989. Reproduced by kind permission of the author.

John Everett Millais, letter to Charles Collins dated 31 May 1853, in *The Life and Letters of Sir John Everett Millais*, edited by John Guille Millais (abridged edition, 1905).

Sue Montgomery, 'The Dancing Brigadier', from the *Racing Post*, 8 November 1989. Reproduced by kind permission of the author and the *Racing Post*.

George Moore, *Esther Waters* (1894). Published by Oxford University Press as a World's Classics paperback, 1983.

Roger Mortimer, 'Travelling Form', from *That's Racing*, edited by Peter O'Sullevan and Sean Magee (1992). Reproduced by permission of Stanley Paul Ltd.

William Nack, *Big Red of Meadow Stable* (1975). Originally published in New York in 1975, and subsequently reissued in paperback by Da Capo Press under the title *Secretariat: The Making of a Champion*. Reproduced by kind permission of the author.

Ogden Nash, 'Hark! Hark! The Pari-Mutuels Bark!', from *I'm a Stranger Here Myself* (Victor Gollancz, 1938); 'Mr Judd and his

Snail, a Sorry Tale', from *There's Always Another Windmill* (André Deutsch, 1969). Reproduced by permission of Curtis Brown Ltd.

John Oaksey, 'Moments of Glory which Turned to Nightmare', in *Horse and Hound*, 6 April 1963. The piece was signed with the name 'Audax', pen-name of John Lawrence, later to succeed to his father's title Lord Oaksey. Reproduced by kind permission of the author.

Flann O'Brien, *At Swim-Two-Birds* (Longman Green, 1939). Reproduced by permission of MacGibbon & Kee, an imprint of Harper-Collins Ltd.

Will H. Ogilvie, 'Steeplechasers', from *The Collected Sporting Verse of Will H. Ogilvie* (1932).

George Orwell, *War-time Diary* (1941).

Peter O'Sullevan, 'A Hundred Monkeys', from *Cope's Racegoers' Encyclopaedia 1961* (David Cope Ltd, 1961). Reproduced by kind permission of the author.

Peter O'Sullevan, *Calling the Horses* (Stanley Paul, 1989). Reproduced by permission of Stanley Paul Ltd.

A. B. Paterson, 'The Riders in the Stand', from *Collected Verse* (1953).

Arthur Wing Pinero, *Dandy Dick* (1887).

Peter Porter, 'Phar Lap in the Melbourne Museum', from *Collected Poems* (1983). Reprinted by permission of Oxford University Press (copyright © Peter Porter, 1983).

Jamie Reid, *A Licence to Print Money* (1992). Reproduced by permission of Macmillan London Ltd.

Riff and Raff [A. M. Harbord and 'Fitz'], *They're Off!, or, The Rough's Guide to the Turf* (1936). Reproduced by permission of Hutchinson Ltd.

Alan Ross, 'Stallion and Teaser' and 'Death of a Trainer', from *Blindfold Games* (1986). Reproduced by permission of Harvill, an imprint of HarperCollins Publishers Ltd.

Damon Runyon, 'Pick the Winner', from *Furthermore* (1938). Reproduced by permission of Constable and Company.

'Saki' [H. H. Munro], 'A Bread and Butter Miss', from *The Toys of Peace* (1919).

Brough Scott, 'My Aintree Nightmare', from the *Sunday Times*, 24 March 1985. Reproduced by kind permission of the author and the *Sunday Times*.

W. C. Sellar and R. J. Yeatman, *Horse Nonsense* (Methuen, 1933). Reproduced by permission of Methuen London (copyright © W. C. Sellar and R. J. Yeatman, 1933).

Michael Silley, 'Raymond Glendinning', from *Yet More Comic and Curious Verse*, edited by J. M. Cohen (1959).

John Steinbeck, 'Needles – Derby Day Choice for President?' in the Louisville *Courier-Journal*, 6 May 1956. Reproduced by permission of the estate of John Steinbeck.

William Makepeace Thackeray, *The Irish Sketch Book* (1843); *Pendennis* (1848–50).

Hunter S. Thompson, 'The Kentucky Derby is Decadent and Depraved' (1970). First published in *Scanlan's Monthly*, June 1970. Reproduced by permission of the author.

Anthony Trollope, *The Duke's Children* (1880). Published by Oxford University Press in the World's Classics series, 1983.

Geoffrey Willans and Ronald Searle, *Whizz for Atomms* (1956). Reissued in *The Compleat Molesworth* (Pavilion Books, 1992). Reproduced by permission of the Tessa Sayle Agency (copyright © Geoffrey Willans and Ronald Searle, 1956).

P. G. Wodehouse, *The Inimitable Jeeves* (1923); *Very Good, Jeeves* (1930); *Ring for Jeeves* (1953); *Eggs, Beans and Crumpets* (1940). Reproduced by permission of the estate of P. G. Wodehouse and of Hutchinson Ltd.

Lord Wyatt of Weeford, speech in the House of Lords, 11 May 1987. Reprinted from *Hansard*: Parliamentary copyright.

Sources and Acknowledgements

W. B. Yeats, 'At Galway Races', from *The Green Helmet and Other Poems* (1910).

William Youatt, *The Horse: Its Breeds, Management, and Diseases* (1831).

Paul Zimmer, 'Forgiving Horses' (1993). Previously unpublished poem, not merely reproduced by kind permission of the author, but written for this book, for a permission fee of one bottle of Calvados.

———————————————

The John Skeaping drawing of horses and jockeys reproduced on each section opening is from a private collection.

Introduction

It is not a truth universally acknowledged that the sport of horse racing has produced a literature worthy of its appeal. In the opinion of Jeffrey Bernard:

> Most books about racing are terrible hack jobs by jumped-up sub-editors who can't write. The rest are dreary rags-to-riches 'autobiographies' about some hard-done-by apprentice who starts life in a rat-infested loft in Newmarket but by sheer talent and force of character becomes a champion jockey, and gets his just reward on his retirement when the Queen summons him to Buckingham Palace and presents him with a silver cigarette box.

On the other hand, Alan Ross introduces his collection *The Turf* thus:

> Anyone compiling an anthology about the Turf soon learns that, after cricket, there is more good writing about racing than on any other sport.

These two views are not necessarily incompatible if a distinction is drawn between run-of-the-mill racing books by those closely involved in the Turf and the way the sport has been used for wider literary purposes. This anthology concentrates on the latter, and in this it is distinct from other collections of racing writing – of which, it must be allowed, the world has not gone short. Rather than approaching its task from the racing end – what are the main topics in the sport, who are the great horses and humans, and who has written anything collectable about these? – *Runners and Riders* looks at racing writing from the literary point of view.

1

In a formula unparalleled in any other sport, horse racing combines the beauty and power of the horse and the speed, spectacle and danger of the race itself with the emotional roller-coaster of betting, the cerebral challenge of the form, the fascination of breeding, and – perhaps of greatest appeal to writers – the broadest imaginable sweep of society. All human life is there, as well as much equine. This sport has attracted many great writers in many different genres. What have they made of it?

There are, of course, large areas of overlap between the two approaches, and if 'insider' writing has special literary merit, in it comes. John Hislop, John Oaksey, Jack Leach and Bill Nack may be racing specialists, but it is the excellence of their work which justifies its inclusion. Thus Oaksey on the 1963 Grand National is here not because that was a famous or significant race, but because of the immediacy and power of his account.

This is not to claim that every single piece in this anthology is of exceptional literary quality: a few extracts – the *Bell's Life* verse preview of the 1837 Derby, for instance – are included to show how racing has been treated in many literary forms (and in that case yielded a 40–1 winner).

The genres in which the sport has most commonly featured are fiction and poetry, and both are extensively represented. Racing is especially well suited to narrative verse, and if when reading 'How We Beat the Favourite' or 'Right Royal' you feel the urge to declaim the lines aloud to whomever may be within earshot, or just to yourself, please do not hold back. Such poetry is best read aloud.

Racing in drama is more difficult to extract. This book contains a large chunk of Howard Brenton's *Epsom Downs*, but other plays in which the sport has a significant role, such as Shirley's *Hyde Park* or Pinero's *Dandy Dick* or Cecil Raleigh and Henry Hamilton's *The Whip*, do not easily lend themselves to having bits picked out of them. This is a particular shame in the case of *The Whip*, first performed at the Theatre Royal, Drury Lane, in 1909, as the climax of the play has the favourite winning at Newmarket – a live horse on stage – after being saved from a train wreck by the villain, whose plotting with the adventuress has been overheard in Madame Tussaud's by one of the comic characters pretending to be a wax effigy!

The Whip displays the humorous possibilities which racing offers and which many 'insider' writers do not appreciate or are incapable of capitalizing upon. But the Turf has caught the attention of some of the best comic writers of the twentieth century, including Beachcomber, Sellar and Yeatman and P. G. Wodehouse – and, perhaps most spectacularly, Nigel Molesworth, as reported by Willans and Searle. A contrast to Molesworth's enthusiasm – 'Bash on the wine gums!' – is the wonderfully urbane wit allied to serious purpose in Guy Griffith and Michael Oakeshott's *A Guide to the Classics*.

Literary quality may be in the eye of the beholder, but there are bound to be accepted classics, and it would be perverse to exclude some of the 'greatest hits' – 'My Old Man', for instance, or 'Lord Hippo' or Banjo Paterson – purely because they had appeared in earlier collections. No anthology ever pleases everyone – least of all the compiler – but the hope here is that encountering the unexpected will soften the blow of excluded favourites. And if you've already read, say, 'The Rocking Horse Winner', please don't skip over it. You may well find it worth reading again.

Runners and Riders is divided into eight sections to reflect connections, however tenuous, between separate pieces. But there is inevitably a good deal of overlap between these compartments, and this is designed to be a book to be dipped into rather than read through from the beginning.

Several volumes of this size could be filled with entertaining and illuminating writing about horse racing, and whittling down all the material unearthed to fit the prescribed size of the book has made the final selection a process of rapidly alternating pleasure and frustration.

Just like racing itself.

1

'This horse-racing business can go too far'

The lure of the Turf

Nearly 2000 years ago the poet Ovid wrote: *Nec te nobilium fugiat certamen equorum* – Never miss a good race meeting; and Ovid, like most poets, knew what was what. It is true that he intended this maxim primarily for lovers, and that when Ovid went to the races he went not to watch the horses but to watch the girls; but the advice is good advice for all that, and indeed Ovid is a conspicuous example of a man who does the right thing for the wrong reason. Ever since that time, with one or two insignificant interruptions due to the Visigoths and other barbarians, the people of Europe, and especially of England, have taken Ovid's advice, for whichever reason. And the English racing season has now for many years – and rightly – provided for all tastes: one may do as one likes at Haydock and Thirsk, but 'Epsom for business and Ascot for pleasure' is a truth that belongs to the national consciousness.

Guy Griffith and Michael Oakeshott,
from *A Guide to the Classics* (1936)

That paragraph was written not by any racing journalist but by Britain's leading Conservative political theorist this century, Michael Oakeshott, and the Cambridge academic Guy Griffith. Unlikely enthusiasts of what Phil Bull famously called 'the great triviality' of the Turf? Scarcely, for racing has woven its spell over all levels and types of society, and academics are not immune.

Nor are those below stairs. Beachcomber (J. B. Morton) chronicled the difficulties which the aristocratic Mr Thake had with his racing-mad valet, Saunders.

My hat! This morning Mrs Bampfylde of all people, my trusted, solid, sane old cook, was in tears. I asked her what was the matter, and she blurted out something about Craigendoran losing at Warwick.

'Don't tell me,' I said, 'that you, too, are mixed up in this new craze of Saunders.' She sniffed and muttered, 'There's always the Lincoln, sir, isn't there?' I said I supposed there was, and left her.

Later on I was rung up, and a voice asked for Saunders. 'Tell 'im it's abaht Gatwick,' said the voice. I said, 'Kindly remember that my chambers are not a stable-yard. My man must find some other means of holding communications with his equine companions.'

I think my manner froze him. I heard him say, 'Blimey, it's the ruddy Duke 'imself,' and he rang off.

This horse-racing business can go too far.

This horse racing business can indeed go too far, and for small punter and big owner alike, the disappointment of losing goes hand in hand with the pleasure of winning. No writer has better expressed the proximity of the pleasure and pain of racing than the nineteenth-century politician and diarist Charles Greville.

23 October 1837

Since Doncaster, I have continued (up to this time) to win at Newmarket, so that my affairs are in a flourishing condition, but, notwithstanding these successes, I am dissatisfied and disquieted in my mind, and my life is spent in the alternations of excitement from the amusement and speculation of the Turf and of remorse and shame at the pursuit itself. One day I resolve to extricate myself entirely from the whole concern, to sell all my horses, and pursue other occupations and objects of interest, and then these resolutions wax faint, and I again find myself buying fresh animals, entering into fresh speculations, and just as deeply engaged as ever. It is the force of habit, a still unconquered propensity to the sport, and a nervous apprehension that if I do give it up, I may find no substitute of equal interest. It is not that there is anything disgraceful in being addicted to that which so many better men have followed and do follow, with quite as much zest, but whether it be from the nature of the occupation, or from my nature, or partly from both, I find that it occupies my mind to the exclusion of worthier and better thoughts. I feel that it degrades and stupefies my understanding, that it renders me less agreeable in society, less useful, less respectable in the world, and that this consciousness together with the want of the cultivation and acquired knowledge, which I might and probably should otherwise have possessed, vex and harass me. I envy those who have no such misgivings, and who are not tormented by any such self-reproaches as these; but I envy still more (if such there be) those who entertaining such scruples and sensible of the pernicious effect which is produced upon their minds, have the resolution to break the chain which binds them, and emancipate themselves at once from such a thraldom, in order to refresh their jaded and debilitated faculties at the fountains of knowledge.

29 May 1838

Just going to Epsom. A year ago was going with the hope of making a fortune and the certainty of winning a great deal of money; now with the great probability of losing a good deal, but I hope and trust *for the last time*. These last few days have been miserably spent; nervous agitation, incapability of application, continual restlessness. Racing is just like dram-drinking – momentary excitement and wretched intervals, full consciousness of the mischievous effects of the habit and equal difficulty in abstaining from it. The wretch who drinks the gin which is his delight and his bane finds a brief oblivion of care and sensation of pleasure in the excitement it provokes and the warmth it diffuses, and the languor and lassitude which follow are only again relieved by recurrence to the same perilous source of comfort. So I, while actually engaged in betting, matching and all the business of the Turf, am stimulated into a sensation of interest and pleasure; but during the *interacts*, which are so much longer than the acts, my spirit groans at the thought of the degrading, the mind-spoiling pursuit and the obstinacy with which my thoughts will rush back (no matter into what channel I try to turn them) to this occupation with all its incidents and consequences.

2 June 1838

Back from Epsom (Marble Hill) yesterday having lost £1400. Very glad it is all over, and hope to keep clear of it for the future, though as long as I have horses (and there is no getting rid of them) I shall never be able to avoid doing as others do. The example is contagious, and good resolutions are forgotten in some momentary impulse.

In 1846 Greville won the Emperor's Plate at Royal Ascot – the predecessor of the Gold Cup – with Alarm.

14 June 1846

It was a moment of excitement and joy when I won this fine piece of plate, in the midst of thousands of spectators; but that past, there returned the undying consciousness of the unworthiness of the pursuit, and the self-reproach that I permit it to exercise the pernicious influence which it does over my mind, filling my thoughts, hopes, and wishes to the exclusion of all other objects and occupations, agitating me, rendering me incapable of application, thought, and reflection, and paralysing my power of reading or busying myself with books of any kind. All this is very bad and unworthy of a reasonable creature.

It's being so cheerful as keeps him going. And keep going he does, at Newmarket in 1848.

7 November 1848

I think I have during the last racing meetings felt more than ever the lassitude, the ennui, the intolerable idleness, the absolute fainéantise of the life of the place. It unhinges, enervates and discomposes my mind. It half paralyses my faculties, it disturbs my temper, and really renders me unfit for society. It makes me shy, stupid and silent. It is a moral and intellectual disease; there is no reason why this should be so, but it is. Then I grow more and more disgusted with the atmosphere of villainy I am forced to breathe, and at the sight of the long processes of fraud and the systematic robberies with which I am perforce made familiar and from which it is not easy to keep oneself undefiled. It is monstrous to see high bred and high born gentlemen of honoured families, themselves marching through the world with their heads in the air, 'all honourable men' living in the best, the greatest and most refined society, mixed up in schemes which are neither more nor less than a system of plunder, stooping to a camaraderie with rascals who pass their lives in fraud, deceit and robbery and who scruple at no means of making money, only taking care to avoid detection and to carry on their machinations with a secrecy essential to success. Sometimes I feel disposed to detail all these things; but it is enough now to record the sensations of shame, disgust, regret and remorse with which they oppress me.

Nigel Molesworth, of St Custard's prep school, also saw both sides of the lure of the sport.

A FEW TIPS FROM THE COARSE

A velvet silence (peotry) enclose the famous PINK dorm of st. custards. Beyond the curtaned window there is no sound except the tread of feet as boys break out down the fire escape and the plop-plop of darts as ye olde matronne sink another treble twenty into the board. Below a gang of mice attack the skool cheese with jelignite. . . .

Suddenly the stillness is broken by a low, musical whisper e.g.

Wot is yore fancy for the 3.30 at Sponger's park, tomow, molesworth?

Instantly the whole dorm is awake. Aktualy it was never silent becos wot with SNORES GRUNTS AND GROANS it would be quieter when they are re-laying the surface of the 7 sisters road than here.

The q. i have been asked, however, catches my interest.

Get out the port and cigars, i sa, and we will diskuss the form. i wate until the decanter is passed hem-hem it is pepsi-cola aktually and give my verdict.

Bees Knees will be having a go. On breeding alone it should be cast-iron. i shall risk half a lb of wine gums on her.

Ta-ran-ta-rah! yell molesworth 2, weedily. 'Come on, lester pigot.

11

This is only one side of a horse

come on, scobie breasly. Come on me yar boo to molesworth 1 he couldn't hurt a flea.

He jump up and down on the soft springs hem-hem of the skool bed until he bounce too high and strike his head on the ceiling cheers cheers.

Which all go to show that apart from backing a county at criket, a foopball team or two, cris chataway, le rouge at the casino and mr grabber for the father's race every boy ort to equip himself for life by knoing a bit about horse racing.

All i kno about this subjekt is contained in my grate work *Snaffles, fetlocks, pasterns and girths* – A CRITICAL EXAMINATION (Grabber 25/- or send a p.o. to the auther direct). This book go to the hart of the matter by considering something you canot hav a horse race without e.g. the HORSE. (see above)

This is only one side of a horse so it hav only two legs, one ear and one eye. However, most horses are aproximately the same on the other side and if they are not it is not safe to hav a fluter on them.

Every horse is said to hav POINTS which is pritty difficult for any animal which is not a hedgehog or comon porcupine. In racing, however, there are only two POINTS about the horse which need

12

concern the eager student – the ears and the tail. If the horse is going to try the ears should be so far back and the tail so far up that they almost meet. When it trot up to the post like that the backer can be sure it is trying, which is something with a horse. It is something with a boy, too, but no one can kno from his ears otherwise we mite get something like this in klass –

MOLESWORTH 1 *stare at a problem in algy scratching his hoary head.*

SIGISMUND THE MAD MATHS MASTER *regard him anxiously through his racing glasses.*

SIGISMUND: there go the galant molesworth upon whom i hav put my shirt (heaven forbid). He is a cert for this algy problem. But wot is this? His ears do not twitch. He sweateth at the mere look of x + y. He screws his pen into his ear he is in a lather. Quick quick i must lay this off on peason who hav an answer book but it will be O.K. unless there is an objektion.

(*He rushes out. molesworth gets the answer from gilibrand and so foils the plot.*)

That is all about horses. Now the q. is how to put your money on. You do this with a bookie or the tote as even a fule kno. Wot every fule do not kno however is which horse to put the money on and bring back a dividend.

To kno this you hav to study form e.g. buy all the papers which say:

> The Dope's Nap – 3.30. BEES KNEES.
> 3.30. FATTY IS A CONFIDENT SELEKTION.
> COARSE WIRE. 3.30. BUMBLE PUPY.
> NEWMARKET. TOOTHBRUSH.*******

This leave you pritty much where you were but it is better than buying a midday edition when all the tipsters agree:

RACING SUMARY. 3.30

PREPOSTEROUS (*Daily Plug*)	DANDRUFF
MENDAX (*The Smugg*)	DANDRUFF****
ON THE BALL (*Daily Shame*)	DANDRUFF
ALCESTES (*Farmer's Joy*)	DANDRUFF

ect.

Everything is right. DANDRUFF hav won over the distance, it hav two ancestors from the national stud, a french owner, trained on meat, sits up in its stable, lest . . . pig . . . up . . . firm going THE LOT. BASH ON THE WINE GUMS. As you are sitting nonchalantly in your club drinking a last pepsi cola you carelessly pick up the ticker tape.

3.30. SPONGER'S PARK. 1. BEES KNEES. 2. CLOT. 3. MORBID. ALSO RAN — DANDRUFF. SKOOL CHEESE. 5 RAN. DANDRUFF 51/1 ON (FAVRITE)

'Hogsnorton.'
'Yes. sir?'
'Bring me another pepsi cola.'
'The '37, sir, or the Club?'
'Wot do it matter? There is only 6d in it.'

Let us stroll over to the padock where the horses are parading. All around is the clamour and bustle of the racecoarse full of gipsies, oafs, cads, snekes tipsters, bullies in fakt it mite just as well be a half-hol at st. custards. See who strolls among them it is ickle-pritty fotherington-Tomas the wonky wet of the skool!

FOTHERINGTON-TOMAS: Hullo clouds hullo sky! How colourful the scene! the colours so gay so alive. But, woe, here is the headmaster GRIMES!

HEADMASTER: Want to buy some jellied eels? Lovely jellied eels (he starteth) Discovered! it is fotherington-tomas!

FOTHERINGTON-TOMAS: Oh wot, sir, can hav brought you to this pass?

GRIMES: the skool doesn't pay all hard work nothing out of it. The boys hav got to be fed and as for the masters they fair eat you out of house and home. (*fotherington-tomas begin to blub*) And then look at the rates on the old place – and the taxes. Can't blame me if i try to make an honest penny down here, there's no disgrace –

FOTHERINGTON-TOMAS: (*blubing harder than ever*) don't go on, sir. Take my money. Here.

GRIMES: don't you want no jellied eels?

FOTHERINGTON-TOMAS: no, no.

GRIMES: Bless you, sonny, you hav a kind face.

As fotherington-Tomas skip away a thick wad of banknotes fall from GRIMES poket. He pick them up agane and begin to GLOAT!

GRIMES: there is one born every minit.

And now we hav aktually got to the padock where the horses are walking round and round and people are looking at them. This is yore first chance to make sure yore selektion is in racing trim. Even at this stage it may be lathering and foaming at the mouth. If, however, its eyes are brite pin-points, it is dancing lite-heartedly on its horseshoes and neighing to itself – it is safe to assume that the stable hav decided to hav a go.
    BASH ON MORE WINE GUMS and return, for the START.
    This is the most exciting moment and fotherington-Tomas jump up and down.
    'Hurrah hurrah how good it is to be alive and the horse is the frend of man!'
At this moment a beer botle fall on his head from the roof of a motor coach and he is borne away. Cheers cheers we can watch the race in peace. THEY'RE OFF! Everyone go mad men shout, gurls fante, molesworth 2 shout ta-ran-ta-ra. Everyone shout and point at each other. IT'S BEES KNEES. DANDRUFF A STREET. FATTY WALKS IT ECT. The race only last ten secs before it is over. And wot hav hapened to the chokolate hoops, raspbery hoops and suede gloves of yore fancy? Alas, it is almost always down the COARSE.
    Boys, keep away from race coarses. Wot is the fun of them. They are crooked and you do not stand a chance. Open the paper and see how grave the world situation is. Look at the H-bombs and disasters and find how you can give yore services to the cause. Open the paper i sa – and wot is the first thing that catch yore eye?
    4.00. COARSE WIRE. NANKIE-POO CAN'T MISS
    BASH ON THE WINE GUMS!!!!!!!!!!

GEOFFREY WILLANS and RONALD SEARLE,
from *Whizz for Atomms* (1956)

From a slightly different academic level comes this beautifully argued but unsigned piece in the New Statesman *in 1920.*

Horse-racing – or, at least, betting – is one of the few crafts that are looked down on by practically everybody who does not take part in it. 'It's a mug's game,' people say. Even betting-men talk like this. There is a street called Mug's Row in a North of England town: it is so called because the houses in it were built by a bookmaker. Whether it was the bookmaker or his victims that gave the street its name we do not know. To call a bookmaker a mug would seem to most people an abuse of language. Yet the only bookmaker the present writer has ever, so to speak, known used to confess himself a mug in the most dismal fashion. He was a mug, however, not because he could not make money, but because he could not keep it. The poor of his suburb, when in difficulties, he declared, used always to come to him instead of going to the clergy, and he was unable to refuse them. But then he was bitter against the clergy. As a young man, he had been a Sunday-school teacher, and, so far as one could gather, he might have gone on being a Sunday-school teacher till the present day if he had not suddenly been assailed with doubts one Sabbath afternoon as he expounded to his pupils the story of David and Goliath. Whether it was that he looked on David as having taken an unsportsmanlike advantage of the giant or whether he doubted that so much could be done with such little stones, he did not make quite clear. Anyhow, from that day on, he never believed in revealed religion. He quarrelled with his clergyman. He broke the Sabbath. He began to drink beer and to go to race-meetings. He rapidly rose from the position of carpenter to that of book-maker, and, were it not for his infernal gift of charity, he would probably now be driving his own car and be hall-marked with a Coalition title. Even as it was, he was much more prosperous than any carpenter. Whenever he produced money, it was in pocketfuls and handfuls. Strange that a bookmaker, who by his trade must be accustomed to miracles, should find it difficult to believe in David and Goliath! He was possibly a man who betted on form, and on form Goliath should undoubtedly have won. David was an outsider. He had no breeding. He would have been surprised if he could have foreseen how his victory would rankle some thousands of years later in the soul of an honest English bookmaker.

It is, however, just these matters of form and breeding that raise horse-racing and betting above the intellectual level of a game of nap. Betting-men who ignore these things are as unintellectual as the average novelist. There are some, for instance, who shut their eyes and bring down a pen or a pencil on a list of names of the horses, in the hope that in this way they may discover a winner. No doubt they may. It is perhaps as good a way as any other. But there is something trivial in such methods. This is mere gambling for the sake of excitement. There is no more fundamental brain-work in it than in a game we saw being played in a railway carriage the other day when a man drew a handful of coins from his pocket and bet his friend half-a-sovereign that there would be more heads than tails lying uppermost. This is a game at which is it possible to lose five pounds in two minutes. It is the sort of game to which a betting-man will resort when *in extremis*, but only then. The ruling passion is strong, however. We have a friend who on one occasion went into retreat in a Catholic monastery. Two well-known bookmakers had also gone into temporary retreat for the good of their souls. Our friend told us that even during the religious services the bookmakers used to bet as to which of the monks would stand up first at the conclusion of a prayer, and that in the solemn hush of the worship he would suddenly hear a hoarse whisper, 'Two to one on Brownie' – a brother with hair of that colour – and the answer, 'I take you, Joe.' One has even heard of men betting as to which of two raindrops on a window pane will reach the bottom first. It is possible to bet on cats, rats or flies. Calvinists do not bet, because they believe that everything that happens is a certainty. The extreme betting-man is no Calvinist, however. He believes that most things are accidents, and the rest catastrophes. Hence his philosophy is almost always that of Epicurus. To him every day is a new day, at the end of which it is his aim to be able to say, like Horace, *Vixi*, or, as the text ought surely to read, *Vici*.

The intellectual betting-man, on the other hand, has a position somewhere between the extremes of Calvinism and Epicureanism. He worships neither certainty nor chance. He reckons up probabilities. When Mr Asquith picked out Spion Kop as the winner of the Derby, he did so because he went about the business of selection not with a pin or a pencil, but with one of the best brains in England. In the course of his long conflicts with the House of Lords he had probably interested himself somewhat profoundly in questions of heredity and pedigree, and he was thus well equipped for an investigation into the records of the parentage and grand-parentage of the various Derby horses. All that the ordinary casual better knows about Spion Kop is that he is the son of Spearmint, which won the Derby in 1906. This, however, would not alone make him an obviously better horse than Orpheus, whose sire, Orby, won the Derby in 1907. The student of breeding must be a feminist, who pays as much attention to the female as to the male line. It was by the study of the female line that the most cunning of the sporting journalists were able to eliminate Tetratema from the list of probable winners. Tetratema, as son of The Tetrarch, was excellently fathered for staying the mile-and-a-half course at Epsom. More than this, as a writer in the *Sportsman* pointed out, 'The Tetrarch himself is by Roi Herode, a fine stayer, and his maternal granddam was by Hagioscope, who rarely failed to transmit stamina.' It is when we turn to Tetratema's mother, Scotch Gift – or is it his grandmother something else? – apparently, that we discover his hereditary vice. This mare our journalist exposed to most scathing and searching criticism, and concluded that 'there can be nothing unreasonable in the inference, based on the records of his family, that the chances are against a Derby winner having descended from the least distinguished of . . . four sisters.' Even so, however, the writer a few sentences later abjures Calvinism, and denies that there is anything certain in what he calls breeding problems. 'It seemed,' he writes, 'wildly improbable at one time that Flying Duchess would produce a Derby winner, for I believe it is correct that two of Galopin's elder brothers ran in a 'bus, and there were two others quite useless. So, on the face of it, the chances were against Galopin, the youngest brother.' We quote these passages as evidence of the immense demand the serious pursuit of horse-racing puts on the intellect. The betting-man must be as well versed in precedents as a lawyer and in genealogical trees as a historian. At school, we always found the genealogical trees the most difficult and bewildering part of history. Yet the genealogical tree of a king is a simple matter compared to that of a horse. All you have to learn about a king is the names of his relations: regarding a horse, however, you must know not only the names but the character, staying-power, and domestic virtues of every male and female with whom he is connected during several generations. If one spent as much labour in disentangling the cousinship of the royal families of ancient Egypt, one would be venerated as a scholar in five continents. Oxford and Cambridge would shower degrees on one. Sir William Sutherland would get one a place on the Civil List. Hence it seems to us that tipping the winners is not, as it is too often regarded, 'anybody's job': it is work that should be undertaken only by men of powerful mind. No man should be allowed to qualify as a tipster unless he has taken a degree at one of the Universities. The ideal tipster would at once be a great historian, a great antiquary, a great zoologist, a great mathematician, and a man of profound common-sense. It is no accident that an ex-Prime Minister was one of the few Englishmen to spot the winner of this year's Derby. Mr Asquith must have gone patiently through all Spion Kop's relations, weighing up the chances whether it was an accident or owing to the weather that such an one fifteen years ago was beaten by a neck in a six-furlong race, studying every incident in every one of their careers, seeing that none of them had ever had a great-uncle a 'bus-horse, bringing out a table of logarithms to decide difficult points . . . We need not be surprised that there are fewer great tipsters than great poets. Shakespeare alone has given us a portrait of the perfect tipster – 'looking before and after . . . in apprehension how like a god!'

It is perhaps, however, when we leave questions of breeding and come to those of form, that we realise most fully the amazing intellectualism of the betting life. In the study of form we are faced by problems that can be solved only by the higher algebra. Thus, if Jehoshaphat, carrying 7 stone, ran third to Jezebel, carrying 8 stone 4lb, in a mile race, and Jezebel, carrying 8st 4lb, was beaten by a neck by Woman and Wine, carrying 7st 9lb, over a mile and a-quarter, and Woman and Wine, carrying 8st 1lb, was beaten by Tom Thumb, carrying 9st in a mile 120 yds, and Tom Thumb, carrying 9st 7lb, was beaten by Jehoshaphat over seven furlongs, we have to calculate what chance Tom Thumb has of beating Jezebel in a race of a mile and a-half on a wet day. There are men to whom such calculations may come easy. To Mr Asquith they are probably child's play. The present writer shrinks from them and, if he were a betting-man, would no doubt in sheer desperation be driven back on the method of pin and pencil. But it is obvious that the sincere betting-man has to make such calculations daily. Every morning the student of form finds his sporting page full of such lists as the following:—

0 0 0 CONCLUSIVE (7–5), Kroonstad – Conclusion. 8th of 9 to Poltava (gave 17lb.) Gatwick May (6f) and 7th of 19 to Orby's Pride (rec 4lb) Kempton May (5f).

3 3 3 RAPIERE (7–4), Sunder – Gourouli. Lost ¾ length and 3 lengths to Bantry (gave 2lb) and Marcia (rec 7lb) Newmarket May (1m), GOLDEN GUINEA (gave 20lb) not in first 9. See BLACK JESS.

0 0 4 ROYAL BLUE (7–0), Prince Palatine – China Blue. See NORTHERN LIGHT.

0 2 0 BLACK JESS (6–11), Black Jester – Diving Bell. Not in first 4 to St. Corentin (gave 12lb) Lingfield last week (7f). Here Ap. (7f) lost 8 lengths to Victory Speech (rec 1lb), RAPIERE (gave 13lb, favourite) ½ length off.

0 LLAMA (6–11), Isard II – Laughing Mirror. Nowhere to Silver Jug (gave 15lb) Newbury Ap. (7f).

Is not a page of Thucydides simpler? Is Persius himself more succinct or obscure? Our teachers used to apologise for teaching us Latin grammar and mathematics by telling us that they were good mental gymnastics. If education is only a matter of mental gymnastics, however, we should recommend horse-racing as an ideal study for young boys and girls. The sole objection to it is that it is so engrossing; it might absorb the whole energies of the child's being. The safety of Latin grammar lies in its dullness. No child is tempted by it into forgetting that there are other duties in life besides mental gymnastics. Horse-racing, on the other hand, comes into one's life with the effect of a religious conversion. It is the greatest monopolist among the pleasures. It affects men's conversation. It affects their entire outlook. The betting-man's is a dedicated life. Even books have a new meaning for him. *The*

Ring and the Book – he asks for no other epic. And it is the most intellectual of epics. That is our point.

New Statesman, 12 June 1920

In P. G. Wodehouse, it is the educative aspect of racing which concerns Jeeves when he is quizzed by Sir Roderick Carmoyle.

'And speaking of winning prizes, what about tomorrow?'

'Tomorrow, Sir Roderick?'

'The Derby. Know anything?'

'I fear not, Sir Roderick. It would seem to be an exceptionally open contest. Monsieur Boussac's Voleur is, I understand, the favourite. Fifteen to two at last night's call-over and the price likely to shorten to sixes or even fives for the SP. But the animal in question is somewhat small and lightly boned for so gruelling an ordeal. Though we have, to be sure, seen such a handicap overcome. The name of Manna, the 1925 winner, springs to the mind, and Hyperion, another smallish horse, broke the course record previously held by Flying Fox, accomplishing the distance in two minutes, thirty-four seconds.'

Rory regarded him with awe.

'By Jove! You know your stuff, don't you?'

'One likes to keep *au courant* in these matters, sir. It is, one might say, an essential part of one's education.'

'Well, I'll certainly have another chat with you tomorrow before I put my bet on.'

'I shall be most happy if I can be of service, Sir Roderick,' said Jeeves courteously, and oozed softly from the room, leaving Rory with the feeling, so universal among those who encountered this great man, that he had established connection with some wise, kindly spirit in whose hands he might place his affairs without a tremor.

from *Ring for Jeeves*

But punters need to start their betting education somewhere. In Peter Carey's Oscar and Lucinda *(winner of the Booker Prize in 1988) Ian*

Wardley-Fish, an undergraduate in nineteenth-century Oxford, introduces the impoverished theology student Oscar Hopkins (the narrator's great-grandfather) to the pleasures of the Turf:

'You know what a bet is,' he said, this time more softly than he had meant.

'Actually,' said Oscar Hopkins, 'no, I don't.'

Wardley-Fish saw that this could go on all day. He did not wish to hurt the chap's feelings (he had a tender face and seemed as though he would be easily hurt) but neither did he wish to miss a day at the track. 'You give money to chaps and if the one you like is the one that wins, why then, they give you double your money back, or treble, or whatever.'

'Bless me.'

Wardley-Fish takes the initiate to Epsom.

It was almost Ascension Day but there was a piercing wind and a low bruised sky. Oscar hunched his shoulders forward as if he wished to roll up his thin body like a sheet of cartridge paper. His temples hurt with cold. The tip of his nose was red. He was so excited he could barely breathe. He took long ungainly steps around the mud and puddles, lifted his head at the scent of pipe tobacco and horse dung, brandy and ladies' eau-de-toilette.

He had never been anywhere like this before. It seemed incredible that this – an entire kingdom – had existed all the time he had lived in Hennacombe. It seemed even more incredible that red-cliffed sleepy little Hennacombe could now exist at all, so much did the racetrack expand, like a volatile gas, to take up every available corner of the living universe. He saw mutton-chopped bookmakers with big bellies ballooning out against their leather bags of money. At this very moment the sea was fizzing across the sand. How good it was not be be near it. The Baptist boys threw stones at rocks somewhere in the myopic haze upon the moors. But he was here. He thought of Mr Stratton, of the damp, long, gloomy room where he and his wife would shortly eat their lunch, and although he was fond of them, and prayed that they might be granted happiness, he preferred to be here, bumping shoulders with gentlemen in grey toppers.

And then he thought of his father, and he stopped the train of thought, uncoupled the engine from the troublesome carriages and reversed at full speed in his mind while, with his body, he pressed urgently forward, following Wardley-Fish towards the next row of stables where he would – in the straw-sweet alleys of this wonderful new world – obtain what he swore was 'first-rate information'.

Oscar knew this was not first-rate information at all. He was still more Plymouth Brethren than he liked to think, and the way he looked at the man who brought this information was not, to any substantial degree, different from the way Theophilus would have looked at the same individual. He was a stunted stable hand with the whiskerless face of a boy. He was pinched up around the nose and eyes and suggested with all his talk, guv'nor, about which horse would 'try' and which would not, the vilest stench of corruption.

Oscar thought this fellow damned. He would no more listen to his advice than he would invite the devil to whisper in his ear.

And yet Wardley-Fish seemed to see none of this. He nodded eagerly and clucked wisely. He leaned towards the ferret-faced informer and Oscar suddenly saw that he was so eager to believe that he would believe anything at all.

Wardley-Fish did not appear to be a man who worked a system. There was no longer anything systematic about him. He was in the grip of a passion which made him, literally, overheat. He was quite pink above the collar and red on the cheeks above his beard. His earlobes were large and fleshy and now they shone so brightly red that Oscar was reminded of the combs of the fowls he had decapitated for Mrs Stratton.

Wardley-Fish unbuttoned his overcoat and, by plunging his hands in his pockets, held the heavy garment out away from his chest. He looked like a rooster. He jiggled sovereigns in his pockets just as he had instructed Oscar not to. The stable hand looked towards this noise expectantly. He suggested that Madding Girl was a 'jam'.

Oscar knew this information was worth nothing, but had he shared this opinion with Wardley-Fish it would not, of course, have been listened to. For this was what Wardley-Fish most enjoyed about the track – the whispered conversations, the passing of 'tips for tips', the grubby low-life corners, the guilt, the fear of damnation, the elation, it all dissolved together in the vaporous spirit of his hip-flask. He took off his overcoat and gave it to Oscar.

'Come on, Odd Bod, we will be just in time to see them in the paddock.'

They ran then, Wardley-Fish in front. He had big buttocks and thick thighs. Oscar could imagine him sitting on a horse. He ran heavily, but quickly. Oscar came behind with his knees clicking painfully, his borrowed coat flapping around him, and was – with his wild red hair in its usual unruly state – such a scarecrow that some ageing Mohawks called out after him. He did not mind. He was intoxicated.

This intoxication was quite different from Wardley-Fish's. Oscar had no guilt at all. He knew that God would give him money at the races and thereby ease the dreadful burden that the Strattons had placed upon themselves. Now they would be released. God would do this just as He had told Moses to divide the land between the tribes of Israel: 'According to the lot shall the possession thereof be divided between the many and the few.' The Almighty would be Oscar's source of 'information'.

'Look at her,' said Wardley-Fish when Madding Girl was brought into the ring. Madding Girl was in a lather of sweat. It had a white foam inside its hind legs. The horse showed a peculiar look in its eye.

'Look at her,' said Wardley-Fish. He took Oscar by the coat sleeve and dragged him so quickly forward that Madding Girl reared, danced sideways, turned, and then backed back, perhaps deliberately, towards them so they had to step back into the whiskered crowd or else have their feet crushed.

'Look at the backside,' said Wardley-Fish.

It was difficult to avoid it.

'That, Odd Bod, is the first thing to look at in a horse, and when the track is wet, it's a day for a powerful bum like that one.'

Oscar remembered how lonely and lacklustre he had felt this morning. He had been cold, and miserable. Now he was warm inside Wardley-Fish's coat. He was a boy comforted by the sweet-sour wrappings of a larger man, the tweed-pricky armour of an elder brother, uncle, father. He was 'looked after' and was content – in the mud of Epsom – as a dog curled inside an armchair.

He grinned at Wardley-Fish.

'See. You have caught the germ,' said Wardley-Fish who saw in the grin the symptoms of his own hot condition. 'You should not be here. I am corrupting you.'

But Oscar did not feel at all corrupted. God had already spoken to him. Sure Blaze would win this race. Tonight he would have the money to pay his buttery account. He would buy long woollen socks and send two guineas and some coffee to Mr and Mrs Stratton. Perhaps he could open an account at Blackwell's. He would like to purchase his own copy of Mr Paley's *Evidences*.

'Look at you,' said Wardley-Fish. 'You look like a grinning scarecrow.'

Oscar frowned. He had no sense of humour about his appearance. In fact he never had any real idea of it. He thought himself 'quite plain and average' in build and physiognomy, and as for clothes, he now imagined himself quite reasonably, if humbly, dressed.

'Of course,' he said at last, 'I am wearing your coat. Doubtless it creates an odd effect.'

Wardley-Fish looked at the Odd Bod's wild red hair, his neat triangular face, his earnest praying-mantis hands clasped on his breast and – just when he began to laugh – saw that Oscar was not joking. The Odd Bod imagined himself quite normal.

When they pushed through the crowd towards the paddock, Wardley-Fish was still laughing. He could not stop himself. He laughed while he made his bets. Oscar watched him, smiling. He thought the laugh to do with betting. Wardley-Fish placed his bets in total disregard for the system, going from bookmaker to bookmaker, laying everything on Madding Girl with tears streaming down his face.

My great-grandfather watched him long enough to see how a bet was made and then, selecting Perce Gully, he laid three guineas on Sure Blaze at 9–1.

My great-grandfather won his first bet. In the case histories of pathological gamblers you find the same story told time and time again.

AT GALWAY RACES

There where the course is,
Delight makes all of the one mind,
The riders upon the galloping horses,
The crowd that closes in behind:
We, too, had good attendance once,
Hearers and hearteners of the work;
Aye, horsemen for companions,
Before the merchant and the clerk
Breathed on the world with timid breath.
Sing on: somewhere at some new moon,
We'll learn that sleeping is not death,
Hearing the whole earth change its tune,
Its flesh being wild, and it again
Crying aloud as the racecourse is,
And we find hearteners among men
That ride upon horses.

W. B. YEATS

IN PURSUIT OF A PUNTER'S PARADISE

At the height of the Olympic Games a sportswriter could be sent dizzy by the sheer diversity of activities about which he can misinform the public. They say that on certain extraordinary days at the modern Games there may even be more different sports on offer than there are drugs. That seems a pretty wild bet. But I can testify that too much exposure to such a multi-racial throng of sweating egos – to all the thousands who are running, jumping, throwing, swimming, lifting, grappling, shooting, kicking, punching and doing Lord knows what else in the name of ideals that long ago crumbled under the obsession with winning at any cost – can make a man long for a simpler amusement and especially for one less burdened with an unconvincing pretence of purity.

That is why, in the middle of the Moscow Olympics of 1980, an American friend and I decided that we were in sore need of the decompression chamber of a day at the races. He was at that time a columnist with *Newsweek*, the international magazine, and had transport and a Russian driver constantly at his disposal, so the expedition should have been straightforward enough. Unfortunately, the driver's lack of English was compounded by an eccentric conviction that he had some kind of psychic gift for divining where he was meant to go almost before his employer had begun trying to give him instructions.

Thus we were soon hurtling off on a marathon journey through grey streets towards distant suburbs, travelling purposefully but in a direction that deeply troubled my American companion, Pete Axthelm, who prides himself on being able to home in on a betting window from a range of 50 miles. He kept attempting to confirm that the determined local at the wheel understood that our target was the racetrack but eventually lost all faith in the effectiveness of his words and gestures. In desperation, he rose out of his seat into a crouch and began to give a passable impersonation of Angel Cordero riding a hectic finish up the stretch at Aqueduct. The driver appeared to feel that Pete was making excessive use of the whip but otherwise he had no difficulties with the extravagant mime and his expression reprimanded us for doubting his powers of comprehension and navigation. Some miles further on a sense of self-satisfaction was radiating from him in waves and then, quite suddenly, we were sweeping through a gateway and he was permitting himself a restrained wave of triumph at the horses all around us.

They were, however, the wrong horses and we were very much in the wrong place. We were in lush parkland for a start, not the dusty, decaying arena we had been warned to expect at Moscow's Hippodrome. The animals on hand were heftier and sleeker than we imagined Russian Flat racers would be and the humans aboard them were wearing fancy riding habits, with not a set of colours in sight.

We had, of course, been brought to the site of the Olympic equestrian competitions. Clearly our driver reasoned that two journalists who were covering the Games and had urgent business with horses must want to be here. He could not possibly realise how much of a misconception that was. We were in no mood for the formal disciplines of show-jumping or the minuet measures of dressage, and even the clatter and splash and derring-do of the cross-country phase of the three-day event wouldn't satisfy. What we needed was the track, with its separate world of brief, vibrant dramas and earthy escapism, always pervaded by an irresistible hint of something faintly roguish in the air. All right, if you insist on less fancy justification and more owning up, we wanted four-legged creatures we could bet on.

As it turned out, there was nothing faint or obscure about the roguishness we encountered when we did finally reach the Hippodrome. Emptying our pockets seemed to be official policy. The fact that the lady who took our wagers did her reckoning on an abacus was disconcerting enough but it was much more disturbing to discover that selecting winners was almost irrelevant as far as the prospects of profit were concerned. We hit three in a row and were still just marginally in front. We did not investigate the details of the tax applied to our bets in that far-off era before *glasnost* and *perestroika* but it had to be on a scale to make the Levy Board drool. Still, even that inconvenience was a tolerable penalty to pay for the pleasures of the afternoon. Next day Seb Coe, Steve Ovett or some of the other great athletes who enabled the Olympics to rise above their problems (which, you will remember, included little aggravations like a US boycott) might be enthralling us again. But for the moment we were glad to be away from de Coubertin's Games and back at the punting game.

I have made similar defections in many corners of the globe, slipping away from a touring England football team in Australia to scuffle with the bookmakers at the Warwick Farm course in Sydney, interrupting coverage of Super Bowl preparations in San Diego to cross the Mexican border and engage the enemy at Agua Caliente in Tijuana, briefly deserting the World Cup in Argentina to sample the Buenos Aires equivalent of Sandown, using a heavyweight championship fight in Caracas, Venezuela, as an excuse to visit a track that offered breathtaking views but not a glimpse of a winner. And, of course, dozens of assignments in the States have encouraged me to play truant at Aqueduct and Belmont, Santa Anita, Hialeah, Gulfstream, Churchill Downs, Saratoga and those two smaller Maryland battlegrounds, Laurel Park and Bowie.

Through my working experience of a score of other sports there runs the seductive pull of the running horse. Sometimes it has dragged me toward penury but I remain happy to be a fully paid-up member of that vast brotherhood who believe that poverty is at its most bearable when endured because of a temporary loss of rapport with the form-book ... There are few languages more international than the lamentation of the losers at a racecourse. It is, I learned long ago, an Esperanto of small-scale suffering that knows no boundaries.

Inevitably, now and again human frailty will manifest itself and one of us will crack, turn heretic and try to infect the rest of the flock. I was exposed to that threat once on a bus pulling away from Belmont (surely a fellow can indulge a sudden enthusiasm for bus travel without arousing the cheap suspicion that a string of slaughtered favourites had anything to do with it). One of the other enthusiasts that day was a young black man who scarcely waited for the driver to get out of first gear before he let the earphones of his Sony Walkman fall around his neck and began to unload a resonant but unfailingly polite monologue on a muted audience. I felt obliged to put his utterances on record at the time and, as a tragic example of lost faith, they are worth repeating.

'Gentlemen, listen to me, you have been to a FOOL'S PARADISE,' he informed us, leaving no doubt about which words were in dramatic capitals. 'At Belmont Park the poor man DON'T HAVE A SHOT. It is a conspiracy of millionaires. Stay home, keep your money in your pocket, put it under the mattress, do anything but don't bring it to the FOOL'S PARADISE. Men have lost everything here. Men have lost THEIR WIVES at Belmont.'

At that point, I distinctly recall, the spirits of the company rose. But another black traveller, who was sitting next to the misguided evangelist, decided he had heard enough. He was of philosophical mien and had been cradling his grizzled and distinguished head in a large hand during the sermon. When he spoke it was through his fingers. 'I wanna bet,' he said with quiet, unhurried authority, 'you gonna be back here tomorrow along with the rest of us.'

Personally, I don't pass up too many opportunities to go racing at Belmont. Perhaps I am haunted by the thought of what I missed by allowing journalistic obligations to keep me away from the place on Saturday June 9, 1973. I was in New York on that day of the 105th running of the Belmont Stakes, the third leg of the US Triple Crown, but instead of being drawn out towards those 430 magical acres on the inner edge of Long Island I stayed among the canyons of Manhattan and have regretted it ever since. There was, it is true, considerable consolation in the fact that one man with whom I had a professional appointment, Andre Laguerre, the late, irreplaceably great Editor of *Sports Illustrated* magazine, was not only a lifelong and knowledgeable devotee of the Turf but sufficiently generous to invite a visiting Brit to hang around his office and watch the race live on television. As a result, I had a direct, contemporaneous experience of what Secretariat did that afternoon. Yet, though that in itself was unforgettable, it wasn't at all the same as being one of the 68,000 who watched the big red horse in the flesh while he surged through what may well have been the greatest mile-and-a-half ever galloped by a thoroughbred.

In June of this year I was in the Press Box for the 21st running of the Belmont and seeing Easy Goer win by eight lengths in the second-fastest time the race has produced was a tremendous thrill, especially as it came only four days after witnessing Nashwan's pulverising brilliance at Epsom. But to appreciate how miraculous Secretariat's run was we need only remember that in annihilating his nearest challenger by 31 lengths he covered the 12 furlongs in 2 mins 24 sec. dead, two full seconds inside Easy Goer's time, and shattered the world record out of recognition. The official account from 1973 tells us that the wind was against Secretariat in the backstretch. The wind should have known better. For a couple of minutes at least, he was a greater force of nature than it was.

None of us can ever expect to see the like of that again. But let's go on climbing up into the stands, just in case.

HUGH MCILVANNEY (1989)

THE HIGHER MOTIVE

The lower classes are such fools
They waste their money on the pools.
I bet, of course, but that's misleading.
One must encourage bloodstock breeding.

BERNARD FERGUSSON

We went racing together many more times that year and other years after I had worked in the early mornings, and Hadley enjoyed it and sometimes she loved it. But it was not the climbs in the high mountain meadows above the last forest, nor nights coming home to the chalet, nor was it climbing with Chink, our best friend, over a high pass into new country. It was not really racing either. It was gambling on horses. But we called it racing.

Racing never came between us, only people could do that; but for a long time it stayed close to us like a demanding friend. That was a generous way to think of it. I, the one who was so righteous about people and their destructiveness, tolerated this friend that was the falsest, most beautiful, most exciting, vicious, and demanding because she could be profitable. To make it profitable was more than a full-time job and I had no time for that. But I justified it to myself because I wrote about it, even though in the end, when everything I had written was lost, there was only one racing story that survived, because it was out in the mails.

I was going to races alone more now and I was involved in them and getting too mixed up with them. I worked two tracks in their season when I could, Auteuil and Enghien. It took full-time work to try to handicap intelligently and you could make no money that way. That was just how it worked out on paper. You could buy a newspaper that gave you that.

You had to watch a jumping race from the top of the stands at Auteuil and it was a fast climb up to see what each horse did and see the horse that might have won and did not, and see why or maybe how he did not do what he could have done. You watched the prices and all the shifts of odds each time a horse you were following would start, and you had to know how he was working and finally to get to know when the stable would try with him. He always might be beaten when he tried; but you should know by then what his chances were. It was hard work but at Auteuil it was beautiful to watch each day they raced when you could be there and see the honest races with the great horses, and you got to know the course as well as any place you had ever known. You knew many people finally, jockeys and trainers and owners, and too many horses and too many things.

In principle I only bet when I had a horse to bet on but I sometimes found horses that nobody believed in except the men who trained and rode them that won race after race with me betting on them. I stopped finally because it took too much time, I was getting too involved and I knew too much about what went on at Enghien and at the flat-racing tracks too.

When I stopped working on the races I was glad, but it left an emptiness. By then I knew that everything good and bad left an emptiness when it stopped. But if it was bad, the emptiness filled up by itself. If it was good you could only fill it by finding something better. I put the racing capital back into the general funds and I felt relaxed and good.

ERNEST HEMINGWAY, from *A Moveable Feast* (1964)

Apart from fresh air, excitement, and learning how to lose money, the racegoer gets a tremendous kick out of talking racing after it is all over, which gives me the opportunity to tell the story of the dinner party at Newmarket, in case there are still a couple of people who haven't heard it.

An American arrived at an owner's house at Newmarket on the eve of the Guineas with a letter of introduction from a mutual friend and was invited to dinner. Towards the end of the meal, the lady on his right suddenly realised that somebody wasn't talking, so she turned to the American and asked: 'Do you like horses?'

'No,' replied the visitor.

Undeterred the lady said: 'What sport are you interested in?'

'I like to shoot,' replied the visitor.

'What do you like to shoot?' she asked.

'Horses,' said the visitor.

Racing, as this story shows, is a peculiar sport – people seem either to love it or hate it, and the funny thing is that those that dislike it feel entitled to run it down whenever the subject is brought up. Racing is an athletic contest between horses. I suppose some people object to it because they think people go to the races to bet – this is only a half-truth, as sometimes the worst betting race on the card causes the most interest and excitement if a couple of exceptionally good horses are in it.

One of my great incentives to go racing is to meet the people.

Racing people seem to have more than their fair share of fun, and accept hazards in the most amusing way. There is a humorous fatalism among the professionals, very well expressed by the instructions given to a steeplechase jockey years ago by the stable boy: 'Don't be afraid of dying; just let him run.'

Besides the people who go racing, I also like the stories. Such as the one told to me by Tommy Reece the billiards player, the inventor of the anchor and pendulum strokes. At the now defunct Derby meeting (I mean the town, not the race), his supposedly deadly enemy but really great friend, Melbourne Inman, had bought an animal that had been put on the racecard to be sold after a selling race, win, lose or draw. It had finished in the ruck and Inman had given sixty guineas for it.

Knowing that Tommy Reece knew everything about racing, except how to find winners, the optimistic new owner went to him and asked: 'What do I do now?'

Tommy said: 'Go and find the boy who was looking after it, give him a couple of quid, and ask if your horse has got any special peculiarities or faults.'

Away went Inman, found the boy, and did the necessary. 'Now,' says he, 'has it got any faults?'

'Well,' said the boy, 'it's got two. One is that if you turn it out in a field it will take you a long time to catch it again.'

Inman said: 'Well, I don't mind that much, as I don't suppose I'll have to do the job myself. What's the other one?'

'The other one is that when you've caught it, it's no bloody good.'

JACK LEACH, from *Sods I Have Cut on the Turf* (1961)

The American novelist John Steinbeck succumbed to the lure of racing at the 1956 Kentucky Derby.

At this sacred moment, in this place of pilgrimage, I have several towering but gossamer convictions. During Derby Week, Louisville is the capital of the world. This lively, lovely city has a temporary population of foster-citizens second only to China. I am also sure that if the national elections took place today, our next president would be a horse.

Yesterday an airplane set us down in the grassy, rolling country crawling with spring and buttered all over with sunshine. And the grass is really blue or I am crazy.

This is my first Derby. I have had to learn the ground rules. As the horses are bred and raised and trained, so must the spectator get into a condition, a process pleasant but inexorable. Within five minutes of landing at Standiford Field we went into training. There was breakfast in a garden glittering with flowers and people. Under a huge tree, which I am sure was not moved in the night before, a long white table staggered under sausages and scrambled eggs and grits and fried apples, while on another table bottles bloomed amidst a groundcover of frosty glasses.

These people of Louisville have a persistent, gentle courtesy which more than compensates for the harshness of the training. From breakfast we went hurriedly to luncheon in another sunny garden and then, so that we might not interfere with our rapidly improving condition, we whisked to the track to see the Friday races.

I like horses as much as the next person, but there is one thing I must admit about them. They are just plain beautiful. They may well be the most beautiful thing in the world. I wish we could improve our own breed as we have improved theirs.

At the track on Friday I got my betting arm limbered up while the youth and beauty and gallantry of four worlds strolled back and forth, the flower of '21' and the Stork Club and Toots Shor's mingling easily with buckskin-clad Kentucky riflemen. Good Lord! these women are handsome. If they can't improve the breed, we are lost.

I broke even at the track, a clear capital gain, and then parties and parties and beautiful parties in houses and with people whose names sound like chapter-headings in my grammar-school American history. What nice people and what ardent hosts they are. And all the time our condition was improving. We wanted to be ready when the 3-year-olds were ready.

And now the moment has come after a week of tempo increasing toward a lightly governed anarchy. Early this morning people began trooping through the tunnel under the track and spreading out inside the field bringing lunches and pillows and folding chairs and small radios and packs of cards to while away the hours. And now they are massed in bright-colored clothing. There must be a hundred thousand of them, like a monster garden of frantic flowers.

In the stands and boxes acres of lovely women in lovely dresses, and hats – this is fungus year for hats. In shape they go from common mushrooms through toadstools to Amanita muscaria.

The boys are here, the nervous horse players who never knew a horse. They wear a uniform, snap-brim hat, sports coat of many colors and field glasses. Their eyes are peering into the future 10 minutes away when they will be rich – or bums. And the happy freaks are here claiming attention and a frowzy eminence with white fur derbys and jeweled teeth and rhinestone sun glasses and along with them the furtive brotherhood who do not quite trust their invisibility.

The bars are choked, the passages clogged, and the long lines to the betting windows are getting impatient with fear that they may not get their money in on time. There is a great rhythm of restless feet on the wooden stands and then – the bugle and the color guards and the National Anthem. 'My Old Kentucky Home' – lonesome music in the multitude.

Now the horses come out, sleek and memorable, perfect as birds, specialized as snakes. They move along the track, some dancing, some shy, but all seeming to know their own importance and beauty.

By the time this is written, there will be few people in the nation who will not have seen the race on television or heard it on radio, and they will all have felt to some extent the bursting emotion at Churchill Downs. Every step of the great Needles will have been discussed – how he dawdled along trailing the field for two-thirds of the course, then fired himself like a torpedo past the screaming while a balloon of tension swelled and burst and it was all over.

Now there is a languor. Over a hundred thousand hearts are more spent than Needles' heart, and some of them split and their owners on the way to the hospital or the morgue.

I am fulfilled and weary. This Kentucky Derby, whatever it is – a race, an emotion, a turbulence, an explosion – is one of the most beautiful and violent and satisfying things I have ever experienced. And I suspect that, as with other wonders, the people one by one have taken away from it exactly as much good or evil as they brought to it.

What an experience. I am glad to have seen and felt it at last.

Louisville *Courier-Journal*, 6 May 1956

Once the horse moved man's physical body and his household goods and his articles of commerce from one place to another. Nowadays all it moves is a part or the whole of his bank account, either through betting on it or trying to keep owning and feeding it.

So, in a way, unlike the other animals which he has domesticated – cows and sheep and hogs and chickens and dogs (I don't include cats; man has never tamed cats) – the horse is economically obsolete. Yet it still endures and probably will continue to as long as man himself does, long after the cows and sheep and hogs and chickens, and the dogs which control and protect them, are extinct. Because the other beasts and their guardians merely supply man with food, and someday science will feed him by means of synthetic gases and so eliminate the economic need which they fill. While what the horse supplies to man is something deep and profound in his emotional nature and need.

It will endure and survive until man's own nature changes. Because you can almost count on your thumbs the types and classes of human beings in whose lives and memories and experience and glandular discharge the horse has no place. These will be the ones who don't like to bet on anything which involves the element of chance or skill or the unforeseen. They will be the ones who don't like to watch something in motion, either big or going fast, no matter what it is. They will be the ones who don't like to watch something alive and bigger and stronger than man, under the control of puny man's will, doing something which man himself is too weak or too inferior in sight or hearing or speed to do.

These will have to exclude even the ones who don't like horses – the ones who would not touch a horse or go near it, who have never mounted one nor ever intend to; who can and do and will risk and lose their shirts on a horse they have never seen.

So some people can bet on a horse without ever seeing one

outside a Central Park fiacre or a peddler's van. And perhaps nobody can watch horses running forever, with a mutuel window convenient, without making a bet. But it is possible that some people can and do do this.

So it is not just betting, the chance to prove with money your luck or what you call your judgment, that draws people to horse races. It is much deeper than that. It is a sublimation, a transference: man, with his admiration for speed and strength, physical power far beyond what he himself is capable of, projects his own desire for physical supremacy, victory, onto the agent – the baseball or football team, the prize fighter. Only the horse race is more universal because the brutality of the prize fight is absent, as well as the attenuation of football or baseball – the long time needed for the orgasm of victory to occur, where in the horse race it is a matter of minutes, never over two or three, repeated six or eight or ten times in one afternoon.

WILLIAM FAULKNER, from 'Kentucky: May: Saturday', in *Sports Illustrated*, 16 May 1955

2

'Gallant slaves and cheery martyrs'

The horses

The arrival of the yearlings towards the end of the season changes the mood in the yard completely. There are generally a good few races still to be won, but the new intake brings with it a set of different tasks and a set of different hopes. When the yearlings started to arrive in the autumn of 1986, the 1987 season was already beginning. They came from the sales, from various private deals, some directly from private studs, and they got to Castle Stables during the final weeks of the racing season and the first few weeks of the close season.

As the 1986 season wound down, many of the fillies left the yard 'on their holidays' as the lads put it: they were sent away from the yard to be turned out in a field during the day at a stud farm, strolling about, picking at the grass, and enjoying the change of rhythm and the relaxation away from the stresses of training.

It would be nice to do the same with the colts, but it doesn't work. If you turn a bunch of colts out together, they get stroppy, pick fights, and end up hurting each other. So the colts stayed in the training yard, doing exercise designed to keep them ticking over and in good heart as the feed and good care put on the muscle and aided the growing bones.

The last few weeks of every year are all about the yearlings. Every year a new wave of hope is set in motion with these unnamed little dream-bearers, the Nureyev colt and the little Lomond filly and the rest of them. In an unsuccessful year, they mean a fresh start; in a year full of winners they bring hopes of plenty more of the same. The yard began the job of preparing them for the great leap forward, the day when they are ridden for the first time, and for the still more momentous event when, if things went well, they would actually race. For most of them, this would happen sometime during the next racing season, when they would be two-year-olds. But right now, they were half-ton, million-quid babies, and they didn't know the first thing about anything.

And so the yard set about the task of 'breaking them' as the rather cruel jargon has it. It sounds a brutal procedure, but, naturally, you do not get terribly far with thoroughbred horses if your start brutalizing them. Castle Stables has a special team of experienced lads to break in the yearlings: it is a tough and ticklish job. You want a lad who knows when to be gentle and when to be a bit of a bully: such people are a major asset for David Kitcher. Kitcher is one of John Dunlop's five head lads. The autumn is his busy time, because he is also in charge of the yearling team.

The first step is to get a bit into the horse's mouth: a breaking bit is gentle and jangly: it gives the horse something to mouth and fidget with, something that accustoms him to feeling something in his mouth. One of the breaking team will walk behind him, holding him with reins about ten feet long. The lad will look as if he is ploughing a field. Gradually he will teach the horse to lunge: that is, walk and trot in circles at the bidding of long reins. One of the reins will be tucked in behind the horse: it will be the first time the horse has felt pressure from behind, the first time he has been asked for real obedience from a human, and, naturally, some of them are pretty spooky about the business.

But the real Wild West bit comes when the horses are fitted with a roller for the first time. A roller is simply a piece of padding that fits round where the saddle will go in the fullness of time, but they don't like it a bit. They go completely crazy, bucking and rearing and doing anything they can think of to get rid of the horrible thing. But there is no shifting it. They are stuck with it for the next 24 hours; it remains strapped on as they eat and as they sleep. In the end, according to theory, they should be completely used to it. Needless to say, many remain deeply suspicious about the idea. They will remain 'cold-backed' for days, or weeks, which means they will play up every time you put on a roller, or, later, a saddle. 'Oh, I've had some awkward ones,' Kitcher said. 'But it's never been impossible. Some you just have to give more time to. Some will play about a good bit, but they always come. In the end, they always come.'

Once they have accepted the roller, they are asked to lunge in it. After a while, the roller is swapped for a saddle, but nobody sits in it just yet. Everything is done softly-softly. All horse people know that when you take six steps forward, you generally have to take five steps back: nothing happens quickly. If you get impatient with horses, you have no place in the horse business. Patience is the cardinal virtue for a trainer and for a lad; that and understanding. Such virtues are important for all horse people, but they are doubly desirable in racing: racehorses are just not bred to be charming, placid beasts. Charm and placidity are not the qualities that win races. A difficult horse might be difficult because of his champion's temperament. On the other hand, he might possess those qualities because he is just a bit of a sod, and talent-less to boot. There is no telling, not yet.

When you have a horse that is more or less happy being lunged in its saddle, you move on to the pretty stage: you take your horse walking in Arundel Park. Each horse is taken out on its own, with no distractions, with a lad walking behind and guiding him gently and tactfully with the long reins. Past the folly, along the avenues of magnificent trees, in the windblown autumn. Raymond Baker has been a member of the yearling team since 1951: 'Done 'em all, Shirley Heights, Snaafi Dancer, the lot. And I'll tell you something, they're a lot better today than they used to be. They've all seen more, been handled more, they've got more used to people. They are a lot less wild. But really I don't mind if they're not all good – I like to see a horse with a bit of spirit to it. I like 'em to have a nice scream and a roar.'

It is at this time of the year that everyone in the yearling team gives thanks that he does not work in Newmarket: Newmarket, with more than 2,000 horses in training at more than 40 training establishments, all of them sharing the same training grounds. You want a yearling to settle down, to relax, to acquire confidence: the fewer distractions he has, the better. Newmarket is a town of spooking horses: if one spooks, they all spook: the herd instinct is based on the principle of safety in numbers.

When you are bringing on a yearling, you find safety in solitude and quiet. Every member of Dunlop's yearling team walks for miles around the empty, rolling spaces of Arundel Park, with his charge slowly getting used to moving at the prompting of some invisible being behind him.

At this stage, the invisible being is still walking like a ploughman. But soon he will be sitting on top. The horse is taught to get used to the idea of feeling a little weight on his back: in the box, his lad will start to lean across him, and to half-lie across his back. The horses get more used to humans every day, and to the weird things that humans do to them: by this time, with a bit of luck, the horse will take this latest oddity without worrying too much about it.

And then, finally, we come to the exciting bit: when a rider sits on a horse for the first time, and gently, gingerly takes up the reins. It is normally about two weeks from the circus act with the roller to the quiet, dignified moment when the animal is first ridden. The performance varies as much as the horses vary, but it normally happens in a quiet, almost anticlimactic manner. If the horse takes this latest event in his stride, then it shows that all the work of preparation has been done to perfection. And that you have a particularly nice horse.

The horses then get used to being ridden in the indoor school, that aircraft hangar in the park. They slowly grow accustomed to trotting and to turning. They will never be required to learn the extravagant gymnastic turns of dressage horses, showjumpers and polo ponies: they must learn merely to find balance and rhythm as they work in shallow loops and generous circles. They learn to organize themselves, to keep count of their legs as they go around the corners, to listen to the rider. The rider's skill can help a horse immensely: a bad, unbalanced rider will throw a horse's balance out, a good one will help him to find it.

All this work is done under Kitcher's eyes. The horses trot gently around him, getting used to being ridden, and getting used to working in large groups of horses, getting used, in fact, to being a racehorse in training. After a couple of weeks of this, they are allowed outside again: this time not with a ploughman, but a real rider. For the first time, they are treated like grown-up horses. They trot up the long cantering paths – at least, they are supposed to trot, though many want to try disorganized canters and sprawly gallops until dissuaded by their riders. A further fortnight on, they will be performing manoeuvres out in the park, trotting in circles and S-bends. The horse is learning to handle himself, learning the essentials of balance, learning basic obedience. But only basic obedience is required. Races are won with a flying atavistic gallop: you do not want to school that out of a horse.

As the yearlings were going through their hoops, Dunlop and Kitcher were sizing them up, already looking for next year's winners, for the Derby hope of two years hence. 'There are some that stick out from day one,' Kitcher said. 'Some that always look nice movers. But you don't know, you see. You really don't know. They come in real scrawny, and by the time they are two-year-olds, they are like a different horse. You might like one right from the start – you never really know, not till you get them out on the racetrack.'

Which brings me, inevitably, to Snaafi Dancer. After Shirley Heights, he is, perhaps, the most famous horse to have been trained at Castle Stables. In its way, the Snaafi Dancer saga is the classic racing story of all time. The horse arrived in a fanfare of trumpets: at the time it was the most expensive yearling ever bought. It was bought by Sheikh Mohammed and it cost an unbelievable $10.2 million. It was the prestige horse, the horse to send a reputation soaring.

There was one slight problem. The horse was useless. 'Rather a sweet little horse, actually,' Dunlop said. 'But unfortunately no bloody good.'

Jeremy Noseda, Dunlop's number three, said: 'The older he got, the worse-looking he got. In fact, even when he arrived he didn't look *that* good. And by spring he was a horrible-looking brute.'

'Mind you,' Kitcher said, 'Moon Madness didn't look much as a yearling. You wouldn't say, there's a nice-looking horse. But he just grew into it, until he became a lovely-looking horse.'

'Everyone I've spoken to said Shirley Heights was the most scrawny-looking thing,' Noseda said. 'No one wanted to do him.'

'Well, he didn't have the best of characters,' Kitcher said. 'He was moody, he had a fillyish sort of a temperament. He messed about all the time. Never wanted to do much. But he just had this engine in him.'

'And Snaafi Dancer didn't,' I said.

'He didn't. We realized that very early on,' Noseda said. 'On the canters, he never looked good. We said, oh, he's just lazy; when he's working, he'll show us something. Then he had problems with his feet. Then he started galloping, and he showed nothing. You'd try to convince yourself that one day he'd spark, we all did. The amount of things he had wrong with him, it was unbelievable. He was club-footed, then he got cow-hocked. He had little ears and horrible eyes.'

'Horses are so seldom black and white,' Dunlop said later. 'There is always hope. But after his first winter Snaafi Dancer really was bitterly disappointing. The writing was on the wall by spring.'

'There don't seem to be any rules in this game,' I said.

'That there are not. No rules, absolutely no rules where horses are concerned. A lot of people think there are. Horses will always give these people a very nasty shock.'

Snaafi Dancer never saw a racetrack. He just didn't like galloping. Eventually he went to stud. But there was only one thing wrong. Snaafi Dancer didn't like mares either. No rules.

SIMON BARNES, from Horsesweat and Tears

The horse enters into the spirit of the race as thoroughly as does his rider, and, without whip or spur, will generally exert his energies to the utmost to beat his opponent. It is beautiful to see him advancing to the starting-post, every motion evincing his eagerness. The signal is given, and he springs away – he settles himself in his stride – the jockey becomes a part and portion of him, every motion of the arms and body corresponding with, and assisting the action of the horse. On he goes, eager, yet husbanding his powers. At length, when he arrives at that distance from which the rider knows that he will *live home* at the top of his speed, the hint is given, and on he rushes. Then the race in reality begins, and every nerve is strained to head his competitor. Then, too, comes the art of the rider, to keep the horse within his pace, and with admirable *give and take*, add to the length of every stride. Then, perhaps, the spur, skilfully applied, may be necessary to rouse every dormant energy. A sluggish lurching horse may need more punishment than the humane observer would think justifiable. But the natural ardour of the race-horse, roused at the moment of the grand struggle, by the moderate application of the whip and spur, will bring him through if he can win.

Forrester will afford sufficient illustration of the natural emulation of the courser. – He had won many a hardly contested race; at length, over-weighted and over-matched, the rally had commenced. His opponent, who had been waiting behind, was gaining upon him; he overtook him, and they continued quite close to within the distance. It was a point that could scarcely be decided. But Forrester's strength was failing. He made one desperate plunge – seized his antagonist by the jaw to hold him back, and could scarcely be forced to quit his hold. In like manner, a horse belonging to Mr Quin, in 1753, finding his adversary gradually passing him, seized him by the leg, and both riders were obliged to dismount, in order to separate the animals. Let us here pause and ask, would the butcherly whipping and cutting which seems so often to form the expected and necessary conclusion of the race – the supposed display of the skill of the rider – the exultation of the thoughtless or unfeeling spectator – would these have carried such horses over one additional inch of ground? They would have been thrown abroad – they would have shortened their stroke – and perhaps would have become enraged and suspended every exertion. The horse is as susceptible of pleasure and pain as ourselves. He was committed to us for our protection and our use; he is a willing, devoted servant. Whence did we derive the right to abuse him? Interest speaks the same language. Many a race has been lost by the infliction of wanton cruelty.

WILLIAM YOUATT, from *The Horse* (1831)

Somewhat different from the 'willing, devoted servant' described by Youatt is the Derby candidate Buttercup, whose exploits – or lack of them – were chronicled in the 1930s in the Daily Express *by Beachcomber.*

April 10

A Cert for the Derby

It may seem to you early for me to speak with any certainty about the Derby, but I can assure you that I am on to a good thing. You remember Buttercup, the horse of which such great things were expected two or three years ago? Buttercup is going to win this year's Derby. I say this with the utmost certainty, since he has been bought for £8 10s 3d by Dr Strabismus (Whom God Preserve), of Utrecht. The doctor points out that the great thing in training a horse is to give it rest, and Buttercup has done nothing for two years but eat grass at peace and occasionally perform light country work.

The doctor has had a suitable stable constructed near Brooklands, which he claims to be the best air in England for horses. Also the neighbourhood is conducive to speed. This stable is ventilated and electrically heated, and Buttercup will have a special diet and a special programme for each day. The doctor has promised to give me news of the horse from time to time. Meanwhile, I regard him, in such hands, as a certainty. After all, 'Scientific training is what brings out the best in a gee,' as Ruskin said to Pater.

Later: Buttercup was let out of his stable to-day, and within three minutes had kicked an American tourist in the face, smashed a churn, knocked over a dog kennel, and trampled a flower-bed to bits. 'Such activities,' writes Dr Strabismus (Whom God Preserve) of Utrecht, 'argue either extreme physical fitness or the race-winning temperament (see Stöfflganger's *Psychology of Horses*: Bk 8, Ch. 14).'

Experts who have seen Buttercup confess themselves puzzled.

Sid Cokerby, whose hat was eaten by this restive mount, commented thus: 'He is a horse to be watched.'

April 13

Dr Strabismus (Whom God Preserve), of Utrecht, had arranged yesterday for Buttercup to be given a preliminary canter, in order to see how the beast was shaping. Accordingly the horse was led into a field, and Walter, the doctor's manservant, mounted and dug his spurs in. The local clergyman, a grocer's boy, and the secretary of the Girls' Guild of Social Service were among the excited spectators. The doctor, who had been reading up racing jargon, said laughingly, 'Come and watch my plating juvenile. It's a useful filly, but none too tractable at the ditch. The filly's a good stayer, and is well fancied.'

For the first ten yards the pace was killing, but after that Buttercup threw Walter, and ran off in the other direction. He was finally brought back by a village policeman, and when they had removed the remains of a gate from his neck, he bit the grocer's boy. He was then led back to his stable, frothing considerably.

April 20

The latest news of this dark horse, which is becoming less and less dark, is reassuring. Buttercup was exercised yesterday for half an hour, during which time he jumped a barrel, stove in a barn-door, and lay down and whinneyed repeatedly. He still shows a tendency to shy whenever anybody comes near him, and the doctor is considering whether it might not be possible to have him ridden by a dummy in the Derby. During a canter in the afternoon Buttercup turned down the village street and ran into the barber's shop. The barber, who was shaving a curate, cut his chin in two places, while the horse ate the shaving soap before willing hands could drag him forth into the street.

April 29

In the words of a stable-boy this horse is 'becoming more and more favourite for the Derby.' Dr Strabismus (Whom God Preserve), of Utrecht, is himself supervising the training, and feeds the horse every morning on a diet of his own invention, consisting of mashed arrowroot, wallflower seed, wet cement and celery. It was decided to give Buttercup a good test gallop yesterday. The doctor led him out, and a friend of his, a Mr Wallis, mounted him, and rode him thirty-nine miles. The speed was not remarkable, and the horse appeared very tired at the end of the day, but he is obviously a stayer. Not every racehorse does thirty-nine miles at a stretch in training. 'A classic horse,' said the doctor yesterday.

May 4

Some days ago the streets were full of women bearing trays filled with imitation buttercups. A card announced that they were collecting for the Buttercup Fund, and I have received more than one letter protesting against the methods employed by Dr Strabismus (Whom God Preserve), of Utrecht, in order to obtain extra luxuries for his Derby colt and at the same time give the horse publicity.

'What is the Sport of Kings coming to?' asks one indignant writer.

It is nothing to do with me. It is a matter for the Turf authorities to deal with.

May 9

'The future favourite for the Derby,' writes Dr Strabismus (Whom God Preserve), of Utrecht, 'is progressing steadily. So mettlesome is the nag that yesterday he kicked his loose-box to matchwood and stunned a stable-boy.'

Mr Edgar Wallace, who has been visiting the doctor, saw Buttercup being fed yesterday, and exclaimed, 'What a remarkable animal!' The doctor, speaking in the town hall, said that by now the betting on Buttercup ought to be in the ratio of 6 to 5 each way. When questioned closely as to his meaning he shouted at the top of his voice, 'I'll take evens, and be hanged to Tattersall's.'

It is thought that the hot weather and the strain of training such a horse may be telling on the doctor.

Later: Buttercup has disappeared.

May 31

Buttercup Mystery Solved

The Buttercup mystery has been solved in a most unexpected manner. Somewhere among the London streets a rather weary horse draws an ancient cab slowly along, in the hope of some old-fashioned person engaging it for a ride. On the seat sits Mr Joe Barlow, a cabman of fifty-eight years experience and the proud owner of the horse, which he bought from the Destitute Horses Home for five and sevenpence, cash down. This horse, which was found wandering along the Brompton Road early yesterday morning in an exhausted condition, pricks up its ears at the sound of the word Buttercup. This is evidently its name.

And so the horse that was once a Derby favourite now drags a seedy four-wheeled cab; for age spares none of us not even great horses. Where is Bucephalus, that had a city built in his honour? Where is Marengo, the good white horse of Napoleon? Where, think you, is the huge monster upon which Chaliapin burst on London? And where is the Buddha's Kantaka, and the delightful Rosinante, who knew the uplands of Estremadura? Tachebrune, too, where is he – the horse that Ogier rode so nobly?

But I will not tire you. I will conclude this epic of Buttercup at once; only remarking that the Doctor is now released to devote all his energies to the coming eclipse.

July 26

Buttercup Disqualified

Buttercup has only run in one race lately, a local affair in a meadow belonging to the vicar. Mrs Dodgett, the vicar's wife, presented a morocco leather pocket-case as the prize, and there were seven entries. The Doctor followed the race through his glasses, and applauded heartily as Buttercup drew away. Two of the other horses stopped to quarrel over a truss of hay that had dropped from a wagon, and the postman got in the way of a third. The remaining four had the field, except for an allotment in the east corner, to themselves; and if they had not all gone in the wrong direction the race would have been over sooner.

When it was seen that the four horses had gone the wrong way, the local milkman, Mr Hedge, dropped the tape and the starter's pistol (he was judge, starter, and timekeeper) and, racing into a barn, came back with a long whip. By this time two of the nags were back in their stables. The third – a pony belonging to a retired Army captain's son – turned at the sound of the whip, and reached the winning-post a good three lengths ahead of the milkman, who, when he recovered his breath, declared Tippy the winner.

Buttercup was found an hour later in the next village, with his head in another horse's nosebag. He was disqualified.

In awarding the prize, Mrs Dodgett commented on the speed of the winner.

Sherwood Anderson's short story 'I'm A Fool' is a familiar racetrack tale. Less well known is another tale in his 1924 collection Horses and Men, *'The Man Who Became A Woman', in which the narrator is a 'swipe' (groom) for racehorses – in this case trotting horses – competing in meetings at country fairs. As this extract illustrates, the story contains a rich evocation of the relationship between horse and man.*

When you go out with the horses there is one job that always takes a lot of time. In the late afternoon, after your horse has been in a race and after you have washed him and rubbed him out, he has to be walked slowly, sometimes for hours and hours, so he'll cool out slowly and won't get muscle-bound. I got so I did that job for both our horses and Burt did the more important things. It left him free to go talk or shoot dice with the other niggers and I didn't mind. I rather liked it and after a hard race even the stallion, O My Man, was tame enough, even when there were mares about.

You walk and walk, around a little circle, and your horse's head is right by your shoulder, and all around you the life of the place you are in is going on, and in a queer way you get so you aren't really a part of it at all. Perhaps no one ever gets as I was then, except boys that aren't quite men yet and who like me have never been with girls or women – to really be with them, up to the hilt, I mean. I used to wonder if young girls got that way too before they married or did what we used to call 'go on the town.'

If I remember it right though, I didn't do much thinking then. Often I would have forgotten supper if Burt hadn't shouted at me and reminded me, and sometimes he forgot and went off to town with one of the other niggers and I did forget.

There I was with the horse, going slow slow slow, around a circle that way. The people were leaving the fair grounds now, some afoot, some driving away to the farms in wagons and Fords. Clouds of dust floated in the air and over to the west, where the town was, maybe the sun was going down, a red ball of fire through the dust. Only a few hours before the crowd had been all filled with excitement and everyone shouting. Let us suppose my horse had been in a race that afternoon and I had stood in front of the grandstand with my horse blanket over my shoulder, alongside of Burt perhaps, and when they came into the stretch my owner began to call, in that queer high voice of his that seemed to float over the top of all the shouting up in the grandstand. And his voice was saying over and over, 'Go, pick it boy, pick it boy, pick it boy,' the way he always did, and my heart was thumping so I could hardly breathe, and Burt was leaning over and snapping his fingers and muttering, 'Come, little sweet. Come on home. Your Mama wants you. Come get your 'lasses and bread, little Pick-it-boy.'

Well, all that was over now and the voices of the people left around were all low. And Pick-it-boy – I was leading him slowly around the little ring, to cool him out slowly, as I've said, – he was different too. Maybe he had pretty nearly broken his heart trying to get down to the wire in front, or getting down there in front, and now everything inside him was quiet and tired, as it was nearly all the time those days in me, except in me tired but not quiet.

You remember I've told you we always walked in a circle, round and round and round. I guess something inside me got to going round and round and round too. The sun did sometimes and the trees and the clouds of dust. I had to think sometimes about putting down my feet so they went down in the right place and I didn't get to staggering like a drunken man.

And a funny feeling came that it is going to be hard to describe. It had something to do with the life in the horse and in me. Sometimes, these late years, I've thought maybe negroes would understand what I'm trying to talk about now better than any white man ever will. I mean something about men and animals, something between them, something that can perhaps only happen to a white man when he has slipped off his base a little, as I suppose I had then. I think maybe a lot of horsey people feel it sometimes though. It's something like this, maybe – do you suppose it could be that something we whites have got, and think such a lot of, and are so proud about, isn't much of any good after all?

It's something in us that wants to be big and grand and important maybe and won't let us just be, like a horse or a dog or a bird can. Let's say Pick-it-boy had won his race that day. He did that pretty often that summer. Well, he was neither proud, like I would have been in his place, or mean in one part of the inside of him either. He was just himself, doing something with a kind of simplicity. That's what Pick-it-boy was like and I got to feeling it in him as I walked with him slowly in the gathering darkness. I got inside him in some way I can't explain and he got inside me. Often we would stop walking for no cause and he would put his nose up against my face.

I wished he was a girl sometimes or that I was a girl and he was a man. It's an odd thing to say but it's a fact. Being with him that way, so long, and in such a quiet way, cured something in me a little. Often after an evening like that I slept all right and did not have the kind of dreams I've spoken about.

FORGIVING HORSES

The anger of bad bets flurries like
Spring snow in the grand stand.
All eyes are on the jockey
Down on all fours in the muck,
Sputtering rage at the shrill horse
Splayed painfully over the hurdle.

But I look at the suffering animal
And forgive it, as now I am able
To pardon the childhood memory
Of a young mare come suddenly
Around a barn to terrorize me,
Shoving me with its muzzle,
Putting its teeth hard on
My shoulder as I shrieked.

PAUL ZIMMER

Phil Bull, who died in 1989, is one of the few racing characters to whom the adjective 'legendary' can be justifiably applied. Founder of the Timeform organisation and the shrewdest brain the sport has produced this century, Bull was also a writer of great clarity and wit, who himself wrote many of the entries in Timeform's Best Horses *and* Racehorses *annuals, now the foundation stones of any racing library. His essay on Nasrullah from* Best Horses of 1943 *is characteristically trenchant.*

I made it pretty clear this time last year that I regarded Nasrullah as head and shoulders above the other colts of his age. I gave him a long and rather enthusiastic write up, and I fear that, in spite of his having failed in each of his classic ventures, in spite of his bad temper, his mulish antics, in spite of his exasperating unwillingness to do the job etc., etc., I fear that I am going to give him another write up. I know he doesn't deserve it, but I can't help it.

The rumours of Nasrullah's temperamental traits, to which I referred in my notes on him last year, proved to have only too painful a basis in fact. On not a single occasion last year did he visit the racecourse and leave it without his performance having some blemish upon it. His display on the way down to the post for the Chatteris Stakes was a disgrace. He refused to leave the paddock, he refused to break into a trot, he refused to respond to the blandishments of the friendly hack sent out on to the course to kid him; he refused to do anything except behave like a spoilt child. And all the time Gordon sat on his back, flapping the reins at him with a patience that would have done credit to Job. Could the catcalls and cries of derision which greeted this unthorough-bred-like behaviour have been heard by Nearco across at the Beech House Stud, and could their origin have been explained to him, it might have had a serious effect on his fertility. Why, he might have asked himself, should I put myself to the trouble and humiliation of siring good horses if they are to disport themselves in this degrading fashion? No doubt Gordon itched to give the brute a resounding crack across the quarters to let him know that the champion jockey was on his back. He must have been sorely tempted. If resistance to temptation strengthens the moral fibre, as the Christians say it does, Gordon must have felt a monument of moral hickory by the time he arrived at the post. Anyhow, he got there eventually, and set off back with the others. Gordon kept him behind as far as the Dip and then gave him his head. In a couple of shakes Nasrullah ran into a three lengths lead, where-upon he dropped his bit and veered away to the left allowing the pacemaker Response to run up to within half a length of him as they passed the post. The photographs of the finish shows that Gordon has given up riding, and Nasrullah has given up racing. Nasrullah gave up first, and he went by the post an unwilling rather than clever winner.

Blinkers were tried on him in the Two Thousand, and setting off to the post early, with his stable mate Baman to lead him, he was much more tractable. But his behaviour in the race was no better. Gordon had him tracking the leaders on the bit until coming down the hill into the Dip, where he gave him his head. So well was he going that in the ordinary way one would have expected him to go on and win comfortably. Instead, as soon as he struck the front his desire to race vanished. The sparkle went out of his stride; there was no response to Gordon's calls and he merely followed the others up the hill in listless fashion to finish fourth. No doubt it had come to his knowledge that I had obtained the very nice bet of 500 to 400 a place only about him! His display in the Derby was cut to the same pattern. When he struck the front running in the Dip he immediately signified his unwillingness to continue by swerving to the right, incidentally crowding Merchant Navy on to Pink Flower and ruining whatever chances these two might have had. Gordon kept him in the lead for a few strides, but he wasn't having any, and not until the race was almost over did he take hold of his bit again to run on and finish third.

To me, the root of Nasrullah's case is simply that he is a genuine racehorse only to the point where he finds himself in front. Long before the Derby was run – after Nasrullah's first race of the season in the Chatteris Stakes in fact – I had come to the firm conclusion that the only method of handling him which would give real prospects of success was the ultra patient method: nursing him until the very last moment before releasing his phenomenal speed in one short burst which would take him to the front so near the post that the race would be over before he was seized with the inevitable attack of reluctance. Of course, it's an easy matter to ride races from the stand, and one ought surely to think twice before offering criticism of a jockey who has the unenviable task of riding such a wayward animal as Nasrullah; but I cannot help wishing that Gordon had ridden the same race on him in the Derby and the Two Thousand as he rode on Chanda in the last race on Derby day. Rightly or wrongly, I must express the opinion that he would have been successful in *both* classics had he done so. Not in the St Leger, though. Here I believe Nasrullah's failure was due to the inability to stay the distance. Beary, who rode him on this occasion, had him well in the rear early on and brought him into a challenging position gradually, but when he called upon him for an effort after leaving the Dip there was nothing forthcoming. The horse never struck the front and although I do not know whether the jockey confirms my impressions I should say that he raced honestly enough but simply didn't have the necessary stamina.

His two other races Nasrullah won. In neither did he give a polished or pleasing performance. In the Caversham Stakes, prior to the St Leger, he consented to beat Triumvir a couple of lengths, giving him a mere four pounds. After going clear in a few strides on the hill he dropped his bit as usual and went by the post in a slovenly manner. Similarly in the Champion Stakes. Gordon waited on him longer this time than in any of his previous races. He allowed Kingsway to lead until half way up the hill before unloosing his challenge. Even so, Nasrullah's head went up, the fire went out of his stride as soon as he was clear, and Kingsway was going up to him again as the post was reached.

Well, there you are, that was Nasrullah as I saw him last year. You've only got to look at his racefigures, to see that he was a racehorse of exceptional ability. Personally, I have to announce that I still persist, with a pig-headed obstinacy equal only to that of Nasrullah himself, in the firm opinion that (up to $1\frac{1}{2}$ miles,) the son of Nearco was head and shoulders above his contemporaries *in ability*. Yes, I know that other qualities go to the making of a great racehorse – courage, determination, the will to race, tractability and so forth – I grant all that; my confession of belief in Nasrullah is confined to his ability. To say that he was a *model* thoroughbred would be tantamount to a libel on the breed; to say that he was a *great* racehorse, would be to ignore his failings; but to say that he *could have been* a great racehorse, if he had cared to, is quite a permissible expression of opinion.

His photograph shows a good head with small ears; a strong neck, well developed withers and excellent depth from withers to brisket; a fair shoulder and a fine, well ribbed-up body; plenty of muscle over the humerus, and full, well developed gaskins, strong straight hocks and pretty good legs, generally. A high class, quality colt, possessing also range and size. He is more impressive in the flesh than in his photograph. None of his rivals of last season could beat him in appearance and none possessed a more delightful action or more space devouring stride when at full stretch. He now stands at The Great Barton Stud under the management of Major Fleming at a fee of 198 sovs. If conformation and innate ability count for anything he may make the name for himself as a stallion which his unfortunate temperament prevented his making for himself as a racehorse.

Nasrullah did indeed make his name as a stallion, becoming one of the most influential sires of recent times. Among his offspring were Musidora, Never Say Die, the Preakness and Belmont Stakes winner Nashua, and Bald Eagle, as well as Never Bend, sire of Mill Reef, and Bold Ruler, sire of Secretariat.

A very different sort of racehorse is immortalised in Will H. Ogilvie's famous poem 'Steeplechasers'.

STEEPLECHASERS

Tucked away in winter quarters,
Gainsborough's sons and Buchan's daughters,
Blue of blood, clean-lined and handsome,
Priced beyond a prince's ransom,
Where no danger can befall them
Rest till next year's Classics call them;
And the limber-lean-of-head ones,
Hardy, hefty, humble-bred ones,
Booted, bandaged to the knee,
Ready for whate'er may be,
Gallant slaves and cheery martyrs,
Stand once more before the starters.

Piggotts, Masons, Leaders, Dullers
Witch the world in mud-splashed colours,
Brushing through the birchwood switches,
Cramming at the open ditches,
Grinning when the guard-rails rattle
In the fore-front of the battle.
Gordons, Anthonys and Reeses
Bow their heads against the breezes,
Hail upon their faces whipping,
Wet reins through their fingers slipping
As they drive their 'chasers crashing
Through the fence-tops, irons clashing.

So they forge through wind and weather
To the creak of straining leather
Lashing at the leaps together,
With the fluttering flags to guide them,

Taking what the Fates provide them,
Danger calling, Death beside them. –
'Tis a game beyond gainsaying
Made by gods for brave men's playing.

WILL H. OGILVIE

The Irish writer Percy French, perhaps best known nowadays for 'The Mountains of Mourne', wrote of a less gallant mount.

SWEET MARIE

I've a little racin' mare called Sweet Marie,
And the temper of a bear has Sweet Marie.
But I've backed the mare to win, and on her I've all my tin,
So we'll take a trial spin, Sweet Marie.

   Hould your hoult, Sweet Marie,
   If you bolt, Sweet Marie,
   Sure, you'll never win the Farmers' Cup for me;
   And if you don't pull it through, faith, I'm done and so are
      you,
   For I'll trade you off for glue, Sweet Marie.

Now, the colours that I chose for Sweet Marie
Were lavender and rose for Sweet Marie,
Och, but now, no thanks to you, sure I'm quite another hue,
For I'm only black and blue, Sweet Marie,
   Hould your hoult, Sweet Marie,
   If you bolt, Sweet Marie
   Sure you'll never win the Farmers' Cup for me,
   Every daisy in the dell ought to know me mighty well,
   For on every one I fell, Sweet Marie.

Now we're started for the Cup, my Sweet Marie
Weight for age and owners up, my Sweet Marie
Owners up just now I own, but the way you're waltzing roun'
Sure, 'twill soon be owners down, Sweet Marie.

   Hould your hoult, Sweet Marie:
   Pass the colt, Sweet Marie.

Och, you've gone and lost the Farmers' Cup for me.
You're a stayer too, I find: but you're not the proper kind
For you stay too far behind, Sweet Marie.

PERCY FRENCH

Fifty Years of My Life by Sir John Astley, published in 1894, is surely the most engaging of nineteenth-century Turf memoirs, and one of the most readable racing books ever written. Among Astley's enthusiasms so infectiously described in this book is his horse Drumhead, on whom he won a match against Caledon Alexander on the Newmarket July Course in 1879: 'I weighed 16 stone 6 lbs, and Alec 16 stones.' Drumhead won by three lengths.

Deary me! there was some cheering, and amid roars of laughter we shook hands. I know I hurried off to the luncheon tent for a glass, for what with the excitement, and the mighty effort of standing up in one's tiny stirrups for a mile and a half, I was real thirsty.

Astley's relationship with his mount found unusual expressions.

Good old Drumhead! he was the very kindest and quietest of horses. I once gave him some whisky before he ran at Shrewsbury, as I thought he didn't struggle quite as gamely as he ought, and the old boy liked the cordial so well, that he followed me round the paddock in hopes of another suck at the bottle . . .

To show the mutual confidence that existed between us, I have often sat on his quarters and smoked my baccy whilst he was laying down in his box.

But there are times when the racehorse, for all its beauty and grace, has less of a claim on the affections. On 25 April 1941 George Orwell wrote in his diary:

C, of my section of the Home Guard, a poulterer by trade but at present dealing in meat of all kinds, yesterday bought 20 zebras which are being sold off by the Zoo. Only for dog meat, presumably, not human consumption. It seems rather a waste . . . There are said to be still 2000 racehorses in England, each of which will be eating 10–15 lbs of grain a day, i.e. these brutes are devouring *every day* the equivalent of the bread ration of a division of troops.

Seeing old racehorses in their retirement can be one of the greatest pleasures for a racing fan. Sue Montgomery describes her single sighting of Brigadier Gerard in the flesh.

I saw the Brigadier's exploits only on television. Even the black-and-white images of nearly two decades age were enough to show something out of the ordinary, but my own, treasured, memory of the great horse came far later.

Two years ago I was staying at an hotel just outside Newmarket. My bedroom overlooked a small, walled paddock, the Brigadier's retirement home. He was then 19 and looked marvellous for his age.

One morning, with the first frost of winter, came the magic. The ground was white and the Brigadier was mooching stiffly about in the thin, fitful November dawn. Then suddenly, as I watched, he began to dance. He arched his neck and described a series of small circles, figures of eight and pirouettes at the trot and canter, tossing his head and pointing his toes on the glistening grass.

And as he played alone, motivated by something only he could sense, the years fell away. There, in an instant, was the grace, elegance and power that had carried him to victory 17 times, and I could see the magnificent young horse he once had been.

The moment passed, and Brigadier Gerard stood still again, dropped his head and began to graze. But it was a moment of pure delight, and one I shall never forget.

Racing Post, 8 November 1989

STALLION AND TEASER

For him, who is above preliminaries,
It is no more than the seigneurial

Raising of hooves round a mane,
A brief thrusting. He strolls off,
Lordly as the sun, indifferent now
To the mare, her bride's eyes dying.
But for that other, amiable,
Grey around the lip, who never
Quite made it, civilities
Of courtship are what he must settle for –
Eyes hazy with love-light, the nuzzle
Of arched necks, legs quivering
As if caressed by cool breezes. She bridles,
Looses her urine. And removed from her,
Pawing stubble in the distance,
He must comfort himself with a suitor's
Dwindling euphoria, remembering
Her shiver, sweat drying on his skin.

ALAN ROSS

AT GRASS

The eye can hardly pick them out
From the cold shade they shelter in,
Till wind distresses tail and mane;
Then one crops grass, and moves about
– The other seeming to look on –
And stands anonymous again.

Yet fifteen years ago, perhaps
Two dozen distances sufficed
To fable them: faint afternoons
Of Cups and Stakes and Handicaps,
Whereby their names were artificed
To inlay faded, classic Junes –

Silks at the start: against the sky
Numbers and parasols: outside,
Squadrons of empty cars, and heat,
And littered grass: then the long cry

Hanging unhushed till it subside
To stop-press columns on the street.

Do memories plague their ears like flies?
They shake their heads. Dusk brims the shadows.
Summer by summer all stole away,
The starting-gates, the crowds and cries –
All but the unmolesting meadows.
Almanacked, their names live; they

Have slipped their names, and stand at ease,
Or gallop for what must be joy,
And not a fieldglass sees them home,
Or curious stop-watch prophesies:
Only the groom, and the groom's boy,
With bridles in the evening come.

PHILIP LARKIN

---

*Although the horse you back may get stuffed, it falls to few to undergo a
more literal stuffing. One such was the great Australian champion Phar
Lap.*

PHAR LAP IN THE MELBOURNE MUSEUM

A masterpiece of the taxidermist's art,
Australia's top patrician stares
Gravely ahead at crowded emptiness.
As if alive, the lustre of dead hairs,
Lozenged liquid eyes, black nostrils
Gently flared, otter-satin coat declares
That death cannot visit in this thin perfection.

The democratic hero full of guile,
Noble, handsome, gentle Houyhnhnm
(In both Paddock and St Leger difference is
Lost in the welter of money) – to see him win
Men sold farms, rode miles in floods,
Stole money, locked up wives, somehow got in:
First away, he led the field and easily won.

It was his simple excellence to be best.
Tough men owned him, their minds beset
By stakes, bookies' doubles, crooked jocks.
He soon became a byword, public asset,
A horse with a nation's soul upon his back –
Australia's Ark of the Covenant, set
Before the people, perfect, loved like God.

And like God to be betrayed by friends.
Sent to America, he died of poisoned food.
In Australia children cried to hear the news
(This Prince of Orange knew no bad or good).
It was, as people knew, a plot of life:
To live in strength, to excel and die too soon,
So they drained his body and they stuffed his skin.

Twenty years later on Sunday afternoons
You still can't see him for the rubbing crowds.
He shares with Bradman and Ned Kelly some
Of the dirty jokes you still can't say out loud.
It is Australian innocence to love
The naturally excessive and be proud
Of a thoroughbred bay gelding who ran fast.

PETER PORTER

3

'Lunatics, criminals, idiots, charmers, bastards and exceptionally nice people'

The humans

There's lots of guys in this world with MBAs or BMWs, and many, probably, with both, but none of them ever thought to brush their hair before meeting a racehorse.

Thus country singer-cum-private detective Kinky Friedman, in Musical Chairs, *expressing the peculiar effect on some people of the closeness of racehorses. It is a commonplace that the people in racing command as much interest as the horses, if not more, and few writers have expressed this as graphically as Jeffrey Bernard.*

I once went to an evening meeting at Windsor, got absolutely pissed, lost every penny in my pocket, and had no idea how to get back to London after the last. I was almost the final person to leave the racecourse and, standing desolately in the car-park, I suddenly saw a beautiful white Rolls Royce slowly approaching. I stood in its way and signalled to it to stop. It stopped. The owner, as suave as a film-star, asked what he could do for me. I said, 'I'm pissed and potless. Will you please take me to the Dorchester immediately and buy me a drink.' I'd never seen him before and I've never seen him since, but he was absolutely charming. He recognised someone who'd done their bollocks and was feeling thirsty. He drove me straight to the American Bar and stood me a huge one. We never introduced ourselves. He just filled me up and then gave me the taxi fare to get back to Soho.

That is typical of what happens at the races. You wouldn't find it at a football game or a cricket match. The racing world is stuffed with lunatics, criminals, idiots, charmers, bastards and exceptionally nice people. When you're on form and don't mind losing a few notes, a day at the races is one of the most magical days you can imagine, and the lure of the ever-changing racing circus soon becomes irresistible. . . .

It's a fairly well-known fact that racing doesn't attract many grey people. Racing folk tend to be either the salt and mustard of the earth or they're utterly ghastly. But there used to be some wonderful-looking women at the racetrack. Where are they now? Discussing the serious shortage with a trainer at Newbury that day I was fascinated by the way – and it's simply a habit not an insult – he referred to them as though they were horses. I had observed this before though, come to think of it. I once asked Fred Winter what he thought of a certain trainer's mistress and he said, 'Oh, she's very moderate.' The trainer I spoke to that Saturday described one woman there as being 'of little account'. My day ended with buying a drink for one whom Mr Winter and his colleagues would describe as 'Promising, useful, scope'.

Although no writer has created a more memorable collection of racetrack characters than Damon Runyon, his greatest philosophical insight comes in 'A Nice Price', a story concerning betting not on horses but on the Harvard–Yale boat race. Sam the Gonoph has learned that one book-maker is quoting 3–1 on that Yale win the race:

'I do not know anything about boat races,' Sam says, 'and the Yales may figure as you say, but nothing between human beings is one to three. In fact,' Sam the Gonoph says, 'I long ago come to the conclusion that all life is six to five against.'

Runyon's story 'Pick The Winner', published in the 1938 collection Furthermore, *is characteristic of his appeal.*

PICK THE WINNER

What I am doing in Miami associating with such a character as Hot Horse Herbie is really quite a long story, and it goes back to one cold night when I am sitting in Mindy's restaurant on Broadway thinking what a cruel world it is, to be sure, when in comes Hot Horse Herbie and his ever-loving fiancée, Miss Cutie Singleton.

This Hot Horse Herbie is a tall, skinny guy with a most depressing kisser, and he is called Hot Horse Herbie because he can always tell you about a horse that is so hot it is practically on fire, a hot horse being a horse that is all readied up to win a race, although sometimes Herbie's hot horses turn out to be so cold they freeze everybody within fifty miles of them.

He is following the races almost since infancy, to hear him tell it. In fact, old Captain Duhaine, who has charge of the Pinkertons around the race tracks, says he remembers Hot Horse Herbie as a little child, and that even then Herbie is a hustler, but of course Captain Duhaine does not care for Hot Horse Herbie, because he claims Herbie is nothing but a tout, and a tout is something that is most repulsive to Captain Duhaine and all other Pinkertons.

A tout is a guy who goes around a race track giving out tips on the races, if he can find anybody who will listen to his tips, especially suckers, and a tout is nearly always broke. If he is not broke, he is by no means a tout, but a handicapper, and is respected by one and all, including the Pinkertons, for knowing so much about the races.

Well, personally, I have nothing much against Hot Horse Herbie, no matter what Captain Duhaine says he is, and I certainly have nothing against Herbie's ever-loving fiancée, Miss Cutie Singleton. In fact, I am rather in favour of Miss Cutie Singleton, because in all the years I know her, I wish to say I never catch Miss Cutie Singleton out of line, which is more than I can say of many other dolls I know.

She is a little, good-natured blonde doll, and by no means a crow, if you care for blondes, and some people say that Miss Cutie Singleton is pretty smart, although I never can see how this can be, as I figure a smart doll will never have any truck with a guy like Hot Horse Herbie, for Herbie is by no means a provider.

But for going on ten years, Miss Cutie Singleton and Hot Horse Herbie are engaged, and it is well known to one and all that they are to be married as soon as Herbie makes a scratch. In fact, they are almost married in New Orleans in 1928, when Hot Horse Herbie beats a good thing for eleven C's, but the tough part of it is the good thing is in the first race, and naturally Herbie bets the eleven C's right back on another good thing in the next race, and this good thing blows, so Herbie winds up with nothing but the morning line and is unable to marry Miss Cutie Singleton at this time.

Then again in 1929 at Churchill Downs, Hot Horse Herbie has a nice bet on Naishapur to win the Kentucky Derby, and he is so sure Naishapur cannot miss that the morning of the race he sends Miss Cutie Singleton out to pick a wedding ring. But Naishapur finishes second, so naturally Hot Horse Herbie is unable to buy the ring, and of course Miss Cutie Singleton does not wish to be married without a wedding ring.

They have another close call in 1931 at Baltimore when Hot Horse Herbie figures Twenty Grand a standout in the Preakness, and in fact is so sure of his figures that he has Miss Cutie Singleton go down to the city hall to find out what a marriage licence costs. But of course Twenty Grand does not win the Preakness, so the information Miss Cutie Singleton obtains is of no use to them and anyway Hot Horse Herbie says he can beat the price on marriage licences in New York.

However, there is no doubt but what Hot Horse Herbie and Miss Cutie Singleton are greatly in love, although I hear rumours that for a couple of years past Miss Cutie Singleton is getting somewhat impatient about Hot Horse Herbie not making a scratch as soon as he claims he is going to when he first meets up with her in Hot Springs in 1923.

In fact, Miss Cutie Singleton says if she knows Hot Horse Herbie is going to be so long delayed in making his scratch she will never consider becoming engaged to him, but will keep her job as a manicurist at the Arlington Hotel, where she is not doing bad, at that.

It seems that the past couple of years Miss Cutie Singleton is taking to looking longingly at the little houses in the towns they pass through going from one race track to another, and especially at little white houses with green shutters and yards and vines all around and about, and saying it must be nice to be able to live in such places instead of in a suitcase.

But of course Hot Horse Herbie does not put in with her on these ideas, because Herbie knows very well if he is placed in a little white house for more than fifteen minutes the chances are he will lose his mind, even if the house has green shutters.

Personally, I consider Miss Cutie Singleton somewhat ungrateful for thinking of such matters after all the scenery Hot Horse Herbie lets her see in the past ten years. In fact, Herbie lets her see practically all the scenery there is in this country, and some in Canada, and all she has to do in return for all this courtesy is to occasionally get out a little crystal ball and deck of cards and let on she is a fortune teller when things are going especially tough for Herbie.

Of course Miss Cutie Singleton cannot really tell fortunes, or she will be telling Hot Horse Herbie's fortune, and maybe her own, too, but I hear she is better than a raw hand at making people believe she is telling their fortunes, especially old maids who think they are in love, or widows who are looking to snare another husband and other such characters.

Well, anyway, when Hot Horse Herbie and his ever-loving fiancée come into Mindy's, he gives me a large hello, and so does Miss Cutie Singleton, so I hello them right back, and Hot Horse Herbie speaks to me as follows:

'Well,' Herbie says, 'we have some wonderful news for you. We are going to Miami,' he says, 'and soon we will be among the waving palms, and revelling in the warm waters of the Gulf Stream.'

Now of course this is a lie, because while Hot Horse Herbie is in Miami many times, he never revels in the warm waters of the Gulf Stream, because he never has time for such a thing, what with hustling around the race tracks in the daytime, and around the dog tracks and the gambling joints at night, and in fact I will lay plenty of six to five Hot Horse Herbie cannot even point in the direction of the Gulf Stream when he is in Miami, and I will give him three points, at that.

But naturally what he says gets me to thinking how pleasant it is in Miami in the winter, especially when it is snowing up north, and a guy does not have a flogger to keep himself warm, and I am commencing to feel very envious of Hot Horse Herbie and his ever-loving fiancée when he says like this:

'But,' Herbie says, 'our wonderful news for you is not about us going. It is about you going,' he says. 'We already have our railroad tickets,' he says, 'as Miss Cutie Singleton, my ever-loving fiancée here, saves up three C's for her hope chest the past summer, but when it comes to deciding between a hope chest and Miami, naturally she chooses Miami, because,' Herbie says, 'she claims she does not have enough hope left to fill a chest. Miss Cutie Singleton is always kidding,' he says.

'Well now,' Herbie goes on, 'I just run into Mr Edward Donlin, the undertaker, and it seems that he is sending a citizen of Miami back home to-morrow night, and of course you know,' he says, 'that Mr Donlin must purchase two railroad tickets for this journey, and as the citizen has no one else to accompany him, I got to thinking of you. He is a very old and respected citizen of Miami,' Herbie says, 'although of course,' he says, 'he is no longer with us, except maybe in spirit.'

Of course such an idea is most obnoxious to me, and I am very indignant that Hot Horse Herbie can even think I will travel in this manner, but he gets to telling me that the old and respected citizen of Miami that Mr Donlin is sending back home is a great old guy in his day, and that for all anybody knows he will appreciate having company on the trip, and about this time Big Nig, the crap shooter, comes into Mindy's leaving the door open behind him so that a blast of cold air hits me, and makes me think more than somewhat of the waving palms and the warm waters of the Gulf Stream.

So the next thing I know, there I am in Miami with Hot Horse Herbie, and it is the winter of 1931, and everybody now knows that this is the winter when the suffering among the horse players in Miami is practically horrible. In fact, it is worse than it is in the winter of 1930. In fact, the suffering is so intense that many citizens are wondering if it will do any good to appeal to Congress for relief for the horse players, but The Dancer says he hears Congress needs a little relief itself.

Hot Horse Herbie and his ever-loving fiancée, Miss Cutie Singleton, and me have rooms in a little hotel on Flagler Street, and while it is nothing but a fleabag, and we are doing the landlord a favour by living there, it is surprising how much fuss he makes any time anybody happens to be a little short of the rent. In fact, the landlord hollers and yells so much any time anybody is a little short of the rent that he becomes a very great nuisance to me, and I have half a notion to move, only I cannot think of any place to move to. Furthermore, the landlord will not let me move unless I pay him all I owe him, and I am not in a position to take care of this matter at the moment.

Of course I am not very dirty when I first come in as far as having any potatoes is concerned, and I start off at once having a little bad luck. It goes this way a while, and then it gets worse, and sometimes I wonder if I will not be better off if I buy myself a rope and end it all on a palm tree in the park on Biscayne Boulevard. But the only trouble with the idea is I do not have the price of a rope, and anyway I hear most of the palm trees in the park are already spoken for by guys who have the same notion.

And bad off as I am, I am not half as bad off as Hot Horse Herbie, because he has his ever-loving fiancée, Miss Cutie Singleton, to think of, especially as Miss Cutie Singleton is putting up quite a beef about not having any recreation, and saying if she only has the brains God gives geese she will break off their engagement at once and find some guy who can show her a little speed, and she seems to have no sympathy whatever for Hot Horse Herbie when he tells her how many tough snoots he gets beat at the track.

But Herbie is very patient with her, and tells her it will not be long now, because the law of averages is such that his luck is bound to change, and he suggests to Miss Cutie Singleton that she get the addresses of a few preachers in case they wish to locate one in a hurry. Furthermore, Hot Horse Herbie suggests to Miss Cutie Singleton that she get out the old crystal ball and her deck of cards, and hang out her sign as a fortune teller while they are waiting for the law of averages to start working for him, although personally I doubt if she will be able to get any business telling fortunes in Miami at this time because everybody in Miami seems to know what their fortune is already.

Now I wish to say that after we arrive in Miami I have very little truck with Hot Horse Herbie, because I do not approve of some of his business methods, and furthermore I do not wish Captain Duhaine and his Pinkertons at my hip all the time, as I never permit myself to get out of line in any respect, or anyway not much. But of course I see Hot Horse Herbie at the track every day, and one day I see him talking to the most innocent-looking guy I ever see in all my life.

He is a tall, spindling guy with a soft brown Vandyke beard, and soft brown hair, and no hat, and he is maybe forty-odd, and wears rumpled white flannel pants, and a rumpled sports coat, and big horn cheaters, and he is smoking a pipe that you can smell a block away. He is such a guy as looks as if he does not know what time it is, and furthermore he does not look as if he has a quarter, but I can see by the way Hot Horse Herbie is warming his ear that Herbie figures him to have a few potatoes.

Furthermore, I never know Hot Horse Herbie to make many bad guesses in this respect, so I am not surprised when I see the guy pull out a long flat leather from the inside pocket of his coat and weed Herbie a bank-note. Then I see Herbie start for the mutuels windows, but I am quite astonished when I see that he makes for a two-dollar window. So I follow Hot Horse Herbie to see what this is all about, because it is certainly not like Herbie to dig up a guy with a bank roll and then only promote him for a deuce.

When I get hold of Herbie and ask him what this means, he laughs, and says to me like this:

'Well,' he says, 'I am just taking a chance with the guy. He may be a prospect, at that,' Herbie says. 'You never can tell about people. This is the first bet he ever makes in his life, and furthermore,' Herbie says, 'he does not wish to bet. He says he knows one horse can beat another, and what of it? But,' Herbie says, 'I give him a good story, so he finally goes for the deuce. I think he is a college professor somewhere,' Herbie says, 'and he is only wandering around the track out of curiosity. He does not know a soul here. Well,' Herbie says, 'I put him on a real hot horse, and if he wins maybe he can be developed into something. You know,' Herbie says, 'they can never rule you off for trying.'

Well, it seems that the horse Herbie gives the guy wins all right and at a fair price, and Herbie lets it go at that for the time being, because he gets hold of a real good guy, and cannot be bothering with guys who only bet deuces. But every day the professor is at the track and I often see him wandering through the crowds, puffing at his old stinkaroo and looking somewhat bewildered.

I get somewhat interested in the guy myself, because he seems so much out of place, but I wish to say I never think of promoting him in any respect, because this is by no means my dodge, and finally one day I get to talking to him and he seems just as innocent as he looks. He is a professor at Princeton, which is a college in New Jersey, and his name is Woodhead, and he has been very sick, and is in Florida to get well, and he thinks the track mob is the greatest show he ever sees, and is sorry he does not study this business a little earlier in life.

Well, personally, I think he is a very nice guy, and he seems to have quite some knowledge of this and that and one thing and another, although he is so ignorant about racing that it is hard to believe he is a college guy.

Even if I am a hustler, I will just as soon try to hustle Santa Claus as Professor Woodhead, but by and by Hot Horse Herbie finds things getting very desperate indeed, so he picks up the professor again and starts working on him, and one day he gets him to go for another deuce, and then for a fin, and both times the horses Herbie gives him are winners, which Herbie says just goes to show you the luck he is playing in, because when he has a guy who is willing to make a bet for him, he cannot pick one to finish fifth.

You see, the idea is when Hot Horse Herbie gives a guy a horse he expects the guy to bet for him, too, or maybe give him a piece of what he wins, but of course Herbie does not mention this to Professor Woodhead as yet, because the professor does not bet enough to bother with, and anyway Herbie is building him up by degrees, although if you ask me, it is going to be slow work, and finally Herbie himself admits as much, and says to me like this:

'It looks as if I will have to blast,' Herbie says. 'The professor is a nice guy, but,' he says, 'he does not loosen so easy. Furthermore,' Herbie says, 'he is very dumb about horses. In fact,' he says, 'I never see a guy so hard to educate, and if I do not like him personally, I will have no part of him whatever. And besides liking him personally,' Herbie says, 'I get a gander into that leather he carries the other day, and what do I see,' he says, 'but some large, coarse notes in there back to back.'

Well, of course this is very interesting news, even to me, because large, coarse notes are so scarce in Miami at this time that if a guy runs into one he takes it to a bank to see if it is counterfeit before he changes it, and even then he will scarcely believe it.

I get to thinking that if a guy such as Professor Woodhead can be going around with large, coarse notes in his possession, I make a serious mistake in not becoming a college professor myself, and naturally after this I treat Professor Woodhead with great respect.

Now what happens one evening, but Hot Horse Herbie and his ever-loving fiancée, Miss Cutie Singleton, and me are in a little grease joint on Second Street putting on the old hot tripe à la Creole, which is a very pleasant dish, and by no means expensive, when who wanders in but Professor Woodhead.

Naturally Herbie calls him over to our table and introduces Professor Woodhead to Miss Cutie Singleton, and Professor Woodhead sits there with us looking at Miss Cutie Singleton with great interest, although Miss Cutie Singleton is at this time feeling somewhat peevish because it is the fourth evening hand running she has to eat tripe à la Creole, and Miss Cutie Singleton does not care for tripe under any circumstances.

She does not pay any attention whatever to Professor Woodhead, but finally Hot Horse Herbie happens to mention that the professor is from Princeton, and then Miss Cutie Singleton looks at the professor, and says to him like this:

'Where is this Princeton?' she says. 'Is it a little town?'

'Well,' Professor Woodhead says, 'Princeton is in New Jersey, and it is by no means a large town, but,' he says, 'it is thriving.'

'Are there any little white houses in this town?' Miss Cutie Singleton asks. 'Are there any little white houses with green shutters and vines all around and about?'

'Why,' Professor Woodhead says, looking at her with more interest than somewhat, 'you are speaking of my own house,' he says. 'I live in a little white house with green shutters and vines all around and about, and,' he says, 'it is a nice place to live in, at that, although it is sometimes a little lonesome, as I live there all by myself unless,' he says, 'you wish to count old Mrs Bixby, who keeps house for me. I am a bachelor,' he says.

Well, Miss Cutie Singleton does not have much to say after this, although it is only fair to Miss Cutie Singleton to state that for a doll, and especially a blonde doll, she is never so very gabby, at that, but she watches Professor Woodhead rather closely, as Miss Cutie Singleton never before comes in contact with anybody who lives in a little white house with green shutters.

Finally we get through with the hot tripe à la Creole and walk around to the fleabag where Hot Horse Herbie and Miss Cutie Singleton and me are residing, and Professor Woodhead walks around with us. In fact, Professor Woodhead walks with Miss Cutie Singleton, while Hot Horse Herbie walks with me, and Hot Horse Herbie is telling me that he has the very best thing of his entire life in the final race at Hialeah the next day, and he is expressing great regret that he does not have any potatoes to bet on this thing, and does not know where he can get any potatoes.

It seems that he is speaking of a horse by the name of Breezing Along, which is owned by a guy by the name of Moose Tassell, who is a citizen of Chicago, and who tells Hot Horse Herbie that the only way Breezing Along can lose the race is to have somebody shoot him at the quarter pole, and of course nobody is shooting horses at the quarter pole at Hialeah, though many citizens often feel like shooting horses at the half.

Well, by this time we get to our fleabag, and we all stand there talking when Professor Woodhead speaks as follows:

'Miss Cutie Singleton informs me,' he says, 'that she dabbles somewhat in fortune telling. Well,' Professor Woodhead says, 'this is most interesting to me, because I am by no means sceptical of fortune telling. In fact,' he says, 'I make something of a study of the matter, and there is no doubt in my mind that certain human beings *do* have the faculty of foretelling future events with remarkable accuracy.'

Now I wish to say one thing for Hot Horse Herbie, and this is that he is a quick-thinking guy when you put him up against a situation that calls for quick thinking, for right away he speaks up and says like this:

'Why, Professor,' he says, 'I am certainly glad to hear you make this statement, because,' he says, 'I am a believer in fortune telling myself. As a matter of fact, I am just figuring on having Miss Cutie Singleton look into her crystal ball and see if she can make out anything on a race that is coming up to-morrow, and which has me greatly puzzled, what with being undecided between a couple of horses.'

Well, of course, up to this time Miss Cutie Singleton does not have any idea she is to look into any crystal ball for a horse, and furthermore, it is the first time in his life Hot Horse Herbie ever asks her to look into the crystal ball for anything whatever, except to make a few bobs for them to eat off, because Herbie by no means believes in matters of this nature.

But naturally Miss Cutie Singleton is not going to display any astonishment, and when she says she will be very glad to oblige, Professor Woodhead speaks up and says he will be glad to see this crystal gazing come off, which makes it perfect for Hot Horse Herbie.

So we all go upstairs to Miss Cutie Singleton's room, and the next thing anybody knows there she is with her crystal ball, gazing into it with both eyes.

Now Professor Woodhead is taking a deep interest in the proceedings, but of course Professor Woodhead does not hear what Hot Horse Herbie tells Miss Cutie Singleton in private, and as far as this is concerned neither do I, but Herbie tells me afterwards that he tells her to be sure and see a breeze blowing in the crystal ball. So by and by, after gazing into the ball a long time, Miss Cutie Singleton speaks in a low voice as follows:

'I seem to see trees bending to the ground under the force of a great wind,' Miss Cutie Singleton says. 'I see houses blown about by the wind,' she says. 'Yes,' Miss Cutie Singleton says, 'I see pedestrians struggling along and shivering in the face of this wind, and I see waves driven high on a beach and boats tossed about like paper cups. In fact,' Miss Singleton says, 'I seem to see quite a blow.'

Well, then, it seems that Miss Cutie Singleton can see no more, but Hot Horse Herbie is greatly excited by what she sees already, and he says like this:

'It means this horse Breezing Along,' he says. 'There can be no doubt about it. Professor,' he says, 'here is the chance of your lifetime. The horse will be not less than six to one,' he says. 'This is the spot to bet a gob, and,' he says, 'the place to bet it is downtown with a bookmaker at the opening price, because there will be a ton of money for the horse in the machines. Give me five C's,' Hot Horse Herbie says, 'and I will bet four for you, and one for me.'

Well, Professor Woodhead seems greatly impressed by what Miss Cutie Singleton sees in the crystal ball, but of course taking a guy from a finnif to five C's is carrying him along too fast, especially when Herbie explains that five C's is five hundred dollars, and naturally the professor does not care to bet any such money as this. In fact, the professor does not seem anxious to bet more than a sawbuck, tops, but Herbie finally moves him up to bet a yard, and of this yard twenty-five bobs is running for Hot Horse Herbie, as Herbie explains to the professor that a remittance he is expecting from his New York bankers fails him.

The next day Herbie takes the hundred bucks and bets it with Gloomy Gus downtown, for Herbie really has great confidence in the horse.

We are out to the track early in the afternoon and the first guy we run into is Professor Woodhead, who is very much excited. We speak to him, and then we do not see him again all day.

Well, I am not going to bother telling you the details of the race, but this horse Breezing Along is nowhere. In fact, he is so far back that I do not recollect seeing him finish, because by the time the third horse in the field crosses the line, Hot Horse Herbie and me are on our way back to town, as Herbie does not feel that he can face Professor Woodhead at such a time as this. In fact, Herbie does not feel that he can face anybody, so we go to a certain spot over on Miami Beach and remain there drinking beer until a late hour, when Herbie happens to think of his ever-loving fiancée, Miss Cutie Singleton, and how she must be suffering from a lack of food, so we return to our fleabag so Herbie can take Miss Cutie Singleton to dinner.

But he does not find Miss Cutie Singleton. All he finds from her is a note, and in this note Miss Cutie Singleton says like this: 'Dear Herbie,' she says, 'I do not believe in long engagements any more, so Professor Woodhead and I are going to Palm Beach to be married to-night, and are leaving for Princeton, New Jersey, at once, where I am going to live in a little white house with green shutters and vines all around and about. Good-bye, Herbie,' the note says. 'Do not eat any bad fish. Respectfully, Mrs Professor Woodhead.'

Well, naturally this is most surprising to Hot Horse Herbie, but I never hear him mention Miss Cutie Singleton or Professor Woodhead again until a couple of weeks later when he shows me a letter from the professor.

It is quite a long letter, and it seems that Professor Woodhead wishes to apologize, and naturally Herbie has a right to think that the professor is going to apologize for marrying his ever-loving fiancée, Miss Cutie Singleton, as Herbie feels he has an apology coming on this account.

But what the professor seems to be apologizing about is not being able to find Hot Horse Herbie just before the Breezing Along race to explain a certain matter that is on his mind.

'It does not seem to me,' the professor says, as near as I can remember the letter, 'that the name of your selection is wholly adequate as a description of the present Mrs Professor Woodhead's wonderful vision in the crystal ball, so,' he says, 'I examine the programme further, and finally discover what I believe to be the name of the horse meant by the vision, and I wager two hundred dollars on this horse, which turns out to be the winner at ten to one, as you may recall. It is in my mind,' the professor says, 'to send you some share of the proceeds, inasmuch as we are partners in the original arrangement, but the present Mrs Woodhead disagrees with my view, so all I can send you is an apology, and best wishes.'

Well, Hot Horse Herbie cannot possibly remember the name of the winner of any race as far back as this, and neither can I, but we go over to the Herald office and look at the files, and what is the name of the winner of the Breezing Along race but Mistral, and when I look in the dictionary to see what this word means, what does it mean but a violent, cold and dry northerly wind.

And of course I never mention to Hot Horse Herbie or anybody else that I am betting on another horse in this race myself, and the name of the horse I am betting on is Leg Show, for how do I know for certain that Miss Cutie Singleton is not really seeing in the crystal ball just such a blow as she describes?

THE HORSE

George Eliot was so like a horse
That bookies on the Gatwick course
Shouted the odds against her when
She came there with some gentlemen;
And there was always quite a stir
When punters put their shirt on her.

But doubt creeps in. 'The Mill on the Floss'
Was never written by a hoss.

BEACHCOMBER (J. B. Morton)

Raymond Glendinning
Though not quite sure what was winning,
Had definitely seen
That the course was wide and green.

MICHAEL SILLEY

*That clerihew depends on mis-spelling the name of Raymond Glenden-
ning. A later and much greater race commentator is Peter O'Sullevan,
whose voice has been inextricably linked with most of the big racing
occasions of recent memory. In 1961 he wrote the following caprice for*
Cope's Racegoers' Encyclopaedia, *an annual published by the bookmaking firm run by Alfred Cope.*

A HUNDRED MONKEYS

If it hadn't been for Alfred Cope I would have abandoned the idea
on the spot. There was still time. And apprehension was rapidly
getting the better part of valour.

I mean anyone who tries to tip winners most days of the week
can make a big enough fool of himself already without trying to
ride one. Especially if his disability as a horseman is on a par with
mine. And lack of skill apart, as if this wasn't enough, there
was the no slight matter of excessive weight – represented by an
undesirable frontage, fostered more by the need for consolatory
than self-congratulatory refreshment.

'Poor form of amateur rider'; I could visualise my dear colleagues' headings already. I was resolved. I would withdraw. After
all, what was a £25 fine compared with the alternative self-
inflicted indignity?

I would diet, practise assiduously, and postpone the whole venture until better qualified. Meanwhile I was indisposed.

It was while walking to the weighing-room to put resolution
into effect that I met Mr Cope. Removing his horn-rimmed spec-

tacles, as if they were no longer trustworthy, he confessed – as though apologising to himself – that he had read my column that morning. And he had inferred, no doubt mistakenly, that I was to ride in a race here at Epsom this very afternoon.

'I am,' I said, his conciliatory tone suddenly dispelling caution, 'I am'.

Mr Cope's composed reaction was such as can only be achieved by one inured to shock by a lifetime's experience of the racing world. With masterly diplomacy – suggesting simultaneously an obligation to place the House of Cope at a disadvantage and a reluctance to part a client from his money – he said, 'You can have 100–1 if you would like a bet'.

'Monkeys', I remember replying with hilarious abandon, 'a hundred monkeys'.

Thus committed, events developed so swiftly as to defy coherent recollection. There was the agony of apprehension in the dressing room as perspiring jockey's valet, Ernie Hales, requested 'try holding your breath' – I hadn't exhaled for three minutes – as he strove to fasten the top button of my breeches... There was Scobie Breasley's tender enquiry as to the present rates for passenger freight insurance.

I remember wishing I knew the answer to the child's query – 'what's that one going to do, Mummy?' – during my uncomfortable progress, on wafer thin soles, over the hot tarmac between weighing-room and waiting car... the voice of ITV paddock commentator Robin Hastings 'they are all very calm here except Peter O'Sullevan who is sweating freely'... Cyril Mitchell's request for 'the other leg' before he deftly manoeuvred me into the saddle. And the shock of landing on it.

I remember Alec Marsh's gleeful 'I hope you will find no grounds for criticising the start'... and the reflection that the cry 'they're off' might have singular significance. But it didn't. We started 'on terms' as they say.

After two furlongs I'd resolved to give up smoking; after half a mile to forswear drink and, approaching Tattenham Corner, to give up riding. But not for nothing was I familiar with *The Rae Johnstone Story*. I recalled how he assessed the opposition at this stage and I looked up to count five white behinds ahead. Fool I was not to have worn binoculars, instead of goggles, to bring them closer. But my gallant partner, eager to be home and shed his burden, was doing that. Each time I switched numb fingers to a new grip – if only they'd plaited the reins instead of his mane – we overtook another.

Now I knew all the sensations of being a jellyfish. One to beat and we were upsides. Such a hive of desperate activity too (surely Sir Gordon had retired?) and I remembered how I had praised jockeys for sitting 'mouse-still' on a dying partner. Here was a unique situation. It was the rider who was dying. And victory so near. I pinched myself to affirm reality, missed and evidently tweaked my partner. For he lunged at the line, placing our unity in further peril in the process, so that when I heard the loudspeaker announcement 'photo-finish', I knew we'd won.

Considering that I had beaten most of their naps, I must say my colleagues on the Press put on a very brave show. I had never experienced such an unrestrained feeling of affection for all my fellow creatures – though I must say I thought the *Daily Sketch*'s Norman Pegg could have phrased his question – 'have you ever been on a horse before in your life?' – with more becoming tact.

Geoffrey Gilbey had, he said, taken photographs of me 'in a great variety of positions'. I thought Lester Piggott was overdoing it a bit when he observed, drily, 'It's a good thing for the rest of us you can't do under twelve stone'.

And I never heard the end of Lord Rosebery's remark which began 'Well you may not be much of a writer but . . .' because at that moment an imperious tap on the shoulder commanded my attention. This was surely the ultimate accolade – an invitation to the Royal Box. Probably it was the Duke himself. I looked up expectantly. But he wasn't the Duke of Edinburgh and he looked very like my sports editor, Bob Findlay. 'Wake up,' he said. 'Wake up, you've got ten minutes to turn in some "copy" '.

Well, I suppose that's as near as I'll get to a hundred monkeys. But as Mr Cope reflected, 'It would have been very annoying if the Tote had paid 200/1'.

Jack Leach, who won the Two Thousand Guineas on Adam's Apple in 1927, wrote one of the great racing books – and gave it the best title of any book ever published – in Sods I Have Cut on the Turf, *published in 1961. His assessment of the jockeys he rode against is worth recalling.*

It is very difficult to decide which was the greatest feat of jockey-ship I ever saw. There were so many great ones. Steve Donoghue's perfect ride on Humorist in the Derby will always stick in my memory – the way he nursed that frail horse with the big heart, and slipped through on the inside at the critical moment. Humorist died soon afterwards, Steve has gone, and so has the money I won on them. They were all three wonderful while they lasted.

Sometimes when I feel like criticising the jockeys riding today, I first repeat to myself a quotation from Dickens: 'Stranger, pause and ask thyself the question, Canst thou do likewise? If not, with a blush retire.'

Steve was of course a genius as a jockey. Moreover, he was a great charmer, altogether irresponsible, and sometimes irritating, although one always ended up laughing at the peculiar things he did. On one occasion he invited me to dine at the Savoy, and we had just started to examine the menu when Steve was called to the telephone. As he left the table he said, 'I'll be back in a minute.' I next saw him ten days later in Manchester.

I gave up travelling to the race meetings with him; it was too nerve-racking. He hardly ever caught a train until it was on the move, and travelled in the guard's van with a first class ticket more often than not, as he would hop on at the last moment, and then stay talking to the guard until he reached his destination. I remember once having booked a sleeper for Steve from King's Cross to Glasgow when we were going to ride at Ayr. Brownie Carslake, Frank Bullock and Jim Malone had all also booked him one. Steve did not arrive at all, but we found him at the Station Hotel at Glasgow when we got there. Having four sleepers booked at King's Cross he had gone to St Pancras, beat us to Scotland, and said he had slept very well indeed.

Nothing seemed to worry him, and he didn't know what nerves meant. That is why I think Steve was at his best on the big occasions – especially in the Derby. And Steve wasn't lucky, except with his weight. He had to fight his way to the top.

When Steve was on top of the list there were many great jockeys in opposition. I rode some hundreds of races against them all, and always thought Frank Bullock was the best of a good lot. But I was wrong; Gordon Richards made himself from a smash-and-grab rider as a youngster into the greatest jockey the world has ever known. He could *always* do things in a race that other top class jockeys could only do *sometimes*. In fact he had something the others hadn't got. Results count, and there is no doubt that Gordon, by his determination, touch, balance, quickness and all round ability, was the best. The best jockey is the one that makes the fewest mistakes, and Gordon made very few.

Leach described George Lambton's Men and Horses I Have Known, *published in 1924, as 'the best book I have ever read on racing', a valuation which many have shared. Certainly Lambton's work is unparalleled as a description of the racing scene around the turn of the century, and is especially interesting on the 'American invasion' then taking place and on the character and skills of its most famous embodiment, the jockey Tod Sloan.*

Huggins told me some interesting facts concerning the origin of the present style of riding. In the old days there used to be a lot of what they called 'Up Country' race meetings in America. These were very primitive affairs with partially untrained horses and inexperienced riders competing for the races. But often a useful horse was to be picked up at these meetings, and Huggins used to make a practice of sending some good old plater round the country. If anything beat him he would buy it, bring it home, where he usually found that good training and riding would work immense improvement. Then there came a time when the country people began putting up nigger boys on these horses. Huggins, having bought two or three horses that had won, and had been ridden by black boys, took them home, but, instead of finding they were improved by his training, they turned out not to be so good as when he bought them. This puzzled him considerably, and he could not make it out. Then one day, having bought a horse, the black boy who rode him begged to be bought too, as he wanted to go with his horse. Huggins, liking the look of his face, agreed to take the boy. When he got home, he tried his new purchase, and he was beaten easily by the very horse he had defeated up country. The black boy went to Huggins and said, 'You let me ride, you see what will happen'; so the experiment was tried, and the Darkie rolled home. To make a long story short, whatever Huggins put the boy up on was sure to win. It may not be generally known that the American jockeys in those days, who I believe were most beautiful horsemen, rode with even longer stirrups and sat more upright than the English. The black boys got their peculiar seat in this way. No one took the trouble to teach them to ride, they were thrown up on some old broncho with only a rug instead of a saddle, and they used to catch hold of the mane and hang on the best way they could until they had found their balance. You have only to picture the scene in your eye and you will see the origin of the present seat. Huggins soon tumbled to this, and to the advantage it gave the horses. There you will find the beginning of the present style of riding. You cannot oppose it, but you cannot like it. It has spoilt much of the beauty of race riding, but it has come to stay, and we must make the best of it . . .

There is no doubt that the 'American invasion' taught us in England a lot, especially in regard to the plating of horses. Their racing plates were far better made and lighter than ours. I remember Huggins telling me once in July that, in his opinion, having American plates on instead of English made the difference of at least four lengths in a mile race. He added that he would rather run his horse without shoes at all than in English ones. This so impressed me that I asked Sloan to cable to America ordering a box of these plates to be sent over. Meanwhile I ran several of my horses without shoes, with considerable success, but to do this you must have a horse with particularly good feet, and the going must be perfect. I did not get my American plates until the First October Meeting at Newmarket. I was running a sharp little two-year-old called Handspike, belonging to my brother Colonel Charles Lambton; Sloan was riding her.

When I told him that I thought she might just win he said, 'I wish she had our plates on.' 'So she has,' I replied, 'for they arrived last night.' The little man fairly jumped, and, saying 'Please excuse me, I have forgotten something in the weighing room,' he ran off, presumably to get his money on. Having found what he wanted, he came back declaring that he was sure to win, and so he did, beating a field of eighteen by two lengths.

The Americans also taught us that open doors and cool stables were far better than the hot-house atmosphere usually to be found in English stables at that time.

It was Sloan's misfortune to be always surrounded by a crowd of the worst class of people that go racing. Once a man gets into that set, I have hardly ever known him get out of it, even if he wants to. This was the ruin of Sloan, and eventually brought about his downfall.

He was a genius on a horse; off one, erratic and foolish. He threw away a career that was full of the greatest promise. As a jockey, in many ways he reminded me of Fred Archer. He had the same wonderful hands, and was as quick as lightning to take advantage of any opportunity that occurred in a race. Like Archer, once he had been on the back of any horse, he had an almost uncanny intuition into its peculiarities and nature.

A race I remember well was when he rode Knight of the Thistle in the Jubilee. The Knight was a great big good-looking horse, but a loose-made sort of customer, and easily unbalanced, in addition to which he was not too generous. He was owned by Lord William Beresford, who had backed him very heavily for the race, and he started favourite.

In the parade, Sloan seemed like a pea on a drum on this big horse, and knowing that other good jockeys had found him more than a handful, I would not back him. The horse was as obstinate as a mule at the post. During the long delay it looked very much as if he would be left. In the end he got off fairly well, but all Sloan's usual quiet persuasive efforts to induce him to race properly were unavailing. He had to fall back on the whip, and in the end slammed him home by a length. When he rode back to the unsaddling enclosure, Sloan looked quite exhausted.

I had engaged him to ride a two-year-old filly of Horace Farquhar's in the next race. Bill Beresford came to me and said, 'Sloan has asked me to tell you he can't ride for you, as he is so tired.' I tried to get another jockey, but as there was a big field I found every one was engaged. So I went to Sloan and told him he must ride. With his funny American twang he replied, 'That was the meanest horse I've ever ridden. I'm tired to death, and I can't ride any more.' But I insisted and weighed him out. When he came into the paddock he lay on his back in the grass, repeating, 'It's no use: I can't ride.'

Bobette, who was a beautiful little filly, was walking about close by. Sloan, still lying on his back, asked, 'Is that my horse?' When I said, 'Yes,' he was on his feet in a moment, and all his depression and lassitude disappeared. He won the race easily. Sloan was like that: when he was full of life and confidence he could do anything, but when he was down he could do nothing, and would get beaten on the best thing in the world.

THE RIDERS IN THE STAND

There's some that ride the Robbo style, and bump at every
    stride;
While others sit a long way back, to get a longer ride.
There's some that ride as sailors do, with legs, and arms, and
    teeth;
And some ride on the horse's neck, and some ride
    underneath.

But all the finest horsemen out – the men to Beat the Band –
You'll find amongst the crowd that ride their races in
    the Stand.
They'll say 'He had the race in hand, and lost it in the
    straight.'
They'll show how Godby came too soon, and Batden came
    too late.

They'll say Chevally lost his nerve, and Regan lost his head;
They'll tell how one was 'livened up' and something else
    was 'dead' –
In fact, the race was never run on sea, or sky, or land
But what you'd get it better done by riders in the Stand.

The rule holds good in everything in life's uncertain fight;
You'll find the winner can't go wrong, the loser can't go
    right.
You'll ride a slashing race and lose – by one and all you're
    banned!

Ride like a bag of flour, and win – they'll cheer you in the
Stand.

A. B. PATERSON

The finest nineteenth-century novel built around horse racing is Esther
Waters *by George Moore, published in 1894. Silver Braid, star of the
yard run by trainer Barfield ('the Gaffer'), is being prepared for
the Stewards Cup at Goodwood. The horse will be ridden by the stable
apprentice, the 'little carroty-haired boy' nicknamed 'the Demon', but as
the day of the race approaches there is a worry over the jockey's weight.*

The Barfield reckoning was that they had a stone in hand. Mr
Leopold said that Bayleaf at seven stone would be backed to win
a million of money, and Silver Braid, who had been tried again
with Bayleaf, and with the same result as before, had been let
off with only six stone.

More rain had fallen, the hay crop was spoilt, and the prospects
of the wheat harvest were jeopardised, but what did a few bush-
els of wheat matter? Another pound of muscle was worth all the
corn that could be grown between here and Henfield. Let the rain
come down, let every ear of wheat be destroyed, so long as those
delicate forelegs remained sound. These were the ethics at Woodview, and within the last few days they were accepted by the little
town and not a few of the farmers, grown tired of seeing their
crops rotting on the hillsides. The fever of the gamble was in
eruption, breaking out in unexpected places – the station-master,
the porters, the flymen, all had their bit on, and notwithstanding
the enormous favouritism of two other horses in the race – Prisoner and Stoke Newington – Silver Braid was creeping up in the
betting, for reports of trials won had reached Brighton, and with
the result that not more than five-and-twenty to one could now
be obtained.

An alarming piece of news it was that the Demon had gone up
several pounds in weight, and the strictest investigation was made
as to when and how he had obtained the food required to produce
such a mass of adipose tissue. The Gaffer had the boy upstairs and
handed him a huge dose of salts, keeping his eye upon him till he

had swallowed every drop; and, when the effects of the medi-
cine had worn off he was sent for a walk to Portslade in two large
overcoats, accompanied by William to make the running. On his
return a couple of feather beds were ready, Mr Leopold and Mr
Swindles laid him between them, and when he began to cease
sweating Mr Leopold made him a cup of hot tea.

'That's the way the Gaffer used to get the flesh off in the old
days when he rode the winner at Liverpool.'

'It's the Demon's own fault,' said Mr Swindles; 'if he hadn't
been so greedy he wouldn't have had to sweat, and we should
'ave been spared a deal of bother and anxiety.'

'Greedy!' murmured the little boy, in whom the warm tea had
induced a new sweat; 'I haven't had what you might call a dinner
for the last three months. I think I'll chuck the whole thing.'

'Not until this race is over,' said Mr Swindles. 'Supposing I was
to pass the warming-pan down these 'ere sheets. What do you
say, Mr Leopold? They are beginning to feel a bit cold.'

'Cold! I 'ope you'll never go to a 'otter place. For God's sake,
Mr Leopold, don't let him come near me with the warming-pan,
or else he'll melt the little flesh that's left off me.'

'You 'ad better not make such a fuss,' said Mr Leopold; 'if you
don't do what you are told, you'll have to take salts again and go
for another walk with William.'

'If we don't warm up them sheets 'e'll dry up,' said Mr Swindles.

'No, I won't; I'm teeming.'

'Be a good boy, and you shall have a nice cut of mutton when
you get up,' said Mr Leopold.

'How much? Two slices?'

'Well, you see, we can't promise; it all depends on how much
has come off, and 'aving once got it hoff, we don't want to put it
on again.'

'I never did 'ear such rot,' said Swindles. 'In my time a boy's
feelings weren't considered – one did what one considered good
for them,' and while Mr Swindles raised the bedclothes, Mr Leopold strove to engage the Demon's thoughts with compliments
regarding his horsemanship in the City and Sub.

'Oh, Mr Swindles, you are burning me.'

'For 'eaven's sake don't let him start out from under the bedclothes like that! Can't yer 'old him? Burning you! I never even touched you with it; it was the sheet that you felt.'

'Then the sheet is as 'ot as the bloody fire. Will yer leave off?'

'What! a Demon like you afraid of a little touch of 'eat; wouldn't 'ave believed it unless I 'ad 'eard it with my own ears,' said Mr Leopold. 'Come, now, do yer want to ride the crack at Goodwood or do yer not? If you do, keep quiet, and let us finish taking off the last couple of pounds.'

'It is the last couple of pounds that takes it out of you; the first lot comes off jest like butter,' said the boy, rolling out of the way of the pan. 'I know what it will be; I shall be so weak that I shall just ride a stinking bad race.'

Mr Leopold and Mr Swindles exchanged glances. It was clear that they thought there was something in the last words of the fainting Demon, and the pan was withdrawn. But when the boy was put into the scale again it was found that he was not yet nearly the right weight, and the Gaffer ordered another effort to be made. The Demon pleaded sore feet, but he was sent off all the same to Portslade in charge of William.

As the last pounds came off the Demon's little carcass Mr Leopold's face resumed a more tranquil expression, and it began to be whispered that instead of hedging any part of his money he would stand it all out, and one day a market gardener brought up word that he had seen Mr Leopold going into Brighton.

'Old Watkins isn't good enough for him, that's about it. If Silver Braid wins, Woodview will see very little more of Mr Leopold. He'll be for buying one of them big houses on the sea road and keeping his own trap.'

Like all too many steeplechase jockeys, Alan Oughton was forced to retire after a bad injury. He then set up as a trainer at Findon in Sussex, where one of his owners was the writer Alan Ross, who composed this poem after Oughton's death from cancer in 1970.

DEATH OF A TRAINER

In Memory of Alan Oughton

Among fellow jockeys bandy and small
He was straight as a board and tall,
So long to the knees
He could pick up and squeeze
Novices and rogues round all sorts of courses.
Neither bred to the sea nor horses,
The son of a Pompey tailor,
He walked with brisk roll of a sailor,
Tilted, as by saddle or quarter deck,
A curve from hipbone to neck.

Falls caught up with him, of the kind habitual
To riders over sticks, but he seemed at last
Safe in his Findon stables, at his disposal
A handful of jumpers not especially fast
Nor clever, but amenable to discipline
And patience, ridden out on a skyline
Of downland and sea, in lime dawn
Or half darkness, clouds torn
By gales blistering the channel,
Mist thickening beechwoods to flannel.

Busy as a ship, smelling of hay
And leather, of mash and linseed,
The yard seemed that ideal harbour
In which work has the essence of play,
Day-long, night-long, obedient to need,
The summer's sweetness, winter's bleak labour.
But season following season, winner
Following winner, so did pain circle,
Eyes grow strained and the thin body thinner,
Until there was only the long hell.

What I still see is a skeletal guy
Half imagined, half real, between races at Fontwell,
Saddle under one arm, threading his way
Through the weighing room, or wiping jellied eel

From his lips, sawdust running out of him
As he drops in the distance, each limb
Jerky as if on a string, patch
Over one eye, trilby dead straight,
And a gelding quickening to snatch
Up the verdict, just leaving it too late.

ALAN ROSS

The life of a stable lad, so often overlooked as writers concentrate on the glamour and glory of the racecourse, has been graphically captured by Susan Gallier in One of the Lads.

The most squalid racecourse, and the one I would most like to forget, is Folkestone. I was sent on my own, in a hired box, with a hysterical two-year-old filly who was having her first run. We set off in the small hours of the morning, and it was pouring with rain. Down in some remote corner of rural southern England, we arrived at what appeared to be a disused chicken farm – Folkestone racecourse. It was still raining, and the stables, sitting in a sea of mud, surely hadn't had a penny spent on them for decades. The eavestroughs leaked, and little waterfalls streamed down over each doorway. The doors themselves were rotten and held on to the frames by one or two rusty screws which could easily be pulled out with bare hands. I shut my horse in all day, not because she was unduly upset, but to spare her a shower, and also because I was afraid that if she leaned out the door would fall flat into the yard.

I went over to the weighing room to declare her as a participant in her race. The official buildings looked like old Boy Scout huts, painted with many coats of faded, peeling green emulsion paint. The tarmac paths were pitted with ruts full of water, and beside the parade ring, which, I was thankful to see, was at least paved, a feeble little fountain, surrounded by a garden of wilted flowers, dribbled dismally.

In keeping with the miserable mood, my horse's race was a shambles. The box driver agreed to help me saddle her, but he didn't arrive until the jockeys were waiting to mount, by which time I was beginning to panic. The owner had not been able to come, but he had sent a representative, a middle-aged lady in stern tweeds and sensible shoes, who scolded and shoved the box driver aside and saddled the horse very efficiently, herself. She told me that the horse looked a disgrace because the noseband of the bridle was a shade darker than the rest of the leather, and managed to make it sound like a heinous crime. And the rain poured down.

The jockey mounted, and I suggested that he should try to get down to the start as soon as possible, since the filly had been known to run away. (I should, actually, have got special permission from the stewards when I declared her to run, but I didn't know that, at the time, and in any case, I hadn't been told to.) 'Quick!' he said. 'Shove in here!' I attempted to 'shove in' the queue to get out of the gate and onto the track, and was told off by a steward. The jockey began to argue with him, and I squirmed with embarrassment and hurried the horse away. As I feared, she leapt skywards and flew off in the direction of the start with her jockey hauling on the reins for all he was worth. There was a brief shower of dirty water, and she was out of sight.

With a feeling of impending doom, I retired to the stable lads' stand to watch the race. There was a hold-up at the start when one of her rivals attempted an early getaway by climbing over the top of the starting stalls. Waiting about in stalls was one of my filly's least favourite things to do, and I watched with concern to see if she would try to join him. Fortunately she did not, and some minutes later the race got underway; but the hold-up had plainly unnerved many of the young horses, and in the scramble out of the gates two jockeys fell off. So, adding to the general confusion, were a couple of loose horses. My filly finished last. She cantered past the winning post with her head in the air, and continued around the racecourse for a second time, taking the two loose horses with her. By the time her jockey had managed to pull her up, one was romping about in a field of ripe wheat and the other heading for the road.

By this time, I couldn't have cared less. My only wish was to get away from this foul place as soon as possible, but my troubles were by no means over. As I caught the horse and held her while her poor jockey removed his saddle, the Lady In Tweeds reappeared and demanded an explanation for the horse's disastrous performance. I left the jockey to it – he was riding her, after all – and went back to the tumble-down stables in the rain to wash the filly down. Because of the persisting rain, it was impossible to walk the horse cool, so I was obliged to wash her, lead her around in the muddy stable yard until she had stopped blowing, and then try and rub her dry. It took ages, and she stamped and nipped at me bad-temperedly, and I didn't have enough towels to do a proper job. When I finally left her, people who saw me began to tell me that the stewards were appealing for a representative from my stable to report to them. At first, I thought it was a joke. Whatever could the stewards want with me? I decided it would be prudent to check, anyway, and as I picked my way through the puddles and across to the dilapidated shed which housed the weighing room, a feeling of dread overcame me. What now? It had to be something awful.

I knocked upon the appropriate door, and went in to find several scowling, blue-suited officials sitting at a desk, a secretary who was writing down every word said, and the Lady In Tweeds, who suddenly began to look like my old headmistress. Perhaps that was because I now felt like a naughty schoolgirl, summoned to the office. I clasped my hands in front of me, shuffled my feet, and one of the men, whose face I didn't bother to look at, started scolding me for having attempted to go down to the start first without having obtained special permission, and for having argued with the gate man. I didn't bother to correct him, or to try and defend myself; I doubted whether it would have gone down very well, and they certainly would not have believed me. It was quicker and easier to let him have his say, and be done with it. When I had been sufficiently chastised, they let me go. I fled back to the stables, found the box driver, and we agreed to leave without any further ado. The horse spent the entire journey back to Newmarket kicking the box partition, and I had to put on her bridle and stand with her to keep her from damaging either the vehicle or her own legs. It was without any doubt the most horrible day at the races I have ever had, and I vowed never to go near the squalid little place again.

One of the great characters of nineteenth-century racing, Sir John Astley mixed sport and politics when he became MP for North Lincolnshire. While campaigning at Crowle he asked for questions from his audience.

I believe the Permissive Bill was at that time exciting much interest in the country, but I was totally non-plussed, when a truculent looking politician stepped forward and asked me my opinion of Sir Wilfrid Lawson's 'Liquor Bill'; however, I pulled myself together and promptly stated that I didn't know much about Sir W. Lawson's Liquor Bill, but I did know that *mine* was a deuced sight too high that year.

Astley owned horses on a large scale, but ownership had its difficulties.

During the ten years between my marriage in 1858, and my father-in-law's death in 1868, I had run my horses in the name of S. Thellusson (a friend of mine who had some horses in Drewitt's stable), and this I did to avoid Mr Corbett's knowing I was wicked enough to own racehorses. Now it so happened that after Actea had won the Cambridgeshire, I decided to run her in the Liverpool Cup, and as we were staying that week in Lincoln for the county ball, I started by an early train for Liverpool, and my wife was to return home to Elsham by road that same afternoon. As I was getting into the train I bought a *Lincolnshire Chronicle* at the station, that weekly paper having been published that morning, and before I arrived at Retford, my eye fell on this horrible paragraph: 'Col. Astley, who runs his horses in the name of Mr S. Thellusson, much to the delight of his many friends, won the Cambridgeshire last week with Actea.' Well, that was a scorcher! and I felt sure that if Corbett read it, he would take particular care I should never inherit a copper from him. So I cut out and sent the obnoxious paragraph by the guard of a train, giving him a douceur of five shillings to see that the note I sent my wife was delivered to her at Brigg on her way home that evening, and in it, I impressed upon her the paramount importance of her cutting out the mischievous sentence the moment she got home, on the chance of the old squire not having read it.

My note was duly delivered, and on arrival she found her father busily engaged reading the *Chronicle*. With great presence of mind she waited till he left the room, and then cut out the paragraph, and when I arrived the next day (after Actea had been beaten) all seemed serene with the old boy, and I verily believe he never knew of my delinquency, or his will would not have been so kindly worded in my favour. It was a squeak, though, wasn't it?

'They were giants in those days'. That old line kept running through the mind this week as the news of Fulke Walwyn's death sank home.

As a child, when a fanatical interest in racing first nudged me down the slippery slope, the great figures of the game seemed like colossuses. Remote and often rather daunting, they bestrode the stage with an imperiousness and style that has few reflections among the current generation of trainers.

They were the 'Old School' and, although some of that revered institution's prefects are still with us in the likes of Crump, Oliver and Stephenson, the head boy has now gone the way of most of its alumni.

The most daunting of them was Peter Cazalet who only had the pleasure of meeting me once. He probably recalled the occasion with mixed feelings.

He was escorting the Queen Mother round Sandown one afternoon when a sturdy young lad of nine years came running round the corner and head-butted him heavily in the stomach.

'Twas me. I remember it distinctly as it may be the last time I actually ran anywhere.

A large hand hauled me to my feet and I found myself peering up at a bowler hat apparently supported over each eye by a medium-sized handbrush. 'It pays to look where you are going in life, young man.'

Sound enough advice and frequently ignored since. But to a child the figure of Cazalet was too terrifying a spectacle to inspire anything but respect. Affection or admiration were reserved for others. My hero of heroes was – and remains – that most wayward pupil of the Old School, the matchless Ryan Price.

Here was a giant indeed, a man fully justifying that tired tag 'larger than life' that is nowadays trotted out to describe all sorts of unremarkable pygmies.

There was a raffishness to his genius and a quality of being his own man that set him apart entirely. In later years, as a green hack on the *Life*, I was sent to interview him down in Sussex.

On the journey excitement turned to more than mild consternation as I realised that one young journalist was going to be very late indeed. Arriving an hour behind schedule I was expecting a bollocking straight out of the top drawer. Instead I received numerous gin and tonics and a whole morning of the great man's time.

After all the chat I asked if we could go up on to the Downs and see his old warriors in retirement – What A Myth, Major Rose, Charlie Worcester, Persian Lancer and Le Vermontois.

I recall racing up a rough old cart track in a large Merc at what seemed about 60 mph and getting out at the edge of an apparently empty field. But after an ear-splitting shout of 'come on you boys' the place suddenly came to life as the horses responded to that inimitable roar and ambled up over the skyline to greet him.

He loved those horses and his obvious affection for them and gratitude for what they had done for him taught me an important lesson about racing and racing people.

It is important because it helps draw a crucial line between those who love racing and those who love racehorses. To most trainers – and it is usually the best trainers – the horses are more important than the racing. But to many people involved with the turf, the racing is more important than the horses.

To listen to the likes of Price or Walwyn or nowadays Jenny Pitman talking about their horses is almost akin to eavesdropping. Their depth of feeling is unmistakable, a strange, almost hard-hearted sentiment.

I am quite capable of getting worked up about horses – I'll still thump anyone who doesn't appreciate that Rondetto was the greatest chaser of all time – but I will never have the depth of feeling for racehorses as a whole that the great trainers exhibit in their every fibre.

My one meeting with Fulke Walwyn some seven years ago was another vivid illustration of this extraordinary bond. After several very substantial liveners we wandered round the yard. He was 73 and still very much in command and, as we went from box to box, I was forcibly reminded of my meeting with Price a year before.

There is no point in talking about 'the likes of Price and Walwyn' for the simple reason there was never anyone 'like' either of them. That is what made them and what will make us remember them. Giants indeed.

ALASTAIR DOWN in the *Sporting Life Weekender*, 21 February 1991

Roger Mortimer was the author of many wonderful books about racing – notably monumental histories of the Derby and of the Jockey Club. This reminiscence of his early days as a journalist is one of the last articles he wrote before his death in November 1991.

TRAVELLING FORM

At the end of June 1947 I left the Army after seventeen mostly happy if undistinguished years. My last duty was to act as second-in-command at the King's Birthday Parade on Whitehall, an occasion less colourful than usual as we were not yet back to tunics and bearskins. I was mounted on a police horse, a gelding inappropriately named Virile who was extremely well behaved except for a habit of urinating whenever the massed bands struck up *God Save the King*. I remained on friendly terms with Virile and made a point of having a few words whenever I came across him on duty at Epsom or Hurst Park.

Since I was due to get married in the autumn it was clearly advisable to find a job. Ever since my preparatory school days when a glass-eyed usher with a genius for teaching history used to lend me a lively weekly publication called *The Jockey* – the paper's motto was '*The Jockey* is on every winner' – I had been hooked on racing. A former brother-officer of mine called Roger de Wesselow ran a very successful weekly form-book called *Raceform* (*Chaseform* during the winter), as well as a number of other publications connected with the Turf. The most popular of these was a four-page weekly named *The Racehorse*, parts of which were not wholly unreminiscent of that famous late Victorian and Edwardian paper of the Turf and the stage, the *Sporting Times* (far more commonly known as 'The Pink 'Un', from the colour of the paper on which it was printed; at most schools you got into trouble if you were caught reading the Pink 'Un, its particular brand of humour being mildly salacious). Evidently someone somewhere was enter-

99

tained by my column in *The Racehorse* and out of the blue I was invited to join *The Sunday Times* which at that point of time had no racing correspondent. In fact, *The Sunday Times* was not much concerned with racing. The great Lord Kemsley knew as much about the Turf as the average Eskimo does about county cricket, while the editor was over 80 years of age. (I cannot recollect ever having seen him, let alone having spoken to him.) However, *The Sunday Times* paid me a good deal more money than *Raceform* for considerably less work, despite the fact that I was handicapped by knowing absolutely nothing about journalism and its world, however much I thought I knew about racing.

One of my common tasks during my earlier days of journalism was to go racing and provide comments on how each horse had performed for inclusion in the form-books. Sometimes I found myself lumbered with the paddock comments as well so that I was kept on the hop when there were a lot of runners to contend with. Of course, I was never entrusted with the big meetings like Ascot, Epsom, Newmarket, Goodwood, York or Doncaster; to start with I was restricted to the more bucolic jumping fixtures such as Newton Abbot, Plumpton, Wye, Devon and Exeter and Buckfast-tleigh. Some of these meetings have gone up in the world since then, while others have vanished from the fixture list altogether.

At first I was often put under the wing of the late Bob Haines, who was very good at his job and later became a successful commentator. Before the war we had served in the same battalion in Egypt but the rank consciousness of those days, before he obtained a commission in the Essex Regiment, meant that I did not know him at all well. When the 3rd Coldstream was at Alexandria, we both had weekend jobs at the main racecourse, the Sporting Club. There was a lively racing paper published in French. I was a Steward and was quite chuffed when I saw a large photograph in this paper of the Stewards presenting a handsome Gold Cup to a successful owner. I was a good deal less delighted when I read the caption: 'Fellow Sportsmen of Alexandria, the gentlemen in the above photograph are not only highly incompetent, they are also extremely dishonest.' I think only one of these imputations was true. The critic was punished by temporary suspension of his club membership.

One of the biggest differences between racing now and in the immediate post-war years lies in the travelling. There was no question then of jumping into a fast and reasonably reliable car and pelting down a motorway. Motorways did not exist; not many people owned a car; new ones were virtually unobtainable; and in any case petrol was strictly rationed. By and large racegoers had to rely on the train service, which varied in quality: the best trains were extremely good and the meals offered were far superior to those dished out today. (One line to the north boasted a truly excellent claret at a far from exorbitant price.) The trouble was that at certain times, in the holiday season for instance, trains were in short supply and long journeys perched on a suitcase in the corridor were by no means rare.

For a budding journalist, a life that involved spending so much time in trains had the advantage that one got to know the personalities of the racing world far more quickly than is possible today. Also, there were good parties at certain hotels for the major meetings. Of course if you were not one of the swells you had to watch expenses. I think *Raceform* allowed £2 10s for a night away from home. I found the racing regulars friendly and helpful, not least the Press Association team who journeyed from meeting to meeting and whose knowledge of travelling form was unbeatable. Moreover, they were on excellent terms with those railway officials who could make life easier on a train, not least in a restaurant-car after a crowded meeting.

Metropolitan racegoers were well looked after by the railway companies and a run-of-the-mill afternoon at Hurst Park not only catered adequately for the general public but also provided special trains for first-class passengers and members of the Club where racing was taking place. On one occasion, going to Hurst Park in a first-class-only train, I shared a compartment with two colonels from the Cavalry Club and their ladies. Just as the train was moving out of Waterloo a tipster called Healy, who always wore an old Harrovian tie, evaded the watchful attendants on the platform and joined us. The colonels regarded him with some suspicion but he gave no trouble and was soon immersed in the *Sporting Life*. The journey was nearly over when he laid down his paper and addressed his fellow-passengers. 'Ladies and gentlemen,' he stated in ringing tones, 'all I can tell you is this. If General

Advance don't win today, I'll [remainder of his little speech must be censored].'

I think it was in 1948 that I received a note from *Raceform* warning me for duty at Buckfastleigh on Saturday 7 August. I had never been to Buckfastleigh, which expired not many years later. It formed part of what is known as the Devon circuit and racing had just started there again after the war. All I could discover about it was that it was situated not far from Buckfast Abbey. As I could not locate a hotel close to the racecourse I judged it best to take a train from London to Exeter and play it from there. There was a solitary train to Exeter on the Friday and, it being the height of the holiday season and holidays abroad not being then permitted, the train was crammed. I was lucky to get a pitch in the corridor. Restaurant cars were off.

Exeter is not short of modest hotels of a vaguely ecclesiastical flavour, and not being able to find a cab I humped my bag to one of these. I was unable to detect any form of public transport to the races the following day and I was beginning to get desperate when a hotel porter suggested I approach the cook and arrange terms for the loan of her bicycle. A small amount of money changed hands and I became the temporary possessor of a solid-looking machine which the sporting local auctioneer would doubt-less have described as 'absolutely sound, up to fourteen stone, has carried a lady'.

It was a damp, muggy day on the Saturday and there was a lot of pedalling to be done before reaching the racecourse. I started almost at dawn to ensure getting there in time; a bit too early, in fact, as the pay-gates had not been opened when I arrived, although a number of people seemed to have found a way in. Actually, the turnstiles did not start to operate till about an hour before the first contest, at which point a coachload of Devon police arrived, alighted, linked arms and marched through the enclosures, sweeping outside all individuals who had got in with-out the formality of paying. These intruders were coerced into orderly queues and duly paid up at the turnstiles.

I was surprised at the total lack of anything that looked like a permanent building; their absence, combined with the presence of a row of marquees, suggested a point-to-point rather than a meeting under National Hunt Rules. A notice on the racecard apologized for the somewhat primitive conditions and attributed the lack of a grandstand to shortage of labour. Luckily there was a rise in the ground from which a fair view of the racing could be obtained.

To pass the time I walked round the course, which appeared to be well maintained. The fences were well made; I discovered that they had been constructed by German prisoners-of-war incarcerated in the vicinity. The quality of the sport was better than I had expected and there was a total of close on sixty runners for the six races. The standard of the jockeys riding was high; among those taking part was the late Bryan Marshall, destined to win the Grand National on Early Mist and Royal Tan, both trained by Vincent O'Brien. Oddly enough, in fact, there were three jockeys riding at Buckfastleigh that day who were unlucky *not* to win the Grand National. Lord Mildmay, a loyal supporter of the Devon circuit, would surely have won the 1936 National on his 100–1 outsider Davy Jones, a big entire chestnut, if only his reins had not broken at the penultimate fence. Mildmay was probably equally unlucky in 1948 when third on Cromwell. Owing to a previous shoulder injury suddenly reasserting itself, he was quite unable to help Cromwell at all in the closing stages of the race. Dick Francis, only recently out of the RAF and long before he wrote his first book, was second in the first event at Buckfastleigh, an optional selling hurdle. In the 1956 Grand National, riding the Queen Mother's Devon Loch, he had the race apparently at his mercy when just short of the winning post Devon Loch suddenly collapsed, a mystery that has yet to be conclusively solved.

Cromwell was not the only unlucky competitor in the 1948 Grand National. The 100–1 outsider Zahia, a mare trained by Major Geoffrey Champneys, was ridden by Eddie Reavey who won a chase at Buckfastleigh this very afternoon. Zahia had the National well won coming to the last fence but somehow Reavey contrived to go the wrong way, and that was that.

Also riding at Buckfastleigh that day was Johnny Bullock, late of the airborne forces, who won the 1951 Grand National on the mare Nickel Coin. Amateurs in the saddle included Mr J. Seely, who won the three-mile chase and whose son Mr Michael Seely is today a leading racing journalist, and Captain Roly Beech, a dashing 12th Lancer who had won the MC in North Africa.

I was desperately tired when I got back to Exeter and returned the bicycle that had served me so well. I had quite enjoyed my trip to Devonshire. I was never detailed to go there again.

THE STEWARDS

A friend of mine, a man of means,
Trains horses which are not machines.
When in the market they're neglected,
They finish seventh, as expected.
But when their price is nice and short,
They win precisely as they ought.
Uncharitable men complain
And say: 'He's twisted us again.
The bally Stewards must be blind.'
Which is exceedingly unkind.
The acting Stewards, upright men,
All over three-score-years-and-ten,
Will not risk getting indigestion
By asking my good friend a question.
If past their lunch-room you are walking
You'll hear the acting Stewards talking.
Sir Randolph says: 'This beef-steak pud
Is really most uncommon good.'
Lord Crust, whose cough is getting chronic,
Says, 'Someone's drunk my gin-and-tonic.'
While Major Plunge says: 'I've been told
To put my shirt on Rotten Gold;
I heard his trainer, Twisty, say
He's going to have a go today.'
The Stewards lunch till half-past three,
When they commence to have their tea.

GEOFFREY GILBEY

Perhaps the finest piece of all racing fiction, 'My Old Man' was Ernest Hemingway's first published story. When it was included in The Best American Short Stories 1923, *he was just twenty-four years old.*

MY OLD MAN

I guess looking at it, now, my old man was cut out for a fat guy, one of those regular little roly fat guys you see around, but he sure never got that way, except a little towards the last, and then it wasn't his fault, he was riding over the jumps only and he could afford to carry plenty of weight then. I remember the way he'd pull on a rubber shirt over a couple of jerseys and a big sweat shirt over that, and get me to run with him in the forenoon in the hot sun. He'd have, maybe, taken a trial trip with one of Razzo's skins early in the morning after just getting in from Torino at four o'clock in the morning and beating it out to the stables in a cab and then with the dew all over everything and the sun just starting to get going, I'd help him pull off his boots and he'd get into a pair of sneakers and all these sweaters and we'd start out.

'Come on, kid,' he'd say, stepping up and down on his toes in front of the jocks' dressing-room, 'let's get moving.'

Then we'd start off jogging around the infield once, maybe, with him ahead, running nice, and then turn out the gate and along one of those roads with all the trees along both sides of them that run out from San Siro. I'd go ahead of him when we hit the road and I could run pretty stout and I'd look around and he'd be jogging easy just behind me and after a little while I'd look around again and he'd begun to sweat. Sweating heavy and he'd just be dogging it along with his eyes on my back, but when he'd catch me looking at him he'd grin and say, 'Sweating plenty?' When my old man grinned, nobody could help but grin too. We'd keep right on running out towards the mountains and then my old man would yell, 'Hey, Joe!' and I'd look back and he'd be sitting under a tree with a towel he'd had around his waist wrapped around his neck.

I'd come back and sit down beside him and he'd pull a rope out of his pocket and start skipping rope out in the sun with the sweat pouring off his face and him skipping rope out in the white dust with the rope going cloppetty, cloppetty, clop, clop, clop, and the sun hotter, and him working harder up and down a patch of the road. Say, it was a treat to see my old man skip rope, too. He could whirr it fast or lop it slow and fancy. Say, you ought to have seen wops look at us sometimes, when they'd come by, going into town walking along with big white steers hauling the cart. They sure looked as though they thought the old man was nuts. He'd start the rope whirring till they'd stop dead still and watch him, then give the steers a cluck and a poke with the goad and get going again.

When I'd sit watching him working out in the hot sun I sure felt fond of him. He sure was fun and he done his work so hard and he'd finish up with a regular whirring that'd drive the sweat out on his face like water and then sling the rope at the tree and come over and sit down with me and lean back against the tree with the towel and a sweater wrapped around his neck.

'Sure is hell keeping it down, Joe,' he'd say and lean back and shut his eyes and breathe long and deep, 'it ain't like when you're a kid.' Then he'd get up before he started to cool and we'd jog along back to the stables. That's the way it was keeping down to weight. He was worried all the time. Most jocks can just about ride off all they want to. A jock loses about a kilo every time he rides, but my old man was sort of dried out and he couldn't keep down his kilos without all that running.

I remember once at San Siro, Regoli, a little wop, that was riding for Buzoni, came out across the paddock going to the bar for something cool; and flicking his boots with his whip, after he'd just weighed in and my old man had just weighed in too, and came out with the saddle under his arm looking red-faced and tired and too big for his silks and he stood there looking at young Regoli standing up to the outdoors bar, cool and kid-looking, and I says, 'What's the matter, Dad?' 'cause I thought maybe Regoli had bumped him or something and he just looked at Regoli and said, 'Oh, to hell with it,' and went on to the dressing-room.

Well, it would have been all right, maybe, if we'd stayed in Milan and ridden at Milan and Torino, 'cause if there ever were any easy courses, it's those two, 'Pianola, Joe,' my old man said when he dismounted in the winning stall after what the wops thought was a hell of a steeplechase. I asked him once. 'This course rides itself. It's the pace you're going at, that makes riding the jumps dangerous, Joe. We ain't going any pace here, and they ain't any really bad jumps either. But it's the pace always – not the jumps that makes the trouble.'

San Siro was the swellest course I'd ever seen but the old man said it was a dog's life. Going back and forth between Mirafiore and San Siro and riding just about every day in the week with a train ride every other night.

I was nuts about the horses, too. There's something about it, when they come out and go up the track to the post. Sort of dancy and tight looking with the jock keeping a tight hold on them and maybe easing off a little and letting them run a little going up. Then once they were at the barrier it got me worse than anything. Especially at San Siro with that big green infield and the mountains way off and the fat wop starter with his big whip and the jocks fiddling them around and then the barrier snapping up and that bell going off and them all getting off in a bunch and then commencing to string out. You know the way a bunch of skins gets off. If you're up in the stand with a pair of glasses all you see is them plunging off and then the bell goes off and it seems like it rings for a thousand years and then they come sweeping round the turn. There wasn't ever anything like it for me.

But my old man said one day, in the dressing-room, when he was getting into his street clothes, 'None of these things are horses, Joe. They'd kill that bunch of skates for their hides and hoofs up at Paris.' That was the day he'd won the Premio Commercio with Lantorna shooting her out of the field the last hundred metres like pulling a cork out of a bottle.

It was right after the Premio Commercio that we pulled out and left Italy. My old man and Holbrook and a fat wop in a straw hat that kept wiping his face with a handkerchief were having an argument at a table in the Galleria. They were all talking French and the two of them were after my old man about something. Finally he didn't say anything any more but just sat there and looked at Holbrook, and the two of them kept after him, first one talking and then the other, and the fat wop always butting in on Holbrook.

'You go out and buy me a *Sportsman*, will you, Joe?' my old man said, and handed me a couple of soldi without looking away from Holbrook.

So I went out of the Galleria and walked over to in front of the Scala and bought a paper, and came back and stood a little way away because I didn't want to butt in and my old man was sitting back in his chair looking down at his coffee and fooling with a spoon and Holbrook and the big wop were standing and the big wop was wiping his face and shaking his head. And I came up and my old man acted just as though the two of them weren't standing there and said, 'Want an ice, Joe?' Holbrook looked down at my old man and said slow and careful, 'You son of a bitch,' and he and the fat wop went out through the tables.

My old man sat there and sort of smiled at me, but his face was white and he looked sick as hell and I was scared and felt sick inside because I knew something had happened and I didn't see how anybody could call my old man a son of a bitch, and get away with it. My old man opened up the *Sportsman* and studied the handicaps for a while and then he said, 'You got to take a lot of things in this world, Joe.' And three days later we left Milan for good on the Turin train for Paris, after an auction sale out in front of Turner's stables of everything we couldn't get into a trunk and a suitcase.

We got into Paris early in the morning in a long, dirty station the old man told me was the Gare de Lyon. Paris was an awful big town after Milan. Seems like in Milan everybody is going somewhere and all the trams run somewhere and there ain't any sort of a mix-up, but Paris is all balled up and they never do straighten it out. I got to like it, though, part of it, anyway, and say, it's got the best racecourses in the world. Seems as though that were the thing that keeps it all going and about the only thing you can figure on is that every day the buses will be going out to whatever track they're running at, going right out through everything to the track. I never really got to know Paris well, because I just came in about once or twice a week with the old man from Maisons and he always sat at the Café de la Paix on the Opéra side with the rest of the gang from Maisons and I guess that's one of the busiest parts of the town. But, say, it is funny that a big town like Paris wouldn't have a Galleria, isn't it?

Well, we went out to live at Maisons-Laffitte, where just about everybody lives except the gang at Chantilly, with a Mrs Meyers that runs a boarding house. Maisons is about the swellest place to live I've ever seen in all my life. The town ain't so much, but there's a lake and a swell forest that we used to go off bumming in all day, a couple of us kids, and my old man made me a sling shot and we got a lot of things with it but the best one was a magpie. Young Dick Atkinson shot a rabbit with it one day and we put it under a tree and were all sitting around and Dick had some cigarettes and all of a sudden the rabbit jumped up and beat it into the brush and we chased it but we couldn't find it. Gee, we had fun at Maisons. Mrs Meyers used to give me lunch in the morning and I'd be gone all day. I learned to talk French quick. It's an easy language.

As soon as we got to Maisons, my old man wrote to Milan for his licence and he was pretty worried till it came. He used to sit around the Café de Paris in Maisons with the gang; there were lots of guys he'd known when he rode up at Paris, before the war, lived at Maisons, and there's a lot of time to sit around because the work around a racing stable, for the jocks, that is, is all cleaned up by nine o'clock in the morning. They take the first batch of skins out to gallop them at 5.30 in the morning and they work the second lot at 8 o'clock. That means getting up early all right and going to bed early, too. If a jock's riding for somebody too, he can't go boozing around because the trainer always has an eye on him if he's a kid and if he ain't a kid he's always got an eye on himself. So mostly if a jock ain't working he sits around the Café de Paris with the gang and they can all sit around about two or three hours in front of some drink like a vermouth and seltz and they talk and tell stories and shoot pool and it's sort of like a club or the Galleria in Milan. Only it ain't really like the Galleria because there everybody is going by all the time and there's everybody around at the tables.

Well, my old man got his licence all right. They sent it through to him without a word and he rode a couple of time. Amiens, up country and that sort of thing, but he didn't seem to get any engagements. Everybody liked him and whenever I'd come in to the café in the forenoon I'd find somebody drinking with him because my old man wasn't tight like most of these jockeys that have got the first dollar they made riding at the World's Fair in St Louis in nineteen ought four. That's what my old man would say when he'd kid George Burns. But it seemed like everybody steered clear of giving my old man any mounts.

We went out to wherever they were running every day with the car from Maisons and that was the most fun of all. I was glad when the horses came back from Deauville and the summer. Even though it meant no more bumming in the woods, 'cause then we'd ride to Enghien or Tremblay or St Cloud and watch them from the trainers' and jockeys' stand. I sure learned about racing from going out with that gang and the fun of it was going every day.

I remember once out at St Cloud. It was a big two-hundred-thousand-franc race with seven entries and War Cloud a big favourite. I went around to the paddock to see the horses with my old man and you never saw such horses. This War Cloud is a great big yellow horse that looks like just nothing but run. I never saw such a horse. He was being led around the paddock with his head down and when he went by me I felt all hollow inside he was so beautiful. There never was such a wonderful, lean, running-built horse. And he went around the paddock putting his feet just so and quiet and careful and moving easy like he knew just what he had to do and not jerking and standing up on his legs and getting wild-eyed like you see these selling platers with a shot of dope in them. The crowd was so thick I couldn't see him again except just his legs going by and some yellow and my old man started out through the crowd and I followed him over to the jocks' dressing-room back in the trees and there was a big crowd around there, too, but the man at the door in a derby nodded to my old man and we got in and everybody was sitting around and getting dressed and pulling shirts over their heads and pulling boots on and it all smelled hot and sweaty and linimenty and outside was the crowd looking in.

The old man went over and sat down beside George Gardner that was getting into his pants and said, 'What's the dope, George?' just in an ordinary tone of voice 'cause there ain't any use him feeling around because George either can tell him or he can't tell him.

'He won't win,' George says very low, leaning over and buttoning the bottoms of his pants.

'Who will?' my old man says, leaning over close so nobody can hear.

'Foxless,' George says, 'and if he does, save me a couple of tickets.'

My old man says something in a regular voice to George and George says, 'Don't ever bet on anything, I tell you,' kidding like, and we beat it out and through all the crowd that was looking in over to the 100 franc mutuel machine. But I knew something big was up because George is War Cloud's jockey. On the way he gets one of the yellow odds-sheets with the starting prices on and War Cloud is only paying 5 for 10, Cefisidote is next at 3 to 1 and fifth down the list this Foxless at 8 to 1. My old man bets five thousand on Foxless to win and puts on a thousand to place and we went around back of the grandstand to go up the stairs and get a place to watch the race.

We were jammed in tight and first a man in a long coat with a grey tall hat and a whip folded up in his hand came out and then one after another the horses, with the jocks up and a stable-boy holding the bridle on each side and walking along, followed the old guy. That big yellow horse War Cloud came first. He didn't look so big when you first looked at him until you saw the length of his legs and the whole way he's built and the way he moves. Gosh, I never saw such a horse. George Gardner was riding him and they moved along slow, back of the old guy in the grey tall hat that walked along like he was the ringmaster in a circus. Back of War Cloud, moving along smooth and yellow in the sun, was a good-looking black with a nice head with Tommy Archibald riding him; and after the black was a string of five more horses all moving along slow in a procession past the grandstand and the *pesage*. My old man said the black was Foxless and I took a good look at him and he was a nice-looking horse, all right, but nothing like War Cloud.

Everybody cheered War Cloud when he went by and he sure was one swell-looking horse. The procession of them went around on the other side past the *pelouse* and then back up to the near end of the course and the circus master had the stable-boys turn them loose one after another so they could gallop by the stands on their way up to the post and let everybody have a good look at them. They weren't at the post hardly any time at all when the gong started and you could see them way off across the infield all in a bunch starting on the first swing like a lot of little toy horses. I was watching them through the glasses and War Cloud was running well back, with one of the bays making the pace. They swept down and around and come pounding past and War Cloud was way back when they passed us and this Foxless horse in front and going smooth. Gee, it's awful when they go by you and then you have to watch them go farther away and get smaller and smaller and then all bunched up on the turns and then come around towards you into the stretch and you feel like swearing and god-damning worse and worse. Finally they made the last turn and came into the straightway with this Foxless horse way out in front. Everybody was looking funny and saying 'War Cloud' in a sort of sick way and them pounding nearer down the stretch, and then something come out of the pack right into my glasses like a horse-headed yellow streak and everybody began to yell 'War Cloud' as though they were crazy. War Cloud came on faster than I'd ever seen anything in my life and pulled up on Foxless that was going fast as any black horse could go with the jock flogging hell out of him with the gad and they were right dead neck and neck for a second but War Cloud seemed about twice as fast with those great jumps and that head out – but it was while they were neck and neck that they passed the winning post and when the numbers went up in the slots the first one was 2 and that meant Foxless had won.

I felt all trembly and funny inside, and then we were all jammed in with the people going downstairs to stand in front of the board where they'd post what Foxless paid. Honest, watching the race I'd forgot how much my old man had bet on Foxless. I'd wanted War Cloud to win so damned bad. But now it was all over it was swell to know we had the winner.

'Wasn't it a swell race, Dad?' I said to him.

He looked at me sort of funny with his derby on the back of his head. 'George Gardner's a swell jockey, all right,' he said. 'It sure took a great jockey to keep that War Cloud horse from winning.'

Of course I knew it was funny all the time. But my old man saying that right out like that sure took the kick all out of it for me and I didn't get the real kick back again ever, even when they posted the numbers up on the board and the bell rang to pay off and we saw that Foxless paid 67.50 for 10. All round people were saying, 'Poor War Cloud! Poor War Cloud!' And I thought, I wish I were a jockey and could have rode him instead of that son of a bitch. And that was funny, thinking of George Gardner as a son of a bitch because I'd always liked him and besides he'd given us the winner, but I guess that's what he is, all right.

My old man had a big lot of money after that race and he took to coming into Paris oftener. If they raced at Tremblay he'd have them drop him in town on their way back to Maisons, and he and I'd sit out in front of the Café de la Paix and watch the people go by. It's funny sitting there. There's streams of people going by and all sorts of guys come up and want to sell you things, and I loved to sit there with my old man. That was when we'd have the most fun. Guys would come by selling funny rabbits that jumped if you squeezed a bulb and they'd come up to us and my old man would kid with them. He could talk French just like English and all those kind of guys knew him 'cause you can always tell a jockey – and then we always sat at the same table and they got used to seeing us there. There were guys selling matrimonial papers and girls selling rubber eggs that when you squeezed them a rooster came out of them and one old wormy-looking guy that went by with postcards of Paris, showing them to everybody, and, of course, nobody ever bought any, and then he would come back and show the under side of the pack and they would all be smutty postcards and lots of people would dig down and buy them.

Gee, I remember the funny people that used to go by. Girls around supper time looking for somebody to take them out to eat and they'd speak to my old man and he'd make some joke at them in French and they'd pat me on the head and go on. Once there was an American woman sitting with her kid daughter at the next table to us and they were both eating ices and I kept looking at the girl and she was awfully good-looking and I smiled at her and she smiled at me but that was all that ever came of it because I looked for her mother and her every day and I made up ways that I was going to speak to her and I wondered if I got to know her if her mother would let me take her out to Auteuil or Tremblay but I never saw either of them again. Anyway, I guess it wouldn't have been any good, anyway, because looking back on it I remember the way I thought out would be best to speak to her was to say, 'Pardon me, but perhaps I can give you a winner at Enghien today?' and, after all, maybe she would have thought I was a tout instead of really trying to give her a winner.

We'd sit at the Café de la Paix, my old man and me, and we had a big drag with the waiter because my old man drank whisky and it cost five francs, and that meant a good tip when the saucers were counted up. My old man was drinking more than I'd ever seen him, but he wasn't riding at all now and besides he said that whisky kept his weight down. But I noticed he was putting it on, all right, just the same. He'd busted away from his old gang out at Maisons and seemed to like just sitting around on the boulevard with me. But he was dropping money every day at the track. He'd feel sort of doleful after the last race, if he'd lost on the day, until we'd get to our table and he'd have his first whisky and then he'd be fine.

He'd be reading the *Paris-Sport* and he'd look over at me and say, 'Where's your girl, Joe?' to kid me on account I had told him about the girl that day at the next table. And I'd get red, but I liked being kidded about her. It gave me a good feeling. 'Keep your eye peeled for her, Joe,' he'd say, 'she'll be back.'

He'd ask me questions about things and some of the things I'd say he'd laugh. And then he'd get started talking about things. About riding down in Egypt, or at St Moritz on the ice before my mother died, and about during the war when they had regular races down in the south of France without any purses, or betting or crowd or anything just to keep the breed up. Regular races with the jocks riding hell out of the horses. Gee, I could listen to my old man talk by the hour, especially when he'd had a couple or so of drinks. He'd tell me about when he was a boy in Kentucky and going coon hunting, and the old days in the States before everything went on the bum there. And he'd say, 'Joe, when we've got a decent stake, you're going back there to the States and go to school.'

'What've I got to go back there to go to school for when everything's on the bum there?' I'd ask him.

'That's different,' he'd say and get the waiter over and pay the pile of saucers and we'd get a taxi to the Gare St Lazare and get on the train out to Maisons.

One day at Auteuil, after a selling steeplechase, my old man bought in the winner for 30,000 francs. He had to bid a little to get him but the stable let the horse go finally and my old man had his permit and his colours in a week. Gee, I felt proud when my old man was an owner. He fixed it up for stable space with Charles Drake and cut out coming in to Paris, and started his running and sweating out again, and him and I were the whole stable gang. Our horse's name was Gilford; he was Irish bred and a nice, sweet jumper. My old man figured that training him and riding him, himself, he was a good investment. I was proud of everything and I thought Gilford was as good a horse as War Cloud. He was a good, solid jumper, a bay, with plenty of speed on the flat, if you asked him for it, he was a nice-looking horse, too.

Gee, I was fond of him. The first time he started with my old man up, he finished third in a 2,500 metre hurdle race and when my old man got off him, all sweating and happy in the place stall, and went in to weigh, I felt as proud of him as though it was the first race he'd ever placed in. You see, when a guy ain't been riding for a long time, you can't make yourself really believe that he has ever rode. The whole thing was different now, 'cause down in Milan, even big races never seemed to make any difference to my old man, if he won he wasn't ever excited or anything, and now it was so I couldn't hardly sleep the night before a race and I knew my old man was excited, too, even if he didn't show it. Riding for yourself makes an awful difference.

Second time Gilford and my old man started, was a rainy Sunday at Auteuil, in the Prix du Marat, a 4,500 metre steeplechase. As soon as he'd gone out I beat it up in the stand with the new glasses my old man had bought for me to watch them. They started way over at the far end of the course and there was some trouble at the barrier. Something with goggle blinders on was making a great fuss and rearing around and busted the barrier once, but I could see my old man in our black jacket, with a white cross and a black cap, sitting up on Gilford, and patting him with his hand. Then they were off in a jump and out of sight behind the trees and the gong going for dear life and the pari-mutuel wickets rattling down. Gosh, I was so excited, I was afraid to look at them, but I fixed the glasses on the place where they would come out back of the trees and then out they came with the old black jacket going third and they all sailing over the jump like birds. Then they went out of sight again and then they came pounding out and down the hill and all going nice and sweet and easy and taking the fence smooth in a bunch, and moving away from us all solid. Looked as though you could walk across on their backs they were all so bunched and going so smooth. Then they bellied over the big double Bullfinch and something came down. I couldn't see who it was, but in a minute the horse was up and galloping free and the field, all bunched still, sweeping around the long left turn into the straightway. They jumped the stone wall and came jammed down the stretch towards the big water-jump right in front of the stands. I saw them coming and hollered at my old man as he went by, and he was leading by about a length and riding way out, and light as a monkey, and they were racing for the water-jump. They took off over the big hedge of the water-jump in a pack and then there was a crash, and two horses pulled sideways out off it, and kept on going, and three others were piled up. I couldn't see my old man anywhere. One horse kneed himself up and the jock had hold of the bridle and mounted and went slamming on after the place money. The other horse was up and away by himself, jerking his head and galloping with the bridle rein hanging and the jock staggered over to one side of the track against the fence. Then Gilford rolled over to one side off my old man and got up and started to run on three legs with his off hoof dangling and there was my old man laying there on the grass flat out with his face up and blood over the side of his head. I ran down the stand and bumped into a jam of people and got to the rail and a cop grabbed me and held me and two big stretcher-bearers were going out after my old man and around on the other side of the course I saw three horses, strung way out, coming out of the trees and taking the jump.

My old man was dead when they brought him in and while a doctor was listening to his heart with a thing plugged in his ears, I heard a shot up the track that meant they'd killed Gilford. I lay down beside my old man, when they carried the stretcher into the hospital room, and hung on to the stretcher and cried and cried, and he looked so white and gone and so awfully dead, and I couldn't help feeling that if my old man was dead maybe they didn't need to have shot Gilford. His hoof might have got well. I don't know. I loved my old man so much.

Then a couple of guys came in and one of them patted me on the back and then went over and looked at my old man and then pulled a sheet off the cot and spread it over him; and the other was telephoning in French for them to send the ambulance to take him out to Maisons. And I couldn't stop crying, crying and choking, sort of, and George Gardner came in and sat down beside me on the floor and put his arm around me and says, 'Come on, Joe, old boy. Get up and we'll go out and wait for the ambulance.'

George and I went out to the gate and I was trying to stop bawling and George wiped off my face with his handkerchief and we were standing back a little ways while the crowd was going out of the gate and a couple of guys stopped near us while we were waiting for the crowd to get through the gate and one of them was counting a bunch of mutuel tickets and said, 'Well, Butler got his, all right.'

The other guy said, 'I don't give a good goddamn if he did, the crook. He had it coming to him on the stuff he's pulled.'

'I'll say he had,' said the other guy, and tore the bunch of tickets in two.

And George Gardner looked at me to see if I'd heard and I had all right and he said, 'Don't you listen to what those bums said, Joe. Your old man was one swell guy.'

But I don't know. Seems like when they get started they don't leave a guy nothing.

4

'He's going to win big, Herb!'

The race

The horses load into the metal starting gates. Starter George Cassidy stands on a green platform by the rail twenty feet in front of the gate, and watches as the horses move one by one. The assistant starter takes Secretariat into the stall gate, then slams closed the door behind him. The colt stands calmly. They load Pvt. Smiles and My Gallant next to him and Twice a Prince. Then Sham. Anticipating the start, Secretariat drops into a crouch, lowering himself about six inches back on his hindlegs. They are all ready.

It is 5:38.

The five colts vault from the gate head and head, Secretariat leaving with them in three giant strides in which his forelegs and chest rise fully four feet in the air, breaking more sharply than he has ever broken in his life. The crowd is on its feet howling. Secretariat isn't falling back today, not as he usually does at the break, but rather picking up speed quickly and running with My Gallant through the first half dozen strides. He is racing with the field from the first jump. Looking to his left quickly Cordero sees the red horse grabbing the bit and running powerfully against it, and decides not to make an issue of the pace. Taking hold of My Gallant, Cordero drops the colt behind the red horse going to the turn. Other riders follow his lead. Baeza, outrun from the gate on Twice a Prince, lets the colt settle to find his stride. Gargan drops way out of it on Pvt. Smiles. But not Sham. Pincay hustles. He has been told to try for the lead on Sham, so he rouses Sham from the outside post to loom up for the lead. The Belmont Stakes develops with a rush to the turn.

Folding up and keeping his hands still, Turcotte at once takes a snug hold of Secretariat. Glancing right, he sees Sham going for

121

the lead and Cordero taking back on My Gallant. Now he has room on the rail. A hole stays open in front of him. Seeing the space, Turcotte keeps a hold of the colt while chirping to him. Secretariat responds, surging and accelerating to the turn. Sham joins him on the outside. Slipping to the left as the others fall back, Sham comes to the flanks of Secretariat. The crowd stays on its feet. The Belmont is a match race at the first turn. Sham is a head in front of Secretariat as they race past the $1^3/_8$ pole, 220 yards out of the gate, and the jockeys are letting them go. The pair draws away, racing the opening eighth in $0:12^1/_5$. They appear to be on their way to the beat of twelve, to that opening half-mile in 0:48 seconds that is the throne in the Belmont Stakes.

But then they pick up more speed, gathering momentum around the turn. Pincay seeks the lead, and now he moves to make an issue of it. Chirping, he urges Sham to keep pace with Secretariat. Turcotte, seeing Sham thrusting his head in front, and responding with more speed, sits and waits on Secretariat. The battle joined, Secretariat skimming the rail with Sham lapped right on him, the two begin to pull away from My Gallant.

They drive the bend as one. The crowd senses a fight and they roar them on. They're running as if it's a six-furlong sprint: they rush the second eighth in $0:11^2/_5$. Pincay knows they're going too fast, senses Sham working too hard, but he presses on. He is under orders to challenge for the lead. Martin wants the red horse to run at Sham. Sommers's bay moves up faster on the turn, challenging and probing at Secretariat. The red horse forces the pace. He is sailing beside Sham. Pincay is waiting for Turcotte to take back on the red horse. But Turcotte is conceding nothing. He feels his colt is running easily so he gives him his head and lets him roll for the turn.

Together they race the opening quarter in $0:23^3/_5$, sharp time.

Now is the time to take back. Now they can give the colts a breather, time to settle down through two more eighths in 0:12 for that half in 0:48. But Pincay has not given up on gaining the lead. He tries for it again around the turn, urging Sham on. He goes to the lead by a full head. Then he is a neck in front. Then almost a half-length. They power past the $1^1/_8$-pole. It is Sham's longest lead, and he battles to keep it. Secretariat gives him no time to relax. He contests every step of ground. He presses at

Sham, keeping the pressure on him. And presses again. He's not letting him get away. They race the third furlong in 0:11²/₅, still a sprinting pace, far too fast for this distance.

They have nine furlongs to go and they should be galloping. At this moment Turcotte could ease the pressure, but he does not. Turning for the backside, he lets Secretariat come to Sham again. Neither lets up. Unrestrained, they are sizzling along better than twelves to the eighth down the backside. The fractions pile up. Pincay keeps looking and hoping for Turcotte to take back on Secretariat. Turcotte, for himself, looks for Pincay to take back, letting Secretariat roll. He comes back to within a neck of Sham, picking up speed, then closes to a head-bobbing nose of him.

John Finney, standing in a box seat with syndicate member Bertram Firestone, senses what is happening now. As the two colts race to the mile-post at the head of the backstretch, following the half-mile, his eyes turn to the toteboard teletimer. Finney blinks. And so does Lucien, who grows grim as the teletimer flashes frantically its message:

0:46¹/₅.

'They're going too fast!' Finney hollers to Firestone above the din. They have rushed through the fastest opening half-mile in the history of the Belmont Stakes.

What is Turcotte doing? What is he thinking about?

He is not thinking about the clock. He is simply sitting on Secretariat. He does not know how fast he's going. He knows he's rolling, yes – but he thinks the colt is running 12 seconds to the eighth, as Riva Ridge had run the year before, galloping the first half in 0:48. Secretariat is moving so effortlessly under him, not straining but moving well and doing it all on his own. The colt is awesome in the way he runs. He has been on the left lead around the turn, and as he banks and straightens into the backstretch, Turcotte feels the hitch in Secretariat's rhythmic stride: nine jumps into the backside straight, Secretariat has switched to the right lead – machinelike in the ease with which he does it – and levels out into long, smooth and powerful strides. The pressure of the pace becomes intense. Neither colt has eased off an instant from the start.

They race in tandem for the seven-eighths pole. Ahead of them, the backstretch opens to the far turn 800 yards away, wavering in

123

furrows in the heat, wide and flat and empty. Turcotte feels the wind rushing his face, his silks billowing out behind him. Looking to the right, he sees the wet and lathering neck of Sham, whose nose is thrust out in a drive. Turcotte thinks Sham looks as if he's under strain. And he is. Pincay feels the colt not striding well. Ten lengths behind them, My Gallant and Twice a Prince are running head and head down the backside in a race of their own. Baeza, on Twice a Prince, looks ahead and sees the hindlegs of Sham beginning to come apart, swimming and rubbery, and for the first time he might have a chance for the $33,000 in second money. It is only a matter of time, Baeza thinks, before Sham will drop back to him. Cordero has seen Sham in distress, too, and now he's trying hard for second money. So Baeza hollers to Cordero, who is riding next to him.

'I'm going to be second, man!'

'Screw you, man,' Cordero says to Baeza. 'You gotta beat me!'

Their race is on down the backstretch.

Secretariat races the fifth furlong in 0:12, giving him five-eighths of a mile in a sensational 0:58$\frac{1}{5}$. That eighth begins to pry him lose from Sham. Sham is already suffering. They are still running as if in a dash, faster than Spanish Riddle raced five furlongs in the fifth that day, faster than Man o' War and Count Fleet and Citation ran the first five furlongs in the Belmont Stakes. Secretariat is almost a length in front coming to the seven-eighths pole, with 1,540 yards to go. He has just dragged Sham through a second quarter-mile of the Belmont Stakes in 0:22$\frac{3}{5}$, then taken him out a fifth furlong in 0:12. He cannot maintain that clip. Yet, what has been seen is still only preliminary. Now he is delivering the coup de grace, the cruncher. Secretariat rushes through the sixth furlong and under the pressure of it Sham begins to disintegrate almost visibly. The crowd can see it, clamoring and shouting as Secretariat begins to pull away from Sham, opening a length and a half. He is picking up speed again, charging down the backside, his form flawless through the twenty-five-foot sweep of his strides – forelegs folding and snapping at the ground, the hindlegs scooting far under him and propelling him forward, the breathing deep and regular, the head and neck rising and dipping with the thrust and motion of the legs. Having chirped just once to force the pace at the first turn, Turcotte has done nothing since then to bring him where he is. Yet, he is racing through the sixth furlong in 0:11³/₅, the crunching eighth, and opening two and a half lengths on Sham. Sham is finished with that eighth. He has been asked for more than he has. Secretariat sweeps past the three-quarter pole. Eyes swing to the teletimer: 1:09⁴/₅.

There are gasps from the crowd. The reaction is almost universal. Finney is stunned.

'That's suicidal!' he yells to Bert Firestone. By almost one full second it is the fastest six furlongs ever run in the Belmont Stakes, and only 0:1¹/₅ seconds off the course record for that distance. In the box seats, Lucien has seen the splits and his face is rigid. His lips are pursed. His hands are on the box-seat railing. He understands the implications of the running time. So he waits, staring at his red horse bounding around the far turn.

Down on the racetrack, racing official Pat O'Brien stands by the finish line looking at the teletimer and his mind jumps back to that afternoon of June 15, 1957, when Bold Ruler raced through the first half-mile in 0:46⁴/₅ and the three-quarters in a suicidal 1:10²/₅ and almost stopped to a walk in the stretch, finally finishing third. Remembering that, O'Brien sees the sins of the father visited on the son.

Up in the press box, CBS' Gene Petersen hollers to *Racing Form* columnist Herb Goldstein, 'He's going to win big, Herb!'

Goldstein, appalled by the fraction, shouts back: *'He's going too damn fast!'*

Dr William Lockridge, the syndicate member, looks at the time from his place in the dining room at Belmont Park and excitedly climbs up on a chair and then onto the dining room table. The beginnings of pandemonium rock the place.

What is Turcotte doing? Has he gone mad?

He is still sitting cool on the turn, listening as Sham's hoofbeats fade away behind him. Turning around once to see who is coming, he sees them dropping back. Then he turns again.

He wonders how fast he's going. He suspects he is going fast enough. He has not cocked his whip, and he's still thinking he's traveling at the rate of 12 seconds to the eighth. He thinks he has gone the three-quarters in 1:12 and that he is doing the seven-eighths in 1:24 and coming to the mile mark in 1:36. It has all been working so beautifully for Turcotte. Secretariat has killed off Sham and now he's coasting home, far in front and getting farther. The colt is bounding along on his own. He has opened three lengths on Sham. Now four, now five. Then six. Turcotte turns again and sees them all far behind him. Now he is widening the lead to seven as he races on the turn and finishes the seventh furlong in 0:12$^1/_5$, giving him seven-eighths in 1:22, and banks around the turn through the eighth furlong in 0:12$^1/_5$. Once again the crowd's eyes turn to the clocks and roll in their sockets: 1:34$^1/_5$.

It is an incredible fraction, far faster than any horse has ever run the first mile in the Belmont Stakes. Goldstein stands awed by it. O'Brien wonders how Secretariat will be able to stand up at the end. Penny clenches her hands. Lucien remains quiet, still looking solemnly at the racetrack, across the hedge and the lakes and lawns to the far turn, where Turcotte rocks on across the back of Secretariat, listens to the beat of Secretariat's hooves on the racetrack and the sound of the 70,000 people screaming and moiling and echoing 600 yards away. Finney is boggled.

'He can't stand up to this!' he yells to Firestone.

In the announcer's booth, announcer Clive Anderson's voice is rising at the sight of it. Beneath him the crowd has grown deafening loud and rich, and Anderson gropes to articulate what he is witnessing.

'Secretariat is blazing along! The first three-quarters of a mile in 1:09$^4/_5$. Secretariat is widening now. He is moving like a tremendous machine!'

The colt is in front by eight and by ten and now he is opening twelve over Sham, who is beginning to come back to My Gallant and Twice a Prince. Feeling the hopelessness, Pincay has decided not to persevere with Sham. He feels the Sommer colt is in distress and so he coasts rearward. Turcotte wheels Secretariat around the turn. All Turcotte hears is the sound of Secretariat walloping the earth and taking deep breaths of air and then, to the right, the lone voice of a man calling to him from the hedge by the fence.

'You got it, Ronnie! Stay there.'

The poles flash by, one after another, and Secretariat continues widening his lead – to fourteen and then fifteen lengths midway of the turn. Then sixteen. Seventeen. Eighteen. He does not back off. He never slows a moment as he sweeps the turn and races to ever-widening leads, battering at the ground with mechanistic precision.

Finney and Laurin and all the others are watching for some sign that Secretariat is weakening, for some evidence that the pace is beginning to hurt, for the stride to shorten or the tail to slash or the ears to lay back fast to the skull. But there are no signs of weariness. Racing past the three-eighths pole – midway of the turn for home, with 660 yards to go – Secretariat is racing faster than he was past the half-mile pole on the turn. He flashes by the pole one and one eighth miles into the race – 1:46$^1/_5$!

Secretariat has just tied the world record for nine furlongs. He is running now as if in contempt of the clock. Those watching him begin to comprehend the magnitude of effort. He is moving beyond the standard by which the running horse has been traditionally judged, not tiring, not leg weary, not backing up a stroke, dimensionless in scope, and all the time Turcotte asking nothing of him. The crowds continue to erupt. Looking, Turcotte sees the hands shoot up in the grandstand, the thousands on their feet, hundreds lining the rail of the homestretch with the programs waving and the hands clapping and the legs jumping.

He is still galloping to the beat of twelve. Aglide, he turns for home in full flight. He opens twenty-one lengths. He increases that to twenty-two. He is running easily. Nor is the form deteriorating. There remains the pendulumlike stride of the forelegs and the drive of the hindlegs, the pumping of the shoulders and the neck, the rise and dip of the head. He makes sense of all the mystical pageant rites of blood through which he has evolved as distillate, a climactic act in a triumph of the breed, one horse combining all the noblest qualities of his species and his ancestry – of the unbeaten Nearco through Nasrullah and Bold Ruler, of the iron horse Discovery through Outdone and Miss Disco, of the dashing St Simon through Prince Rose and Princequillo and of the staying Brown Bud through Imperatrice by way of Somethingroyal. He defines the blooded horse in his own terms.

He sweeps into the stretch through a tenth furlong in 0:12$^4/_5$, the slowest eighth yet, and Turcotte is still holding him together – his black boots pressed against the upper back, moving with the rocky motion of the legs, his hands feeling the mane blown back against the fingers and the knuckles pressed white against the rubber-thick reins. The teletimer flashes 1:59 for the mile and a quarter, two-fifths faster than his Derby, faster than the Belmont ten-furlong record by a full second.

He is twenty-three lengths in front. He lengthens that to twenty-four. And then to twenty-five, the record victory margin held by Count Fleet since 1943.

He is not backing up yet.

Once again he picks up the tempo in the upper stretch, racing the eleventh furlong in 0:12$^1/_5$, as fast as he has run the opening 220 yards of the race. That furlong gives him a mile and three-eighths in 2:11$^1/_5$, three seconds faster than Man o' War's world record set in the Belmont Stakes fifty-three years before. Obliterating Count Fleet's record, Secretariat opens twenty-six lengths. He widens that to twenty-seven and twenty-eight. He comes to the eighth pole in midstretch, and the whole of Belmont Park is roaring full-throatedly. The television camera sweeps the stands and hands are shooting in the air. No one can remember anything quite like it, not even the oldest veteran. No one applauds during the running of a race, but now the crowds in the box seats and the grandstand are standing as one and clapping as Secretariat races alone through the homestretch. They've come to see a coronation, America's ninth Triple Crown winner, but many are beginning to realize that they are witnessing the greatest single performance in the history of the sport. Veteran horsemen are incredulous. Eyes have turned to and from the teletimer and the horse in disbelief, looking for some signs of stress and seeing nothing but the methodical rock of the form and the reach and snap of the forelegs. For a moment in midstretch, as the sounds envelop him, even Turcotte is caught off guard by the scope of the accomplishment. Passing the eighth pole, he looks to the left at the infield tote and the teletimer, and the first number he sees is 1:09$^4/_5$ for the first three-quarters. He sees these numbers but they fail to register. So he looks ahead again. Then they register and he looks back again, in a delayed double take.

By now he has passed the sixteenth pole, with only seventy-five yards to run, and the crowd senses the record, too. Turcotte looks at the teletimer blinking excitedly and sees 2:19, 2:20. The record is 2:26$^3/_5$. The colt has a chance to break the record in all three classics – an unprecedented feat. So, keeping his whip uncocked, Turcotte pumps his arm and hand-rides Secretariat through the final yards. Sham fades back to last, and Twice a Prince and My Gallant are head and head battling for the place – Cordero and Baeza are riding all out to the wire – but Secretariat continues widening on them.

To twenty-nine lengths.

Turcotte scrubs and pushes on Secretariat and he lengthens the margin to thirty lengths. The wire looms. The teletimer flashes crazily. All eyes are on it and on the horse. Many horsemen have seen Turcotte looking at the timer and now they're looking at it too. He is racing the clock, his only competitor, and he is beating it badly as he rushes the red horse through the final yards. At the end, the colt dives for the wire. The teletimer blinks the last time and then it stops, as though it has been caught in midair – 2:24.

He hits the wire thirty-one lengths in front of Twice a Prince, with Sham finishing last, forty-five lengths behind.

The sounds of the crowd have gathered in the run through the straight and now they burst forth in one stentorian howl. Secretariat has just shattered three records in the Triple Crown, this mile-and-a-half record by two and two-fifths seconds, and Turcotte stands up at the wire and lets him gallop out an extra eighth to the turn. Even easing up he eclipses records through his momentum. Clocker Sonny Taylor catches him going the final eighth in $0:13^3/_5$, giving the colt a mile and five-eighths in an unofficial $2:37^3/_5$, time that would shatter Swaps's world mark by three-fifths of a second. He has strung together a phenomenal run of eighths – $0:12^1/_5$, $0:11^2/_5$, $0:11^2/_5$, $0:11^1/_5$ $0:12$, $0:11^3/_5$, $0:12^1/_5$, $0:12^1/_5$, $0:12$, $0:12^4/_5$, $0:12^1/_5$, $0:12^4/_5$. Incredibly, none of them is slower than $0:12^4/_5$.

Turcotte pulls him to a halt on the turn. Jim Dailey, the outrider who met Gaffney on the colt a year before, meets him now on the bend. He has not seen the teletimer.

'How fast you go?'

'Two twenty-four flat,' Turcotte yells back to him.

'You're crazy.'

'I'm telling you!' says Turcotte.

'Can't be.'

Turcotte turns the horse around at the bend. With Dailey riding a pony beside him, he begins a slow gallop past the stands and the clubhouse. Ovations ripple and accompany him home. Acknowledging them, Turcotte doffs his helmet as he did at the Derby and brings down the house, prompting even more thunderous cheering and applause.

On the racetrack, Hollis Chenery greets Secretariat and Turcotte outside the winner's circle, and Chenery takes hold of the lead shank and brings them into the circle. The reception of the crowd is electric.

They lean over the flower boxes down the victory lane; long, braceleted arms reach out for him. Hands slap his glistening coat. Hands shoot up in fists. Hands are cupped over faces. Hands are holding hands and gesturing elation and awe. The clapping and the shouts of encouragement – to Turcotte and Laurin, to Penny and Secretariat – come in endless waves, and they follow them all through the winner's circle ceremony. Eddie Sweat takes the colt and walks him home, passing the crowds that line the winner's circle, the governors and racing officials, and heading back to the mouth of the tunnel. Thousands of people line the tunnel and send up cheers as Sweat and Secretariat pass. Men and women of all ages holler boisterously to Sweat and clap their hands. Sweat nods his head and smiles and raises his fist in the air. As he makes his way home through the paddock, the crowds are waiting for him everywhere. The colt is sweating heavily as he slants around the walking ring of the paddock, his nostrils moist and warm and flaring. Beads of sweat trickle down his head and neck, his eyes dart left and right. The crowds shout his name over and over as he walks past them.

As Sweat leads the colt around the paddock, he passes trainer Elliott Burch, who is waiting to saddle a horse in the race following the Belmont. His patron, Paul Mellon, owns a share in Secretariat. Burch's face is flushed with excitement. His arms are folded and he turns to follow Secretariat as he goes by. He has never seen such a performance, and he calls out, 'Spectacular! Just sensational!'

Burch is one of many horsemen, young and old, who would claim that they had witnessed, on a sultry afternoon in June, the greatest single performance ever by a running horse, an unprecedented feat of power, grace, and speed. The chorus is large and vocal in their claims of that, and among them are Alfred Vanderbilt and Woody Stephens, Buddy Hirsch and Sherrill Ward, P. G. Johnson and Arthur Kennedy. Charles Hatton is calling Secretariat the greatest horse he has ever seen, in sixty years of covering and observing the American turf, greater even than Man o' War.

'His only point of reference is himself,' Hatton says.

WILLIAM NACK, from *Big Red of Meadow Stable*

Charlie Hatton, famous writer on the Daily Racing Form, *later summed up Secretariat's 1973 Belmont Stakes with one of the most telling sentences in all racing literature:*

He could not have moved faster if he had fallen off the grandstand roof.

Bill Nack's extraordinarily detailed account of the 1973 Belmont contrasts with the minimalist race description of the 1964 Cheltenham Gold Cup by Dominic Behan in his rollicking song 'Arkle'.

ARKLE

It happened in the springtime of the year of sixty-four
When Englishmen were making pounds and fivers by the score.
He beat them on the hollows, he beat them on the jumps
A pair of fancy fetlocks, well he showed them all the bumps.

He's English, he's English, English as you've seen
A little bit of Arab stock and more from Stephen's Green
Take a look at Mill House, throw out your chest with pride
He's the greatest steeplechaser on the English countryside.

Then a quiet man called Dreaper living in the Emerald Isle
Said, 'That horse of yours called Mill House surely shows a bit
    of style.
But I've a little fellow, and Arkle is his name.
Put your money where you put your mouth and then we'll play
    the game.'

Well the racing English gentlemen laughed till fit to burst,
'You tried before, Tom Dreaper, and then you came off worst.

If you think your horse can beat us, you're running short on
   brains.
It's Mill House that you're talking of and not those beastly
   Danes.'

Arkle now is five to two, Mill House is money on,
They're off! and dare believe I do, the champion has it won.
There are other horses in the race to test the great chap's might,
But dearie me! it's plain to see the rest are out of sight.

There are three more fences now to go, he leads by twenty
   lengths.
Brave Arkle's putting in a show – poor chap, he's all but spent!
Mill House sweeps on majestically, great glory in each stride,
He's the greatest horse undoubtedly within the whole world
   wide.

Two to go, still he comes, cutting down the lead,
He's beaten bar the shouting, he hasn't got the speed.
They're on the run-up to the last, 'My God! Can he hold out?
Look behind you, Willie Robinson, man what are you about?'

They're at the last and over, Pat Taaffe has more in hand.
He's passing England's Mill House, the finest in the land.
'My God, he has us beaten, what can we English say?
The ground was wrong, the distance long, too early in the day.'

DOMINIC BEHAN

---

*Thirty years earlier another of the all-time favourites had made his final
racecourse appearance in the Queen Alexandra Stakes at Royal Ascot.*

'They're off!' It was 4.34 p.m. – the start was four minutes late.
Mail Fist, as ever, jumped into the lead. He did his best, but there
were other horses in the race who, aided and abetted by their
riders, thought that it would not be fair that he should always
have the honour of being pacemaker: and they also set off as fast
as they could go, thinking that the old gentleman behind might
crack up and cry 'enough' long before the winning post was
reached. As the field came past the Stands for the first time, rather

more than seven furlongs from the start, Benskin and Mail Fist were leading, followed by Solatium and Loosestrife. Brown Jack was running with Nitsichin several lengths behind the leaders. Quite early on the stretch of the course going down to the Swinley Bottom Loosestrife went on in front with a definite lead. Mail Fist had done his bit and retired gracefully. Solatium followed Loosestrife, and it seemed to some visitors just for a moment that Loosestrife might run away. On the far side of the course Brown Jack moved up, followed by the French horse, Dark Dew. Before the Straight was reached Loosestrife was in trouble and Brown Jack came on in front with Solatium, the latter running a much better race than he had done in the race for the Ascot Stakes earlier in the week.

The bell rang and Brown Jack and Solatium entered the Straight well clear of any other runner. It was certain then that one of the two would win. Solatium, on the rails, hung on most gallantly to Brown Jack. Indeed, he hung on so long that the suspense to me became almost unbearable.

Solatium belongs to a great friend of mine, but how I hoped his horse would fall away beaten so that Brown Jack could win! And then slowly but surely Brown Jack and Donoghue began to draw away; at first by inches and then by feet, and then, quite close to the winning post, they were clear and the race was over. Brown Jack and his friend won by two lengths from Solatium, who had run a most gallant race and had been ridden as ably as a horse could be ridden by Caldwell. Some of the runners were struggling past the winning post after Brown Jack had been pulled up and was returning to the Paddock, and Mail Fist received a special cheer as he went by long after his friend.

I have never seen such a sight anywhere, and especially never at Ascot, as I was privileged to see when Brown Jack went past the winning post. Eminently respectable old ladies in the Royal Enclosure gathered up their skirts and began, with such dignity as they could command in their excitement, to make the best of their way as quickly as they could towards the place where Brown Jack and Donoghue would return after the race. Hats were raised in the air in every enclosure and there were cheers from all parts of the course. Such a scene could be witnessed only in this country, and it has never in my time been witnessed here in such intensity.

The unsaddling enclosure to which Brown Jack was returning for the sixth time after winning this race was surrounded many times deep. Crowds were waiting round the gateway leading from the course to the Enclosure. Police made a lane for the triumphant pair, Brown Jack and Donoghue. The trainer, Ivor Anthony, as shy and bashful as ever, had already gone into the unsaddling enclosure where he was standing stroking his chin and trying to look unconcerned: he had been too nervous to watch the race, and had sat alone under the trees in the paddock until the great roar of cheering told him all was well.

And then at last Brown Jack came in. He looked to the right and to the left as he walked through the lane from the course to his own enclosure. His ears were pricked and he knew full well what was happening and what had happened. He was being patted on both sides from head to tail as he made his progress. 'Half his tail was pulled out,' Sir Harold Wernher told me afterwards. And then when he got to the gateway to his own enclosure he stood still. Donoghue tried to persuade him to go in, but he would not move. His ears were pricked and he was most certainly watching the people still pouring into the Paddock to see his return. He would not disappoint them. When he thought that all had arrived he walked in quietly and received the congratulations of his owner, his owner's wife, and his trainer. Donoghue, in some wonderful way, wormed his way through the people to the weighing room, and after that came the end.

R. C. LYLE, from *Brown Jack* (1934)

HOW WE BEAT THE FAVOURITE

(A Lay of the Loamshire Hunt Cup)

'Ay, squire,' said Stevens, 'they back him at evens;
The race is all over, bar shouting, they say;
The Clown ought to beat her; Dick Neville is sweeter
Than ever – he swears he can win all the way.

'A gentleman rider – well, I'm an outsider,
But if he's a gent who the mischief's a jock?

You swells mostly blunder, Dick rides for the plunder,
He rides, too, like thunder – he sits like a rock.

'He calls "hunted fairly" a horse that has barely
Been stripped for a trot within sight of the hounds,
A horse that at Warwick beat Birdlime and Yorick,
And gave Abd-el-Kader at Aintree nine pounds.

'They say we have no test to warrant a protest;
Dick rides for a lord and stands in with a steward;
The light of their faces they show him – his case is
Prejudged and his verdict already secured.

'But none can outlast her, and few travel faster,
She strides in her work clean away from The Drag,
You hold her and sit her, she couldn't be fitter,
Whenever you hit her she'll spring like a stag.

'And p'rhaps the green jacket, at odds though they back it,
May fall, or there's no knowing what may turn up.
The mare is quite ready, sit still and ride steady,
Keep cool; and I think you may just win the Cup.'

Dark-brown with tan muzzle, just stripped for the tussle,
Stood Iseult, arching her neck to the curb,
A lean head and fiery, strong quarters and wiry,
A loin rather light, but a shoulder superb.

Some parting injunction, bestow'd with great unction,
I tried to recall, but forgot like a dunce,
When Reginald Murray, full tilt on White Surrey,
Came down in a hurry to start us at once.

'Keep back in the yellow! Come up on Othello!
Hold hard on the chestnut! Turn round on The Drag!
Keep back there on Spartan! Back you, sir, in tartan!
So, steady there, easy,' and down went the flag.

We started, and Kerr made strong running on Mermaid,
Through furrows that lead to the first stake-and-bound,
The crack half extended look'd bloodlike and splendid,
Held wide on the right where the headland was sound.

I pulled hard to baffle her rush with the snaffle,
Before her two-thirds of the field got away,
All through the wet pasture where floods of the last year
Still loitered, they clotted my crimson with clay.

The fourth fence, a wattle, floor'd Monk and Bluebottle;
The Drag came to grief at the blackthorn and ditch,
The rails toppled over Redoubt and Red Rover,
The lane stopped Lycurgus and Leicestershire Witch.

She passed like an arrow Kildare and Cock Sparrow,
And Mantrap and Mermaid refused the stone wall;
And Giles on The Grayling came down at the paling,
And I was left sailing in front of them all.

I took them a burster, nor eased her nor nursed her
Until the black bullfinch led into the plough,
And through the strong bramble we bored with a scramble –
My cap was knocked off by a hazel-tree bough.

Where furrows looked lighter I drew the rein tighter
Her dark chest all dappled with flakes of white foam,
Her flanks mud-bespattered, a weak rail she shattered –
We landed on turf with our heads turned for home.

Then crashed a low binder, and then close behind her
The sward to the strokes of the favourite shook,
His rush roused her mettle, yet ever so little
She shortened her stride as we raced at the brook.

She rose when I hit her. I saw the stream glitter,
A wide scarlet nostril flashed close to my knee,
Between sky and water The Clown came and caught her,
The space that he cleared was a caution to see.

And forcing the running, discarding all cunning,
A length to the front went the rider in green;
A long strip of stubble, and then the big double,
Two stiff flights of rails with a quickset between.

She raced at the rasper, I felt my knees grasp her,
I found my hands give to her strain on the bit,

She rose when The Clown did – our silks as we bounded
Brush'd lightly, our stirrups clash'd loud as we lit.

A rise steeply sloping, a fence with stone coping –
The last – we diverged round the base of the hill,
His path was the nearer, his leap was the clearer,
I flogg'd up the straight, and he led sitting still.

She came to his quarter and on still I brought her,
And, up to his girth, to his breast-plate she drew,
A short prayer from Neville just reach'd me, 'The Devil!'
He mutter'd – lock'd level the hurdles we flew.

A hum of hoarse cheering, a dense crowd careering,
All sights seen obscurely, all shouts vaguely heard,
'The green wins!' 'The crimson!' The multitude swims on,
And figures are blended and features are blurr'd.

'The horse is her master!' 'The green forges past her!'
'The Clown will outlast her!' 'The Clown wins!' 'The Clown!'
The white railing races with all the white faces,
The chestnut outpaces, outstretches the brown.

On still past the gateway she strains in the straightway,
Still struggles, 'The Clown by a short neck at most!'
He swerves, the green scourges, the stand rocks and surges,
And flashes, and verges, and flits the white post.

Ay! so ends the tussle – I knew the tan muzzle
Was first, though the ring-men were yelling 'Dead heat!'
A nose I could swear by, but Clark said, 'The mare by
A short head.' And that's how the favourite was beat.

ADAM LINDSAY GORDON

John Masefield is not much in fashion these days, but his lengthy poem
Right Royal, *about the race for 'the English Chasers' Cup on Compton
Course', is heady stuff. Charles Cothill has backed his mount Right Royal
with all he has, to the alarm of his lady, Emmy Crowthorne, but comes
to grief early in the race. However, he remounts and sets off after his
rivals, setting up the poem's stirring ending.*

Now they charged the last hurdle that led to the Straight,
Charles longing to ride, though his spirit said 'Wait.'
He came to his horses as they came to the leap,
Eight hard-driven horses, eight men breathing deep.

On the left, as he leaped it, a flashing of brown
Kicking white on the grass, showed that Thankful was down;
Then a glance, right and left, showed that, barring all flukes,
It was Soyland's, Sir Lopez', or Peterkinooks'.

For Stormalong blundered and dwelt as he landed,
Counter-Vair's man was beaten and Monkery stranded.
As he reached to Red Ember the man on the red
Cried, 'Lord, Charlie Cothill, I thought you were dead!'

He passed the Red Ember, he came to the flank
Of Peterkinooks, whom he reached and then sank.
There were only two others, going level alone,
First the spotted cream jacket, then the blue, white and roan.

Up the street of green race-course they strained for the prize,
While the stands blurred with waving and the air shook with
    cries:
'Now, Sir Lopez!' 'Come, Soyland!' 'Now, Sir Lopez! Now, now!'
Then Charles judged his second, but he could not tell how.

But a glory of sureness leaped from horse into man,
And the man said, 'Now, beauty,' and the horse said, 'I can.'
And the long weary Royal made an effort the more,
Though his heart thumped like drum-beats as he went to the
    fore.

Neck and neck went Sir Lopez and Soyland together,
Soyland first, a short head, with his neck all in lather;
Both were ridden their hardest, both were doing their best,
Right Royal reached Soyland and came to his chest.

There Soyland's man saw him with the heel of his eye,
A horse with an effort that could beat him or tie;
Then he glanced at Sir Lopez, and he bit through his lip
And he drove in his spurs and he took up his whip.

There he lashed the game Soyland who had given his all,
And he gave three strides more, and then failed at the call,
And he dropped behind Royal like a leaf in a tide:
Then Sir Lopez and Royal ran on side by side.

There they looked at each other, and they rode, and were grim;
Charles thought, 'That's Sir Lopez. I shall never beat him.'
All the yells for Sir Lopez seemed to darken the air,
They were rushing past Emmy and the White Post was there.

He drew to Sir Lopez; but Sir Lopez drew clear;
Right Royal clung to him and crept to his ear.
Then the man on Sir Lopez judged the moment had come
For the last ounce of effort that would bring his horse home.

So he picked up his whip for three swift slashing blows,
And Sir Lopez drew clear, but Right Royal stuck close.
Charles sat still as stone, for he dared not to stir,
There was that in Right Royal that needed no spur.

In the trembling of an instant power leaped up within,
Royal's pride of high spirit not to let the bay win.
Up he went, past his withers, past his neck, to his head.
With Sir Lopez' man lashing, Charles still, seeing red.

So they rushed for one second, then Sir Lopez shot out:
Charles thought, 'There, he's done me, without any doubt.
Oh, come now, Right Royal!' And Sir Lopez changed feet
And his ears went back level; Sir Lopez was beat.

Right Royal went past him, half an inch, half a head,
Half a neck, he was leading, for an instant he led;
Then a hooped black and coral flew up like a shot,
With a lightning-like effort from little Gavotte.

The little bright mare, made of nerves and steel springs,
Shot level beside him, shot ahead as with wings.
Charles felt his horse quicken, felt the desperate beat
Of the blood in his body from his knees to his feet.

Three terrible strides brought him up to the mare,
Then they rushed to wild shouting through a whirl of blown air;

Then Gavotte died to nothing; Soyland came once again
Till his muzzle just reached to the knot on his rein.

Then a whirl of urged horses thundered up, whipped and blown,
Soyland, Peterkinooks, and Red Ember the roan.
For an instant they challenged, then they drooped and were
    done;
Then the White Post shot backwards, Right Royal had won.

Won a half length from Soyland, Red Ember close third;
Fourth, Peterkinooks; fifth, Gavotte harshly spurred;
Sixth, Sir Lopez, whose rider said 'Just at the Straight
He swerved at the hurdle and twisted a plate.'

Then the number went up; then John Harding appeared
To lead in the Winner while the bookmakers cheered.
Then the riders weighed-in, and the meeting was over,
And bright Emmy Crowthorne could go with her lover.

For the bets on Right Royal which Cothill had made
The taker defaulted, they never were paid;
The taker went West, whence he sent Charles's bride
Silver bit-cups and beadwork on antelope hide.

Charles married his lady, but he rode no more races;
He lives on the Downland on the blown grassy places,
Where he and Right Royal can canter for hours
On the flock-bitten turf full of tiny blue flowers.

There the Roman pitcht camp, there the Saxon kept sheep,
There he lives out this Living that no man can keep,
This is manful but a moment before it must pass,
Like the stars sweeping westward, like the wind on the grass.

THE BROKEN-LINK HANDICAP

While the snaffle holds, or the long-neck stings,
While the big beam tilts, or the last bell rings,
While horses are horses to train and to race,
Then women and wine take a second place
        For me – for me –

While a short 'ten-three'
Has a field to squander or fence to face!

Song of the G. R.

There are more ways of running a horse to suit your book than
pulling his head off in the straight. Some men forget this. Understand clearly that all racing is rotten – as everything connected
with losing money must be. In India, in addition to its inherent
rottenness, it has the merit of being two-thirds sham; looking
pretty on paper only. Every one knows every one else far too well
for business purposes. How on earth can you rack and harry and
post a man for his losings, when you are fond of his wife, and live
in the same Station with him? He says, 'On the Monday following,'
'I can't settle just yet.' You say, 'All right, old man,' and think
yourself lucky if you pull off nine hundred out of a two-thousand-
rupee debt. Any way you look at it, Indian racing is immoral, and
expensively immoral. Which is much worse. If a man wants your
money, he ought to ask for it, or send round a subscription-list,
instead of juggling about the country, with an Australian larrikin;
a 'brumby,' with as much breed as the boy; a brace of *chumars* in
gold-laced caps; three or four *ekka*-ponies with hogged manes, and
a switch-tailed demirep of a mare called Arab because she has a
kink in her flag. Racing leads to the *shroff* quicker than anything
else. But if you have no conscience and no sentiments, and good
hands, and some knowledge of pace, and ten years' experience of
horses, and several thousand rupees a month, I believe that you
can occasionally contrive to pay your shoeing-bills.

Did you ever know Shackles – b. w. g., 15.1$^3/_8$ – coarse, loose,
mule-like ears – barrel as long as a gatepost – tough as a telegraph-
wire – and the queerest brute that ever looked through a bridle?
He was of no brand, being one of an ear-nicked mob taken into
the *Bucephalus* at £4 10s a head to make up freight, and sold raw
and out of condition at Calcutta for Rs 275. People who lost money
on him called him a 'brumby'; but if ever any horse had Harpoon's
shoulders and The Gin's temper, Shackles was that horse. Two
miles was his own particular distance. He trained himself, ran
himself, and rode himself; and, if his jockey insulted him by giving
him hints, he shut up at once and bucked the boy off. He objected
to dictation. Two or three of his owners did not understand this,

141

and lost money in consequence. At last he was bought by a man who discovered that, if a race was to be won, Shackles, and Shackles only, would win it in his own way, so long as his jockey sat still. This man had a riding-boy called Brunt – a lad from Perth, West Australia – and he taught Brunt, with a trainer's whip, the hardest thing a jock can learn – to sit still, to sit still, and to keep on sitting still. When Brunt fairly grasped this truth, Shackles devastated the country. No weight could stop him at his own distance; and the fame of Shackles spread from Ajmir in the South, to Chedputter in the North. There was no horse like Shackles, so long as he was allowed to do his work in his own way. But he was beaten in the end; and the story of his fall is enough to make angels weep.

At the lower end of the Chedputter race-course just before the turn into the straight, the track passes close to a couple of old brick-mounds enclosing a funnel-shaped hollow. The big end of the funnel is not six feet from the railings on the off-side. The astounding peculiarity of the course is that, if you stand at one particular place, about half a mile away, inside the course, and speak at ordinary pitch, your voice just hits the funnel of the brick-mounds and makes a curious whining echo there. A man discovered this one morning by accident while out training with a friend. He marked the place to stand and speak from with a couple of bricks, and he kept his knowledge to himself. *Every* peculiarity of a course is worth remembering in a country where rats play the mischief with the elephant-litter, and Stewards build jumps to suit their own stables. This man ran a very fairish country-bred, a long, racking high mare with the temper of a fiend, and the paces of an airy wandering seraph – a drifty, glidy stretch. The mare was, as a delicate tribute to Mrs Reiver, called 'The Lady Regula Baddun' – or for short, Regula Baddun.

Shackles' jockey, Brunt, was a quite well-behaved boy, but his nerve had been shaken. He began his career by riding jump-races in Melbourne, where a few Stewards want lynching, and was one of the jockeys who came through the awful butchery – perhaps you will recollect it – of the Maribyrnong Plate. The walls were colonial ramparts – logs of *jarrah* spiked into masonry – with wings as strong as Church buttresses. Once in his stride, a horse had to jump or fall. He couldn't run out. In the Maribyrnong Plate, twelve horses were jammed at the second wall. Red Hat, leading, fell this side, and threw out The Gled, and the ruck came up behind and the space between wing and wing was one struggling, screaming, kicking shambles. Four jockeys were taken out dead; three were very badly hurt, and Brunt was among the three. He told the story of the Maribyrnong Plate sometimes; and when he described how Whalley on Red Hat, said, as the mare fell under him – 'God ha' mercy, I'm done for!' and how, next instant, Sithee There and White Otter had crushed the life out of poor Whalley, and the dust hid a small hell of men and horses, no one marvelled that Brunt had dropped jump-races and Australia together. Regula Baddun's owner knew that story by heart. Brunt never varied it in the telling. He had no education.

Shackles came to the Chedputter Autumn races one year, and his owner walked about insulting the sportsmen of Chedputter generally, till they went to the Honorary Secretary in a body and said, 'Appoint handicappers, and arrange a race which shall break Shackles and humble the pride of his owner.' The Districts rose against Shackles and sent up of their best; Ousel, who was supposed to be able to do his mile in 1–53; Petard, the stud-bred, trained by a cavalry regiment who knew how to train; Gringalet, the ewe-lamb of the 75th; Bobolink, the pride of Peshawar; and many others.

They called that race The Broken-Link Handicap, because it was to smash Shackles; and the Handicappers piled on the weights, and the Fund gave eight hundred rupees, and the distance was 'round the course for all horses.' Shackles' owner said, 'You can arrange the race with regard to Shackles only. So long as you don't bury him under weight-cloths, I don't mind.' Regula Baddun's owner said, 'I throw in my mare to fret Ousel. Six furlongs is Regula's distance, and she will then lie down and die. So also will Ousel, for his jockey doesn't understand a waiting race.' Now, this was a lie, Regula had been in work for two months at Dehra, and her chances were good, always supposing that Shackles broke a blood-vessel – or Brunt moved on him.

The plunging in the lotteries was fine. They filled eight thousand-rupee lotteries on the Broken-Link Handicap, and the account in the *Pioneer* said that 'favouritism was divided.' In plain English, the various contingents were wild on their respective

143

horses; for the Handicappers had done their work well. The Honorary Secretary shouted himself hoarse through the din; and the smoke of the cheroots was like the smoke, and the rattling of the dice-boxes like the rattle of small-arm fire.

Ten horses started – very level – and Regula Baddun's owner cantered out on his hack to a place inside the circle of the course, where two bricks had been thrown. He faced towards the brick-mounds at the lower end of the course and waited.

The story of the running is in the *Pioneer*. At the end of the first mile, Shackles crept out of the ruck, well on the outside, ready to get round the turn, lay hold of the bit and spin up the straight before the others knew he had got away. Brunt was sitting still, perfectly happy, listening to the 'drum-drum-drum' of the hoofs behind, and knowing that, in about twenty strides, Shackles would draw one deep breath and go up the last half-mile like the 'Flying Dutchman.' As Shackles went short to take the turn and came abreast of the brick-mound, Brunt heard, above the noise of the wind in his ears, a whining, wailing voice on the offside, saying – 'God ha' mercy, I'm done for!' In one stride, Brunt saw the whole seething smash of the Maribyrnong Plate before him, started in his saddle and gave a yell of terror. The start brought the heels into Shackles' side, and the scream hurt Shackles' feelings. He couldn't stop dead; but he put out his feet and slid along for fifty yards, and then, very gravely and judicially, bucked off Brunt – a shaking, terror-stricken lump, while Regula Baddun made a neck-and-neck race with Bobolink up the straight, and won by a short head – Petard a bad third. Shackles' owner, in the Stand, tried to think that his fieldglasses had gone wrong. Regula Baddun's owner, waiting by the two bricks, gave one deep sigh of relief, and cantered back to the Stand. He had won, in lotteries and bets, about fifteen thousand.

It was a Broken-Link Handicap with a vengeance. It broke nearly all the men concerned, and nearly broke the heart of Shackles' owner. He went down to interview Brunt. The boy lay, livid and gasping with fright, where he had tumbled off. The sin of losing the race never seemed to strike him. All he knew was that Whalley had 'called' him, that the 'call' was a warning; and, were he cut in two for it, he would never get up again. His nerve had gone altogether, and he only asked his master to give him a good thrashing, and let him go. He was fit for nothing, he said. He got his dismissal, and crept up to the paddock, white as chalk, with blue lips, his knees giving way under him. People said nasty things in the paddock; but Brunt never heeded. He changed into tweeds, took his stick and went down the road, still shaking with fright, and muttering over and over again – 'God ha' mercy, I'm done for!' To the best of my knowledge and belief he spoke the truth.

So now you know how the Broken-Link Handicap was run and won. Of course you don't believe it. You would credit anything about Russia's designs on India, or the recommendations of the Currency Commission; but a little bit of sober fact is more than you can stand.

RUDYARD KIPLING (1888)

He would have withdrawn from the feast had not the noise of voices allayed the smart. Madden had lost five drachmas on Sceptre for a whim of the rider's name: Lenehan as much more. He told them of the race. The flag fell and, huuh, off, scamper, the mare ran out freshly with O. Madden up. She was leading the field: all hearts were beating. Even Phyllis could not contain herself. She waved her scarf and cried: Huzzah! Sceptre wins! But in the straight on the run home when all were in close order the dark horse Throwaway drew level, reached, outstripped her. All was lost now. Phyllis was silent: her eyes were sad anemones. Juno, she cried, I am undone. But her lover consoled her and brought her a bright casket of gold in which lay some oval sugarplums which she partook. A tear fell: one only. A whacking fine whip, said Lenehan, is W. Lane. Four winners yesterday and three today. What rider is like him? Mount him on the camel or the boisterous buffalo the victory in a hack canter is still his. But let us bear it as was the ancient wont. Mercy on the luckless! Poor Sceptre! he said with a light sigh. She is not the filly that she was. Never, by this hand, shall we behold such another.

JAMES JOYCE, from *Ulysses* (1922)

Few fiction writers have so successfully evoked the atmosphere of the race

145

as Dick Francis, who as a former champion jump jockey knew what he was writing about. These are the opening few paragraphs of his very first novel, Dead Cert, *published in 1962.*

The mingled smells of hot horse and cold river mist filled my nostrils. I could hear only the swish and thud of galloping hooves and the occasional sharp click of horse-shoes striking against each other. Behind me, strung out, rode a group of men dressed like myself in white silk breeches and harlequin jerseys, and in front, his body vividly red and green against the pale curtain of fog, one solitary rider steadied his horse to jump the birch fence stretching blackly across his path.

All, in fact, was going as expected. Bill Davidson was about to win his ninety-seventh steeplechase. Admiral, his chestnut horse, was amply proving he was still the best hunter chaser in the kingdom and I, as often before, had been admiring their combined back view for several minutes.

Ahead of me the powerful chestnut hindquarters bunched, tensed, sprang: Admiral cleared the fence with the effortlessness of the really great performer. And he'd gained another two lengths, I saw, as I followed him over. We were down at the far end of Maidenhead racecourse with more than half a mile to go to the winning post. I hadn't a hope of catching him.

The February fog was getting denser. It was now impossible to see much farther than from one fence to the next, and the silent surrounding whiteness seemed to shut us, an isolated string of riders, into a private lonely limbo. Speed was the only reality. Winning post, crowds, stands and stewards, left behind in the mist, lay again invisibly ahead, but on the long deserted mile and a half circuit it was quite difficult to believe they were really there.

It was an eerie, severed world in which anything might happen. And something did.

We rounded the first part of the bend at the bottom of the racecourse and straightened to jump the next fence. Bill was a good ten lengths in front of me and the other horses, and hadn't exerted himself. He seldom needed to.

The attendant at the next fence strolled across the course from the outside to the inside, patting the top of the birch as he went, and ducked under the rails. Bill glanced back over his shoulder and I saw the flash of his teeth as he smiled with satisfaction to see me so far behind. Then he turned his head towards the fence and measured his distance.

Admiral met the fence perfectly. He rose to it as if flight were not only for birds.

And he fell.

Aghast, I saw the flurry of chestnut legs threshing the air as the horse pitched over in a somersault. I had a glimpse of Bill's bright-clad figure hurtling head downwards from the highest point of his trajectory, and I heard the crash of Admiral landing upside down after him.

Automatically I swerved over to the right and kicked my horse into the fence. In mid-air, as I crossed it, I looked down at Bill. He lay loosely on the ground with one arm outstretched. His eyes were shut. Admiral had fallen solidly, back downwards, across Bill's unprotected abdomen, and he was rolling backwards and forwards in a frantic effort to stand up again.

I had a brief impression that something lay beneath them. Something incongruous, which ought not to be there. But I was going too fast to see properly.

As my horse pressed on away from the fence, I felt as sick as if I'd been kicked in the stomach myself. There had been a quality about that fall which put it straight into the killing class.

I looked over my shoulder. Admiral succeeded in getting to his feet and cantered off loose, and the attendant stepped forward and bent over Bill, who still lay motionless on the ground. I turned back to attend to the race. I had been left in front and I ought to stay there. At the side of the course a black-suited, white-sashed First-Aid man was running towards and past me. He had been standing at the fence I was now approaching, and was on his way to help Bill.

I booted my horse into the next three fences, but my heart was no longer in it, and when I emerged as the winner into the full view of the crowded stands, the mixed gasp and groan which greeted me seemed an apt enough welcome. I passed the winning post, patted my mount's neck, and looked at the stands. Most heads were still turned towards the last fence, searching in the

impenetrable mist for Admiral, the odds-on certainty who had lost
his first race for two years.

In George Moore's Esther Waters, *the servants below stairs are anxious
to hear from Mr Leopold, who has been at Goodwood, how 'the Demon'
on Silver Braid beat 'the Tinman' – Fred Archer – to win the big race.*

Nearly everything came down untouched. The Barfields had been
eating and drinking almost all day on the course, and Esther had
finished washing up before nine. But if little was eaten upstairs,
plenty was eaten downstairs; the mutton was finished in a trice,
and Mrs Latch had to fetch from the larder what remained of a
beefsteak pudding. Even then they were not satisfied, and fine
inroads were made into a new piece of cheese. Beer, according to
orders, was served without limit, and four bottles of port were
sent down so that the health of the horse might be adequately
drunk.

While assuaging their hunger the men had exchanged many
remarks regarding the Demon's bad ending, how nearly he had
thrown the race away; and the meal being now over, and there
being nothing to do but to sit and talk, Mr Leopold, encouraged
by William, entered on an elaborate and technical account of the
race. The women listened, playing with a rind of cheese, glancing
at the cheese itself, wondering if they could manage another slice,
and the men sipping their port wine, puffing at their pipes, William
listening most greedily, enjoying each sporting term, and remind-
ing Mr Leopold of some detail ingeniously whenever he seemed
disposed to shorten his narrative. The criticism of the Demon's
horsemanship took a long while, for by a variety of suggestive
remarks William led Mr Leopold into reminiscences of the skill
of certain famous jockeys in the first half of the century. These
disgressions wearied Sarah and Grover, and their thoughts
wandered to the dresses that had been worn that day, and the
lady's-maid remembered she would hear all that interested her
that night in the young ladies' rooms. At last, losing all patience,
Sarah declared that she didn't care what Chifney had said when
he just managed to squeeze his horse's head in front in the last
dozen yards, she wanted to know what the Demon had done to

nearly lose the race – had he mistaken the winning-post and pulled up? William looked at her contemptuously, and would have answered rudely, but at that moment Mr Leopold began to tell the last instructions that the Gaffer had given the Demon. The orders were that the Demon should go right up to the leaders before they reached the half-mile and remain there. Of course, if he found that he was a stone or more in hand, as the Gaffer expected, he might come away pretty well as he liked, for the greatest danger was that the horse might get shut out or might show temper and turn it up.

'Well,' said Mr Leopold, 'there were two false starts, and Silver Braid must have galloped a couple of 'undred yards afore the Demon could stop him. There wasn't two-penny worth of strength in him – pulling off those three or four pounds pretty well finished him. He'll never be able to ride that weight again. He said afore starting that he felt weak; you took him along too smartly from Portslade the last time you went there.'

'When he went by himself he'd stop playing marbles with the boys round the Southwick public-house.'

'If there had been another false start I think it would have been all up with us. The Gaffer was pale, and he stood there not taking his glasses from his eyes. There were over thirty of them, so you can imagine how hard it was to get them into line. However, at the third attempt they were got straight and away they came, a black line stretching right across the course. Presently the black cap and jacket came to the front, and not very long after a murmur went round, "Silver Braid wins." Never saw anything like it in all my life. He was three lengths a'ead, and the others were pulling off. "Damn the boy; he'll win by twenty lengths," said the Gaffer, without removing his glasses. But when within a few yards of the stand – '

At that moment the bell rang. Mr Leopold said, 'There, they are wanting their tea; I must go and get it.'

'Drat their tea,' said Margaret; 'they can wait. Finish up; tell us how he won.'

Mr Leopold looked round, and seeing every eye fixed on him he considered how much remained of the story, and with quickened speech continued, 'Well, approaching the stand, I noticed that Silver Braid was not going quite so fast, and at the very instant the Demon looked over his shoulder, and seeing he was losing ground he took up the whip. But the moment he struck him the horse swerved right across the course, right under the stand, running like a rat from underneath the whip. The Demon threw the whip across and caught him one across the nose, but seeing what was 'appening, the Tinman, who was on Bullfinch, sat down and began riding. I felt as if there was a lump of ice down my back,' and Mr Leopold lowered his voice, and his face became grave as he recalled that perilous moment. 'I thought it was all over,' he said, 'and the Gaffer thought the same; I never saw a man go so deadly pale. It was all the work of a moment, but that moment was more than a year – at least, so it seemed to me. Well, about halfway up the rails the Tinman got level with the Demon. It was ten to one that Silver Braid would turn it up, or that the boy wouldn't 'ave the strength to ride out so close a finish as it was bound to be. I thought then of the way you used to take him along from Portslade, and I'd have given something to've put a pound or two of flesh into his thighs and arms. The Tinman was riding splendid, getting every ounce and something more out of Bullfinch. The Demon, too weak to do much, was sitting nearly quite still. It looked as if it was all up with us, but somehow Silver Braid took to galloping of his own accord, and 'aving such a mighty lot in 'and, he won on the post by a 'ead – a short 'ead.

'I never felt so queer in my life, and the Gaffer was no better; but I said to him, just afore the numbers went up, "It is all right, sir, he's just done it," and when the right number went up I thought everything was on the dance, going for a swim like. By golly, it was a near thing!' At the end of a long silence Mr Leopold said, shaking himself out of his thoughts, 'Now I must go and get their tea.'

5

'Grass and clean air and a sense of cheerfulness'

Days at the races

Val was in the stand at Newmarket, watching the empty track, straining her ears for the sound of the hooves, seeing the small bunch of dust and regular surging turn into a stream of shining muscle and brilliant silk, and then come past in a flash, bay, grey, chestnut, bay, so much waiting for so short a time of thundering life. And then the release of tension, the sweat-streaked beasts with flaring nostrils, the people congratulating or shrugging.

'Who won?' she said to Euan MacIntyre. 'It was so quick, I didn't see.' Though she had cried out with the rest.

'We won,' said Euan. 'He won, The Reverberator. He was great.'

Val flung her arms around Euan's neck.

'We can have a celebration,' said Euan. '25–1, not bad, we knew he would come good.'

'I bet on him,' said Val. 'To win. I put some money on White Nights, each way, because its name was nice, but I bet on him to win.'

'There,' said Euan. 'You see I've cheered you up. Nothing like a gamble and a bit of action.'

'You didn't tell me it was so beautiful,' said Val.

It was a good day, an English day, palely sunny, with patches of mist out at the edges of vision, out at the invisible end of the track, where the horses gathered.

Val had had the idea that racecourses were like the betting shops of her childhood, smelling of beer and fag ends and, it seemed to her, sawdust and male piss.

And this was grass and clean air and a sense of cheerfulness, and the dancing lovely creatures.

'I don't know if the others are here,' said Euan. 'Want to look?'

153

Euan was part of a syndicate, two solicitors, two stockbrokers, who each owned a part of The Reverberator.

They made their way round to the winner's enclosure, where the horse stood and quivered under his rug, a bright bay with white stockings, streaked black with sweat, which rose from him in steam and joined the mist. He smelled marvellous, Val thought, he smelled of hay and health and effort which was – loose, which was free, was natural. She breathed his smell and he ruffled his nostrils and tossed his head.

A. S. BYATT, from *Possession: A Romance* (1990)

I never know, when I'm telling a story, whether to cut the thing down to plain facts or whether to drool on and shove in a lot of atmosphere, and all that. I mean, many a cove would no doubt edge into the final spasm of this narrative with a long description of Goodwood, featuring the blue sky, the rolling prospect, the joyous crowds of pickpockets, and the parties of the second part who were having their pockets picked, and – in a word, what not. But better give it a miss, I think. Even if I wanted to go into details about the bally meeting I don't think I'd have the heart to. The thing's too recent. The anguish hasn't had time to pass. You see, what happened was that Ocean Breeze (curse him!) finished absolutely nowhere for the Cup. Believe me, nowhere.

These are the times that try men's souls. It's never pleasant to be caught in the machinery when a favourite comes unstitched, and in the case of this particular dashed animal, one had come to look on the running of the race as a pure formality, a sort of quaint, old-world ceremony to be gone through before one sauntered up to the bookie and collected. I had wandered out of the paddock to try and forget, when I bumped into old Bittlesham: and he looked so rattled and purple, and his eyes were standing out of his head at such an angle, that I simply pushed my hand out and shook his in silence.

'Me, too,' I said. 'Me, too. How much did *you* drop?'

'Drop?'

'On Ocean Breeze.'

'I did not bet on Ocean Breeze.'

'What! You owned the favourite for the Cup, and didn't back it!'

'I never bet on horse-racing. It is against my principles. I am told that the animal failed to win the contest.'

'Failed to win! Why, he was so far behind that he nearly came in first in the next race.'

'Tut!' said old Bittlesham.

P. G. WODEHOUSE, from *The Inimitable Jeeves*

They rolled the old car up into the park and got out. The Boy passed his arm through Spicer's. Life was good walking outside the white sun-drenched wall, past the loud-speaker vans, the man who believed in a second coming, towards the finest of all sensations, the infliction of pain. 'You're a fine fellow, Spicer,' the Boy said, squeezing his arm, and Spicer began to tell him in a low friendly confiding way all about the 'Blue Anchor'. 'It's not a tied house,' he said, 'they've a reputation. I've always thought when I'd made enough money I'd go in with my friend. He still wants me to. I nearly went when they killed Kite.'

'You get scared easy, don't you?' the Boy said. The loudspeakers on the vans advised them whom to put their money with, and gipsy children chased a rabbit with cries across the trampled chalk. They went down into the tunnel under the course and came up into the light and the short grey grass sloping down by the bungalow houses to the sea. Old bookies' tickets rotted into the chalk: 'Barker for the Odds', a smug smiling nonconformist face printed in yellow: 'Don't Worry I Pay', and old tote tickets among the stunted plantains. They went through the wire fence into the half-crown enclosure. 'Have a glass of beer, Spicer,' the Boy said, pressing him on.

'Why, that's good of you, Pinkie. I wouldn't mind a glass,' and while Spicer drank it by the wooden trestles, the Boy looked down the line of bookies. There was Barker and Macpherson and George Beale ('The Old Firm') and Bob Tavell of Clapton, all the familiar faces, full of blarney and fake good humour. The first two races had been run: there were long queues at the tote windows. The sun lit the white Tattersall stand across the course, and a few horses cantered by to the start. 'There goes General Burgoyne,' a man said, 'he's restless,' starting off to Bob Tavell's stand to cover his bet. The bookies rubbed out and altered the odds as the horses went by, their hoofs padding like boxing gloves on the turf.

'You going to take a plunge?' Spicer asked, finishing his Bass, blowing a little gaseous malted breath towards the bookies.

'I don't bet,' the Boy said.

'It's the last chance for me,' Spicer said, 'in good old Brighton. I wouldn't mind risking a couple of nicker. Not more. I'm saving my cash for Nottingham.'

'Go on,' the Boy said, 'have a good time while you can.'

They walked down the row of bookies towards Brewer's stand: there were a lot of men about. 'He's doing good business,' Spicer said. 'Did you see the Merry Monarch? He's going up,' and while he spoke, all down the line the bookies rubbed out the old sixteen to one odds. 'Ten's,' Spicer said.

'Have a good time while you're here,' the Boy said.

'Might as well patronize the old firm,' Spicer said, detaching his arm and walking across to Tate's stand. The Boy smiled. It was as easy as shelling peas. 'Memento Mori,' Spicer said, coming away card in hand. 'That's a funny name to give a horse. Five to one, a place. What does Memento Mori mean?'

'It's foreign,' the Boy said. 'Black Boy's shortening.'

'I wish I'd covered myself on Black Boy,' Spicer said. 'There was a woman down there says she's backed Black Boy for a pony. It sounds crazy to me. But think if he wins,' Spicer said. 'My God, what wouldn't I do with two hundred and fifty pounds? I'd take a share in the "Blue Anchor" straight away. You wouldn't see me back here,' he added, staring round at the brilliant sky, the dust over the course, the torn betting cards and the short grass towards the dark sea beneath the down.

'Black Boy won't win,' the Boy said. 'Who was it put the pony on?'

'Some polony or other. She was over there at the bar. Why don't you have a fiver on Black Boy? Have a bet for once to celebrate?'

'Celebrate what?' the Boy asked quickly.

'I forgot,' Spicer said. 'This holiday's perked me up, so's I think everyone's got something to celebrate.'

'If I did want to celebrate,' the Boy said, 'it wouldn't be with

Black Boy. Why, that used to be Fred's favourite. Said he'd be a Derby winner yet. I wouldn't call that a lucky horse,' but he couldn't help watching him canter up by the rails: a little too fresh, a little too restless. A man on top of the half-crown stand tic-tacked to Bob Tavell of Clapton and a tiny Jew, who was studying the ten shilling enclosure through binoculars, suddenly began to saw the air, to attract the attention of the Old Firm. 'There,' the Boy said, 'what did I tell you? Black Boy's going out again.'

'Hundred to eight, Black Boy, hundred to eight,' George Beale's representative called, and 'They're off,' somebody said. People pressed out from the refreshment booth towards the rails carrying glasses of Bass and currant buns. Barker, Macpherson, Bob Tavell, all wiped the odds from their boards, but the Old Firm remained game to the last: 'Hundred to six Black Boy': while the little Jew made masonic passes from the top of the stand. The horses came by in a bunch, with a sharp sound like splintering wood, and were gone. 'General Burgoyne,' somebody said, and somebody said: 'Merry Monarch.' The beer drinkers went back to the trestle boards and had another glass, and the bookies put up the runners in the four o'clock and began to chalk a few odds.

'There,' the Boy said, 'what did I tell you? Fred never knew a good horse from a bad one. That crazy polony's dropped a pony. It's not *her* lucky day. Why' – but the silence, the inaction after a race is run and before the results go up, had a daunting quality. The queues waited outside the totes. Everything on the course was suddenly still, waiting for a signal to begin again; in the silence you could hear a horse whinny all the way across from the weighing-in. A sense of uneasiness gripped the Boy in the quiet and the brightness. The soured false age, the concentrated and limited experience of the Brighton slum drained out of him. He wished he had Cubitt there and Dallow. There was too much to tackle by himself at seventeen. It wasn't only Spicer. He had started something on Whit Monday which had no end. Death wasn't an end; the censer swung and the priest raised the Host, and the loudspeaker intoned the winners: 'Black Boy. Memento Mori. General Burgoyne.'

'By God,' Spicer said, 'I've won. Memento Mori for a place,' and remembering what the Boy had said, 'And she's won too. A pony. What a break. Now what about Black Boy?' Pinkie was silent. He told himself: Fred's horse. If I was one of those crazy geezers who touch wood, throw salt, won't go under ladders, I might be scared to –

Spicer plucked at him. 'I've won, Pinkie. A tenner. What do you know about that?'

– to go on with what he'd planned with care. Somewhere from farther down the enclosure he heard a laugh, a female laugh, mellow and confident, perhaps the polony who'd put a pony on Fred's horse. He turned on Spicer with secret venom, cruelty straightening his body like lust.

'Yes,' he said, putting his arm round Spicer's shoulder, 'you'd better collect now.'

GRAHAM GREENE, from *Brighton Rock* (1938)

A GENUINE TIP

I now submit a strange but authentic tale. I suppose, in a sense, it could be called a case of mistaken identity. Judge for yourself, however. Draw your own conclusion. Maybe you've had a similar experience yourself.

Some time ago I paid a visit to Killarney Races. I didn't back a single winner but I enjoyed the racing, the incomparable setting and the glamour of the many delightful females present for the occasion. It was worth the visit for the shapes, colours, and sizes of the many interesting hats on view, not to mention the costumes, the shoes, the handbags and what have you!

I was given several tips but not one obliged. I wasn't disappointed because I don't really go to races to win. I go to enjoy myself and, perhaps too, to find material for my books and newspaper columns and so it was on that lovely May evening with the glitter of lakes and the serenity of soaring mountains in the background that I found the makings of a readable story. I stored it away for a while to let it mature. In this respect certain stories like certain wines improve with age.

With an old friend I partook of several bottles of nourishing beer and, believe it or not, two cream buns apiece which we purchased in the nearby dining area. I have an unbridled yearning for buns and often in city streets when I behold a pastry shop I am drawn indoors like a moth to a light bulb. We savoured our buns and beer in a quiet corner of the stand.

In between we would back our fancies and watch the racing until there came a time when the intake of beer compelled us to forsake the camaraderie of the bar for the gents' toilets.

'Always,' my friend advised, 'it is wise to keep your ears alerted in racecourse toilets for very often a lot more than buttons are slipped by the piddling punters. I have overheard vital pieces of information from time to time and, as a result, have backed many winners I might not otherwise have backed.'

Sure enough as we performed our duties we heard above the gentle cascading of numerous waters the following words of advice given by an elderly chap dressed in tweeds to a younger chap with a thin face and a jockey's slender frame.

'Never mind what her form's been like up to this,' the older of the pair was saying, 'put it all behind you and concentrate on the present time. Put the past firmly behind you and you could be on a red hot favourite instead of a rank outsider.'

'Yes, yes,' the younger man responded eagerly as they tied their fly buttons and headed for the exit.

Motioning me to silence my friend followed the pair out into the evening sunlight. They were still talking when I arrived.

The older man's face was now possessed by a most solemn expression as he looked the younger in the eye. That worthy, to give him his due, was the epitome of attention.

'Don't give her as much as a single stroke,' the older man was counselling, 'or you could unsettle her and all your efforts will be for nothing. There's some will take it alright and be the better for it but this one is bred otherwise so let you handle her with kid gloves.'

'No whip then!' the younger man said with a touch of a wry smile around his pinched mouth.

'No whip,' said the older emphatically, 'she'll go a damned sight better without it.'

Again the younger man responded agreeably. He had a jockey's athletic body, the finely chiselled features, the aquiline nose, in short, all the attributes of the professional horseman. I was about to depart in the direction of the parade ring when my pal fore-stalled me.

'Not yet,' said he, 'not yet.'

I indulged him and waited a while longer but nothing more seemed to be forthcoming. Then suddenly the old man placed a fatherly hand on the younger man's shoulder.

'Don't mind what you're told about her,' he counselled, 'she'll take any fence with you if you don't push her too hard.'

'What's the final word then?' the younger man asked before heading towards the jockeys' room to don his silks.

'The final word!' the older man echoed as he pondered deeply and scratched his chin.

'My final word,' said he, 'is to take her easy in the early stages, hold her up so to speak and then when she gets used to you and used to the course you can start nudging her. Give her a few pats when you come to the straight and you'll make that winning post no bother.'

The pair shook hands, the younger man going his way and the older presumably to the owners' and trainers' enclosure.

My friend, ever an enterprising fellow, followed the older man and waylaid him with the following words: 'Would you tell us her name like a decent man. Neither my friend nor myself has a single winner backed this night.'

The old man looked at him and a puzzled look appeared on his kindly face.

'Whose name?' he asked.

'The name of the mare you were talking to your jockey about.'

The old man threw back his head and laughed loud and long.

'Ah God help you,' said he, 'she's not a mare at all and he's no jockey. He's a neighbour of mine that's after getting married this morning and he just asked me for a few words of advice.'

'Oh,' I said apologetically, 'forgive us.'

'Think nothing of it,' said the old man. 'I'm a veteran of over forty-five years in the marriage stakes so you could say that I know the ropes.'

'I should say so,' I agreed.

'You see,' he said, 'this lady he married hasn't had such good form up to this and what I really tried to get across to him was

160

that the past is past and it's the future performance that matters in all marriages.'

On our way back to the train my friend laid a hand on my arm. There was a smile on his face.

'I was right,' he said.

'In what way?' I asked.

'Well,' said he, 'we went into that toilet looking for a tip and we got a genuine one!'

JOHN B. KEANE

The Kentucky writer Irvin S. Cobb – 'the homespun philosopher of Paducah' – displayed an appropriate degree of local pride when offering this puff for the main event at Churchill Downs in the Kentucky Derby programme in 1936:

Until you go to Kentucky and with your own eyes behold the Derby, you ain't never been nowheres and you ain't never seen nothin'!

But the second part of the American Triple Crown has its supporters also. In 1973 Bob Marisch of the Baltimore Sun *penned this appreciation of the local leg:*

The Derby is a race of autocrat sleekness
For horses of birth to prove their worth to run in the Preakness.
The Preakness is my weakness.

Hunter S. Thompson tasted the Kentucky Derby experience in 1970 with the English illustrator Ralph Steadman, then wrote an account in which autocrat sleekness does not greatly figure.

Derby morning

It was Saturday morning, the day of the Big Race, and we were having breakfast in a plastic hamburger palace called the Ptomaine Village. Our rooms were just across the road in a foul scumbox of a place called the Horn Suburban Hotel. They had a dining room, but the food was so bad that we couldn't handle it anymore. The waitresses seemed to be suffering from shin splints; they moved around very slowly, moaning and cursing the 'darkies' in the kitchen.

Steadman liked the Ptomaine Village because it had fish and chips. I preferred the 'french toast,' which was really pancake batter, fried to the proper thickness and then chopped out with a sort of cookie cutter to resemble pieces of toast.

Beyond drink and lack of sleep, our only real problem at that point was the question of access to the clubhouse. Finally we decided just to go ahead and steal two passes, if necessary, rather than miss that part of the action. This was the last coherent decision we were able to make for the next 48 hours. From that point on – almost from the very moment we started out to the track – we lost all control of events and spent the rest of the weekend just churning around in a sea of drunken horrors. My notes and recollections from Derby Day are somewhat scrambled.

But now, looking at the big red notebook I carried all through that scene, I see more or less what happened. The book itself is somewhat mangled and bent; some of the pages are torn, others are shriveled and stained by what appears to be whiskey, but taken as a whole, with sporadic memory flashes, the notes seem to tell the story. To wit:

Unscrambling Derby Day – 1
Steadman is worried about fire

Rain all nite until dawn. No sleep. Christ, here we go, a nightmare of mud and madness . . . Drunks in the mud. Drowning, fighting for shelter . . . But no. By noon the sun burns, perfect day, not even humid.

Steadman is now worried about fire. Somebody told him about the clubhouse catching on fire two years ago. Could it happen again? Horrible. Trapped in the press box. Holocaust. A hundred thousand people fighting to get out. Drunks screaming in the flames and the mud, crazed horses running wild. Blind in the smoke. Grandstand collapsing into the flames with us on the roof. Poor Ralph is about to crack. Drinking heavily, into the Haig.

Out to the track in a cab, avoid that terrible parking in people's front yards, $25 each, toothless old men on the street with big signs:

Park Here, flagging cars in the yard. 'That's fine, boy, never mind the tulips.' Wild hair on his head, straight up like a clump of reeds.

Sidewalks full of people all moving in the same direction, towards Churchill Downs. Kids hauling coolers and blankets, teenyboppers in tight pink shorts, many blacks . . . black dudes in white felt hats with leopard-skin bands, cops waving traffic along.

The mob was thick for many blocks around the track; very slow going in the crowd, very hot. On the way to the press box elevator, just inside the clubhouse, we came on a row of soldiers all carrying long white riot sticks. About two platoons, with helmets. A man walking next to us said they were waiting for the governor and his party. Steadman eyed them nervously. 'Why do they have those clubs?'

'Black Panthers,' I said. Then I remembered good old 'Jimbo' at the airport and I wondered what he was thinking right now. Probably very nervous; the place was teeming with cops and soldiers. We pressed on through the crowd, through many gates, past the paddock where the jockeys bring the horses out and parade around for a while before each race so the bettors can get a good look. Five million dollars will be bet today. Many winners, more losers. What the hell. The press gate was jammed up with people trying to get in, shouting at the guards, waving strange press badges: Chicago Sporting Times, Pittsburgh Police Athletic League . . . they were all turned away. 'Move on, fella, make way for the working press.' We shoved through the crowd and into the elevator, then quickly up to the free bar. Why not? Get it on. Very hot today, not feeling well, must be this rotten climate. The press box was cool and airy, plenty of room to walk around and balcony seats for watching the race or looking down at the crowd. We got a betting sheet and went outside.

Unscrambling D-Day II
Clubhouse/Paddock bar

Pink faces with a stylish Southern sag, old Ivy styles, seersucker coats and buttondown collars. 'Mayblossom Senility' (Steadman's phrase) . . . burnt out early or maybe just not much to burn in the first place. Not much energy in these faces, not much *curiosity*. Suffering in silence, nowhere to go after thirty in this life, just hang on and humor the children. Let the young enjoy themselves while they can. Why not? The grim reaper comes early in this league . . . banshees on the lawn at night, screaming out there beside that little iron nigger in jockey clothes. Maybe he's the one who's screaming. Bad DT's and too many snarls at the bridge club. Going down with the stock market. Oh Jesus the kid had wrecked the new car, wrapped it around that big stone pillar at the bottom of the driveway. Broken leg? Twisted eye? Send him off to Yale, they can cure anything up there.

Yale? Did you see today's paper? New Haven is under siege. Yale is swarming with Black Panthers . . . I tell you, Colonel, the world has gone mad, stone mad. Why they tell me a goddam woman jockey might ride in the Derby today.

I left Steadman sketching in the Paddock bar and went off to place our bets on the sixth race. When I came back he was staring intently at a group of young men around a table not far away. 'Jesus, look at the corruption in that face!' he whispered. 'Look at the madness, the fear, the greed!' I looked, then quickly turned my back on the table he was drawing. The face he'd picked out to draw was the face of an old friend of mine, a prep school football star in the good old days with a sleek red Chevy convertible and a very quick hand, it was said, with the snaps of a 32 B brassiere. They call him 'Cat Man.'

But now, a dozen years later, I wouldn't have recognized him anywhere but here, where I should have expected to find him, in the Paddock bar on Derby Day . . . fat slanted eyes and a pimp's smile, blue silk suit and his friends looking like crooked bank tellers on a binge. . . .

Steadman wanted to see some Kentucky Colonels, but he wasn't sure what they looked like. I told him to go back to the clubhouse men's rooms and look for men in white linen suits vomiting in the urinals. 'They'll usually have large brown whiskey stains on the front of their suits,' I said. 'But watch the shoes, that's the tip-off. Most of them manage to avoid vomiting on their own clothes, but they never miss their shoes.'

In a box not far from ours was Colonel Anna Friedman Gold-man, *Chairman and Keeper of the Great Seal of the Honorable Order of Kentucky Colonels*. Not all the 76 million or so Kentucky Colonels could make it to the Derby this year, but many had kept the faith and several days prior to the Derby they gathered for their annual dinner at the Seelbach Hotel.

The Derby, the actual race, was scheduled for late afternoon, and as the magic hour approached I suggested to Steadman that we should probably spend some time in the infield, that boiling sea of people across the track from the clubhouse. He seemed a little nervous about it, but since none of the awful things I'd warned him about had happened so far – no race riots, firestorms, or savage drunken attacks – he shrugged and said, 'Right, let's do it.'

To get there we had to pass through many gates, each one a step down in status, then through a tunnel under the track. Emerging from the tunnel was such a culture shock that it took us a while to adjust. 'God almighty!' Steadman muttered. 'This is a . . . Jesus!' He plunged ahead with his tiny camera, stepping over bodies, and I followed, trying to take notes.

Unscrambling D-Day III
The infield

Total chaos, no way to see the race, not even the track . . . nobody cares. Big lines at the outdoor betting windows, then stand back to watch winning numbers flash on the big board, like a giant bingo game.

Old blacks arguing about bets; 'Hold on there, I'll handle this' (waving pint of whiskey, fistful of dollar bills); girl riding piggyback, t-shirt says, 'Stolen from Fort Lauderdale Jail.' Thousands of teenagers, group singing 'Let the Sun Shine In,' ten soldiers guarding the American flag and a huge fat drunk wearing a blue football jersey (No. 80) reeling around with quart of beer in hand.

No booze sold out here, too dangerous . . . no bathrooms either. Muscle Beach . . . Woodstock . . . many cops with riot sticks, but no sign of riot. Far across the track the clubhouse looks like a postcard from the Kentucky Derby.

Unscrambling D-Day IV
'My Old Kentucky Home'

We went back to the clubhouse to watch the big race. When the crowd stood to face the flag and sing 'My Old Kentucky Home,'

Steadman faced the crowd and sketched frantically. Somewhere up in the boxes a voice screeched, 'Turn around, you hairy freak!' The race itself was only two minutes long, and even from our super-status seats and using 12-power glasses, there was no way to see what was really happening. Later, watching a TV rerun in the press box, we saw what happened to our horses. Holy Land, Ralph's choice, stumbled and lost his jockey in the final turn. Mine, Silent Screen, had the lead coming into the stretch but faded to fifth at the finish. The winner was a 16–1 shot named Dust Commander.

Moments after the race was over, the crowd surged wildly for the exits, rushing for cabs and buses. The next day's Courier told of violence in the parking lot; people were punched and trampled, pockets were picked, children lost, bottles hurled. But we missed all this, having retired to the press box for a bit of post-race drinking. By this time we were both half-crazy from too much whiskey, sun fatigue, culture shock, lack of sleep and general dissolution. We hung around the press box long enough to watch a mass interview with the winning owner, a dapper little man named Lehmann who said he had just flown into Louisville that morning from Nepal, where he'd 'bagged a record tiger.' The sportswriters murmured their admiration and a waiter filled Lehmann's glass with Chivas Regal. He had just won $127,000 with a horse that cost him $6,500 two years ago. His occupation, he said, was 'retired contractor.' And then he added, with a big grin, 'I just retired.'

The rest of that day blurs into madness. The rest of that night too. And all the next day and night. Such horrible things occurred that I can't bring myself even to think about them now, much less put them down in print. Steadman was lucky to get out of Louisville without serious injuries, and I was lucky to get out at all. One of my clearest memories of that vicious time is Ralph being attacked by one of my old friends in the billiard room of the Pendennis Club in downtown Louisville on Saturday night. The man had ripped his own shirt open to the waist before deciding that Ralph wasn't after his wife. No blows were struck, but the emotional effects were massive. Then, as a sort of final horror, Steadman put his fiendish pen to work and tried to patch things up by doing a little sketch of the girl he'd been accused of hustling. That finished us in the Pendennis.

HUNTER S. THOMPSON, from 'The Kentucky Derby is Decadent and Depraved'

One of the most enjoyable racing novels to appear since the war is Roger Longrigg's Daughters of Mulberry, *published in 1961, the complicated plot of which revolves around the efforts of old Major Desmond Cook to win enough money from betting to buy the farm of his dreams. The book reaches its climax with the running of an international two-year-old race at Longchamp.*

Cook began plunging through the crowd, dodging among the people who thronged the front of the grandstand. They all had their race-glasses, now, trained down the course towards the start: none of them saw Cook coming. He cannoned off a stout man, ricocheted among a group of cloth manufacturers' wives, side-stepped a pale little boy in a tweed cap and very short blue shorts. A murmur followed him, outraged and astounded: but he charged on, his mind racing and his heart sick with foreboding.

All his money on the wrong bloody horse.

The runners were under orders now, and the crowd buzzed and crackled.

He loped round the corner of the stand, dodging an ambulance man. His heart began to pound, heavily and worryingly. His legs felt like porridge. He struggled on, and came at last to the small barred windows of the Pari-Mutuel. One window had only one man at it: a neat man, making a small, neat bet. Cook clung to the iron rail by the window, panting painfully. His face felt wet and hot and his whole body was sticky with exertion and fatigue. The neat man finished and hurried away and Cook lurched to the window.

'Agh, agh,' he said, trying to control his breathing enough to form words.

A bell rang and there was a low roar from the crowd.

'*Non, monsieur,*' said the face behind the grille.

'*Mais*, damn, *mais –* '

'*C'est embêtant, je le comprends bien, mais c'est ça.*'

The window slapped shut. The runners were off.

'Oh God,' said Cook aloud.

He began running again, back towards the stand, looking for a bookie: any bookie he knew: any bookie who would lay him a bet on Larksong and save something out of the crash.

Then his heart leapt, for he saw Gaudy Carroll trotting along beside the stand.

'Gaudy!' he tried to shout. But only a high, thin wail came out. He made a great effort and shouted again: 'Gaudy!'

But the crowd was humming now, a full ripe harmony from piccolo to tuba.

'Gaudy!' shouted Cook.

But Gaudy's plump figure disappeared round the corner of the stand. Cook ran after him. He saw him for a moment, bobbing along among the fringes of the crowd; he took a huge, shuddering breath and ran on. Then he lost him. He pushed frantically through the dense, unnoticing crowd. The hum was rising to a blare. No Gaudy.

Wildly Cook saw that the horses were nearly half-way.

He looked round, desperately searching for a familiar face in the great slope of faces piled up in the stands above him. Blank white footballs, millions, all backed Larksong, shouting like fools . . . Then he saw Robby Rigby, a bookie from London with a wide yellow face: he'd do it! he'd do it! Robby was a dozen rows up in the stand and Cook began an impetuous, nightmare climb. The soft mass of French bodies walled him from each successive step; he charged and clawed and elbowed, forcing tiny gaps, whimpering and struggling and purple.

'Robby – ' he shouted: but the noise of the crowd was rising to a bellow and his voice was whisked out over the course. He lost his papers and a form-book and his hat; his collar, grubby from the night and morning, was soaked and greyish; his shirt and trousers clung as though he had been dunked in lukewarm tea. 'Robby – '

The noise of the crowd mounted to an inexorable climax. Cook turned helplessly to face the course, and saw Larksong draw ahead of Toffee-Apple to win by half a length.

All round Cook there was happy babel. People kissed; people

laughed. Tension relaxed, glasses went back into cases, the crowd began to move. Cook clung to an outcrop of metal tubing as the people flowed sluggishly down the grandstand. The sweat gathered coldly in the small of his back and he concentrated numbly on his iron handhold: it was painted green, and felt rough to the touch, and was warm. He moved one hand, leaving a dark smear of perspiration where his palm had been. The great soft-bodied crowd broke round him, reforming like interrupted treacle. Green, rough, warm – he clung to the iron, thinking: start again. Have to start again.

Sir John Astley's father

abhorred any allusion to racing, and always declared that a race-course was the sink of iniquity.

And Astley himself got into the occasional scrape.

I must now tell you the story of my watch being borrowed, without my leave, at the Epsom Spring Meeting, in April, 1887. You must know I rather pride myself on my gold watch, made by Barraud and Lund, of Cornhill, for it is a wonderful bit of mechanism, and keeps extraordinary time, and as, in the present state of my finances, I could not replace it, I ought to be more cautious as to the company I wear it in. Well, on the City and Suburban day, after an excellent luncheon at the booth, I was strolling down to the paddock to have a look at the horses, as I have done for very many years, when I want to satisfy myself as to their condition and general appearance (though, mind you, it didn't do me much good when I cast my critical eye over the wretched-looking Hermit, just before he won the Derby). However, I felt contented with all men, and never gave a thought to the safety of my ticker, not even buttoning my coat over my waistcoat; when, all of a sudden, just as I had crossed the tan-covered road, and was not more than fifty yards from the entrance to the paddock, three or four men, pretending to be larking with each other, crossed in front of me, and, to my indignation, two of them ran right up against me. I up with my clenched fists and asked them where they were coming to, and whilst my arms were thus upraised, one of them abstracted my watch from my waistcoat-pocket and twisted the bow off. I never felt him do it, but I *did* feel my watch-chain flap against my tummy, and, looking down, at once realised that my timekeeper was gone.

I made a lunge at the ruffian nearest me, but he darted away, and I after him; fortunately he ran into the arms of a good chap, Mason, who held him till I got up and gripped him by the collar, and was in the act of giving him a good shaking and ordering him to give me back my watch, when, with an amount of acuteness I am proud of, I observed a hand from behind me put forward to meet the paw of the party I had hold of, and, seeing the strange hand closed tightly, I instantly made up my mind the digits would not shut up so quickly unless there was something inside them; so, dropping the first thief, I turned round and made a grab at number two. But he wriggled off like an eel, and I should never have got up to him, had he not stooped to slip under the chains that guard the course, and as he ducked for that purpose, I caught him one in the small of the back, sending him sprawling on his stomach, and before he could rise I was on top of him; then, putting a knee each side of him, I turned him over on his back, and with my right hand secured a good hold of his neck, while with my left I seized his right hand, which was so firmly clasped that I made sure my watch was in it.

He sang out, and when I thumped his head against the turf and bid him keep still and give up my watch, he shrieked: 'I ain't got yer blooming watch, gov'nor! Didn't you see me help you ketch the man as took it? &c. &c.' I, with more knowledge of the mechanism of the human frame than most men possess (when in a hurry), raised my right knee and pressed it on his stomach, and at once established the fact of the sensitive sympathy existing (unknown to most of the faculty, but which I offer to them free, gratis, for confirmation) between the bread-basket of the *genus homo* and the digital organs which convey the bread to the small aperture leading to the store-room or, to put it more plainly, the pressure I contrived to bring to bear on his stomach became so painful that the thief sang out, 'Oh don't, gov'nor! There's yer watch, I picked it off the grass.' As his hand opened, I seized my ticker and put it in a safe receptacle; but would you believe it? all this time not a man lent me a helping hand! Wonderful lucky they didn't help the thief, I thought; and, as the man tried to wrench himself clear, I was obliged to give him a tap between the eyes to keep him quiet. At last a full-blown 'bobby' came up, swelling with importance, and with sparkling intelligence asked, 'What was up?'

I am afraid I was a little rough on him and his *confrères*, and I bid him get another to help him take the gentleman I was in charge of to the lock-up, and this he was man enough to bring off. So I followed and charged the culprit, and was told to attend the police-court at Epsom the next morning, which I did, you may be sure, particularly as the Superintendent of Police had charge of my watch. I narrated the facts to the Bench, and the benevolent old Chairman had the audacity to read me a lesson about taking the law into my own hands – good idea forsooth! He might as well have bid me give the thief another watch, and stand him a drink – and when I explained that had I not been nippy, my watch would have been ticking in another man's pocket by now, the G.O.M. pointed to the prisoner's optics (sure enough they were, 'Two lovely black eyes') and chided me for so painting him. But on my telling him the man was inclined to be obstreperous, and some wag remarking that 'I doubtless put a private mark on the thief, so that I might know him again,' the worthy beak sentenced the culprit to 'three months' hard,' and the Superintendent returned my watch, none the worse, excepting the loss of the bow. The police were very complimentary to me afterwards, and one of considerable rank assured me that, he had never known of a watch being recovered that had once been passed from the snatcher to his confederate. No doubt it was an extraordinary bit of luck my noticing that transfer from one to the other, the while I was busily employed shaking the party that borrowed it. I was told afterwards that this thief was sentenced soon after he came out of prison, to penal servitude for burglary.

The diarist John Evelyn was at Newmarket in July 1670.

Having after dinner rid about that vast level, pestered with heat and swarms of gnats, we returned over Newmarket Heath, the way being most of it a sweet turf and down, like Salisbury Plain, the jockeys breathing their fine barbs and racers, and giving them their heats.

For a mile and a half to the race-course there could be no pleasanter occupation than looking at the happy multitudes who were thronging thither; and I am bound to say, that on rich or poor shoulders I never saw so many handsome faces in my life. In the carriages, among the ladies of Kerry, every second woman was handsome; and there is something peculiarly tender and pleasing in the looks of the young female peasantry, that is perhaps even better than beauty. Beggars had taken their stations along the road in no great numbers, for I suspect they were most of them on the ground, and those who remained were consequently of the oldest and ugliest. It is a shame that such horrible figures are allowed to appear in public, as some of the loathsome ones which belong to these unhappy people. On went the crowd, how-ever, laughing and gay as possible; all sorts of fun passing from car- to foot-passengers as the pretty girls came clattering by, and the 'boys' had a word for each. One lady, with long, flowing, auburn hair, who was turning away her head from some 'boys' very demurely, I actually saw, at a pause of the cart, kissed by one of them. She gave the fellow a huge box on the ear, and he roared out, 'O murther!' and she frowned for some time as hard as she could, whilst the ladies in the blue cloaks at the back of the car uttered a shrill rebuke in Irish. But in a minute the whole party was grinning, and the young fellow who had administered the salute may, for what I know, have taken another without the slap on the face, by way of exchange.

And here, lest the fair public may have a bad opinion of the personage who talks of kissing with such awful levity, let it be said, that with all this laughing, romping, kissing, and the like, there are no more innocent girls in the world than the Irish girls; and that the women of our squeamish country are far more liable to err. One has but to walk through an English and Irish town, and see how much superior is the morality of the latter. That great terror-striker, the Confessional, is before the Irish girl, and, sooner or later, her sins must be told there.

By this time we are got upon the course, which is really one of the most beautiful spots that ever was seen: the lake and mountains lying along two sides of it, and of course visible from all. They were busy putting up the hurdles when we arrived – stiff bars and poles, four feet from the ground, with furze bushes over them. The grand stand was already full; along the hedges sat thousands of the people, sitting at their ease doing nothing, and happy as kings. A daguerreotype would have been of great service to have taken their portraits, and I never saw a vast multitude of heads and attitudes so picturesque and lively. The sun lighted up the whole course and the lakes with amazing brightness, though behind the former lay a huge rack of the darkest clouds, against which the cornfields and meadows shone in the brightest green and gold, and a row of white tents was quite dazzling.

There was a brightness and intelligence about this immense Irish crowd, which I don't remember to have seen in an English one. The women in their blue cloaks, with red smiling faces peering from one end, and bare feet from the other, had seated themselves in all sorts of pretty attitudes of cheerful contemplation; and the men, who are accustomed to lie about, were doing so now with all their might – sprawling on the banks, with as much ease and variety as club-room loungers on their soft cushions, – or squatted leisurely among the green potatoes. The sight of so much happy laziness did one good to look on. Nor did the honest fellows seem to weary of this amusement. Hours passed on, and the gentlefolks (judging from our party) began to grow somewhat weary; but the finest peasantry in Europe never budged from their posts, and continued to indulge in talk, indolence, and conversation.

When we came to the row of white tents, as usual it did not look so brilliant or imposing as it appeared from a little distance, though the scene around them was animated enough. The tents were long humble booths stretched on hoops, each with its humble streamer or ensign without, and containing, of course, articles of refreshment within. But Father Mathew has been busy among the publicans, and the consequence is, that the poor fellows are now condemned for the most part to sell 'tay' in place of whisky: for the concoction of which beverage, huge cauldrons were smoking in front of each hut-door, in round graves dug for the purpose and piled up with black smoking sod.

Behind this camp were the carts of the poor people, which were not allowed to penetrate into the quarter where the quality cars stood. And a little way from the huts again, you might see (for you could scarcely hear) certain pipers executing their melodies and inviting people to dance.

Anything more lugubrious than the drone of the pipe, or the jig danced to it, or the countenances of the dancers and musicians, I never saw. Round each set of dancers the people formed a ring, in the which the figurantes and coryphées went through their operations. The toes went in and the toes went out; then there came certain mystic figures of hands across, and so forth. I never saw less grace or seemingly less enjoyment – no, not even in a quadrille. The people, however, took a great interest, and it was 'Well done, Tim!' 'Step out, Miss Brady!' and so forth, during the dance.

Thimblerig too obtained somewhat, though in a humble way. A ragged scoundrel, the image of Hogarth's Bad Apprentice, went bustling and shouting through the crowd with his dirty tray and thimble; and, as soon as he had taken his post, stated that this was the 'royal game of thimble,' and calling upon 'jintlemin' to come forward; and then a ragged fellow would be seen to approach, with as innocent an air as he could assume, and the bystanders might remark that the second ragged fellow almost always won. Nay, he was so benevolent, in many instances, as to point out to various people who had a mind to bet, under which thimble the pea actually was; meanwhile the first fellow was sure to be looking away and talking to some one in the crowd. But somehow it generally happened, and how of course I can't tell, that any man who listened to the advice of rascal No. 2, lost his money. I believe it is so even in England.

Then you would see gentlemen with halfpenny roulette tables; and again, here were a pair (indeed, they are very good portraits) who came forward disinterestedly with a table and a pack of cards, and began playing against each other for ten shillings a game, betting crowns as freely as possible.

Gambling, however, must have been fatal to both of these gentlemen, else might not one have supposed, that if they were in the habit of winning much, they would have treated themselves to better clothes? This, however, is the way with all gamblers, as the reader has, no doubt, remarked; for, look at a game of loo or *vingt-et-un*, played in a friendly way, and where you, and three or four others, have certainly lost three or four pounds: well, ask at the end of the game who has won? and you invariably find that nobody has. Hopkins has only covered himself; Snooks has neither lost nor won; Smith has won four shillings; and so on. Who gets the money? The devil gets it, I dare say: and so, no doubt, he has laid hold of the money of yonder gentleman in the handsome greatcoat.

But, to the shame of the stewards be it spoken, they are extremely averse to this kind of sport; and presently comes up one, a stout old gentleman on a bay horse, wielding a huge hunting-whip, at the sight of which all fly, amateurs, idlers, professional men, and all. He is a rude customer to deal with, that gentleman with the whip: just now he was clearing the course, and cleared it with such a vengeance, that a whole troop on a hedge retreated backwards into a ditch opposite, where was rare kicking, and sprawling, and disarrangement of petticoats, and cries of 'O murther!' 'Mother of God!' 'I'm kilt!' and so on. But as soon as the horsewhip was gone, the people clambered out of their ditch again, and were as thick as ever on the bank.

The last instance of the exercise of the whip shall be this. A groom rode insolently after a gentleman, and calling him names, and inviting him to fight. This the great flagellator hearing, rode up to the groom, lifted him gracefully off his horse, into the air, and on to the ground, and when there administered to him a severe and merited fustigation: after which he told the course-keepers to drive the fellow off the course, and enjoined the latter not to appear again at his peril.

As for the races themselves, I won't pretend to say that they were better or worse than other such amusements; or to quarrel with gentlemen who choose to risk their lives in manly exercise. In the first race there was a fall; one of the gentlemen was carried off the ground, and it was said *he was dead*. In the second race, a horse and man went over and over each other, and the fine young man (we had seen him five minutes before, full of life and triumph, clearing the hurdles on his grey horse, at the head of the race): – in the second heat of the second race, the poor fellow missed his leap, was carried away, stunned and dying; – and the bay horse won.

I was standing, during the first heat of this race (this is the second man the grey has killed – they ought to call him the Pale Horse), by half a dozen young girls from the gentleman's village, and hundreds more of them were there, anxious for the honour of their village, the young squire, and the grey horse. Oh, how they hurrahed as he rode ahead; I saw these girls – they might be fourteen years old – after the catastrophe. 'Well,' says I, 'this is a sad end to the race.' '*And is it the pink jacket or the blue has won this time?*' says one of the girls. It was poor Mr. C—'s only epitaph: and wasn't it a sporting answer? That girl ought to be a hurdle-racer's wife; and I would like, for my part, to bestow her upon the groom who won the race.

I don't care to confess that the accident to the poor young gentleman so thoroughly disgusted my feeling as a man and a Cockney, that I turned off the race-course short, and hired a horse for sixpence to carry me back to Miss Macgillicuddy.

WILLIAM MAKEPEACE THACKERAY, from *The Irish Sketch Book* (1843)

A very outstanding feature of the British racecourse is its car-park. This is always a miracle of skill in its arrangement. Every car is fitted in, like a Chinese puzzle, so adroitly that none can be removed until the key car has been found and driven away. The key car is placed with unerring instinct – it is always a large Damliar, the owner of which, upholstered like a musical-comedy duchess, is the relict of an extremely prosperous publican.

The owner of the key car can never be found. In point of fact, she is always involved after the last race in an argument with a bookie. The trouble is that she had three-and-sevenpence each way on a horse that ran third in the fifth race at 9 to 2. She had instructed the bookmaker to reinvest the proceeds of this on a horse which eventually dead-heated at 11 to 8 in the last. She is now trying to convince the man with the bag that his method of calculating the result is wrong and that hers is right. Meanwhile, we are waiting to get home.

RIFF and RAFF (A. M. Harbord and 'Fitz'), from *They're Off! or, The Rough's Guide to the Turf* (1936)

6

'Hectic, strenuous, memorably pleasant and over before you know it'

The Derby

Derby Day has always attracted writers and artists, more on account of its social than its sporting significance.

The American writer Bill Bryson paid his first visit to the race in 1990.

THE SPORT OF GIPSIES AND KINGS

The Derby is a little like your first experience of sex – hectic, strenuous, memorably pleasant and over before you know it. If you have never been to the races before, it comes as something of a shock to realise that a day at the track means long periods of standing around in a slow but soaking rain interspersed with very occasional two-minute bursts of activity.

But that doesn't altogether matter because – and here's the second big surprise – you can't see a thing anyway. In my simple way I had thought that all races were essentially a matter of sending some animals around an oval track until they returned to the starting point. But not so at Epsom, where the course is immense and irregular. There the horses set off miles away across the downs, gallop off over the horizon somewhere in the neighbourhood of Dorking, reappear briefly on a distant slope and then disappear again.

It's only over the last couple of hundred yards that you have any hope at all of seeing anything that you could recognise as a horse. Even then, the peculiar geography of the grandstand terrace and a sudden enthusiasm for jumping up and down on the part of the spectators means that you are lucky to get more than a

179

passing glimpse of the top of some jockeys' heads as they sweep across the finishing line.

And so the day goes.

Fortunately racing is only a small part of Derby Day. There is also the gambling and drinking, the vast funfair, the gipsies with their baskets of heather, the fortune-tellers, the wandering crowds, the noise, the tumult, the sense of being part of one of the great rituals of summer. It is impossible not to be captivated by it all.

My preconceptions about the occasion were based almost entirely on a 19th-century painting by, I think, W. P. Frith. It portrayed, as I recall, crowds of beery proles happily mingling with fire-eaters, jugglers and flower sellers while their social superiors stood in elegant clusters looking over the horses for the next race. It is a quintessentially English scene of masters and servants having a happy day in the country simultaneously if not together.

Things aren't quite so picturesque now. These days the downs on Derby Day resemble nothing so much as a refugee camp, with tents and caravans and endless crowds of people sprawled boozily across the undulating landscape. Cars clog every road and the rubbish skips are overflowing by midday. But Frith would instantly recognise the air of cheerful escape, that same beguiling sense of occasion, that hum of excitement that accompanies any great sporting event.

One of the first things to strike you about the Derby is that there are no normal, average people there – the sort of people you see pottering about with hedge trimmers on Sunday mornings or sitting in lay-bys drinking cups of tea. Everyone looks like either an aristocrat or one of the Krays. The only exception to this are the bookies, most of whom look not only normal but decidedly bored, as if they would far rather be sitting in a lay-by somewhere.

In their top hats and tails, the toffs look splendid and yet faintly insufferable. Their whole bearing seems to say: 'I'm rich and important and look at what an interesting thing my barber can do with the back of my hair.' I have never understood this compulsion on the part of the British upper-classes to wear silly clothes whenever the occasion permits. You would think it would be the other way round, that it would be the servants who would be forced to wear the straw boaters and hideous jackets at Henley and the ushers who would be compelled to dress up like funeral home directors at Epsom and Ascot. But no, these are perks reserved for the rich and well-bred.

Outside the grandstand the world was full of East End jack-the-lads with their earrings and cans of lager. The toffs came and went among them, but there was no sense of animosity, even of the bantering kind, which I found surprising, even a little disappointing. It is difficult to see such a ridiculously pompous piece of headgear and not want to go up and knock it off, but no one did and everywhere there was this cheerful, and decidedly endearing, air of good will.

I don't think I have ever been amongst such good-natured people. Everybody – the police, the touts, the course officials – seemed to be having a wonderful day, the only squabbling I saw was between two wobbly Bertie Wooster types who collided outside the members' enclosure and had words, but even that, alas, came to nothing.

With so much time to kill between races I wandered around. I looked in at the Ever Ready Pavilion, where I had been promised that I would be able to rub shoulders with the likes of Roger Moore and Lady Rothermere. (This is of course why I accepted the assignment.) I showed my press pass at the door and was given a large red armband to wear at all times inside the pavilion, presumably so that everyone would realise that I was a grubby little hack and not someone important. I put it in my pocket and was interested to note that Nigel Dempster wasn't wearing his either. I bet he wasn't even asked.

Afterwards, I wandered over to the funfair and had a doughnut and the sort of hot dog that leaves you wondering if this could be the last thing you eat before going on a life-support machine. Nothing much was happening at the funfair, on account of the weather, but there was a whole encampment of gipsy fortune-tellers, all of them evidently related – Gipsy Rose Lee and Gipsy Rosa Lee and Gipsy Rose Marie Lee and Gipsy Marie Rose Lee and Gipsy Priscilla Lee ('The Gipsy Who Has Bean On BBC TV') and at least three dozen others. They all displayed photographs of themselves standing besides startled-looking members of the *Coronation Street* cast.

The Derby began late and in increasingly atrocious weather. I keep calling it the Derby, but of course it isn't that any more. It's the Ever Ready Derby. Nobody ever seems to remark on what a depressingly cheapening effect this sponsorship business has on national institutions. Where will it end – the Texas Home Care Queen Mother, the Campari House of Parliament, the Nissan Bluebird United Kingdom? In any case, I went down to the parade ring to watch the jockeys mount up (they really are astonishingly tiny) and then stayed on to watch from a viewing platform on the roof of a building overlooking the paddock.

I couldn't see a thing but an occasional far off clump of movement, I couldn't hear the track commentator because of all the shouting, I was soaked to the skin and very cold, and I hadn't laid a bet (I was about to until I saw a bookie put a wad of money the size of a Cornish pastie in his pocket and I thought: these men are licensed thieves), but I still found myself jumping up and down and shouting, 'Come on, Farmer Jock! Come on, Farmer Jock!.'

It was only much later that I discovered I had been looking at the wrong page in the programme and that Farmer Jock was in another race. I will do better next year.

Sunday Correspondent, 10 June 1990

Howard Brenton's play Epsom Downs *was first performed at the Round House in London in August 1977 (a few weeks after The Minstrel had given Lester Piggott his eighth Derby victory), with a promising young actor named Simon Callow showing his versatility by playing five roles, including the bookmaker Les Backshaker, a Beer Tent Drunk and the Aga Khan. Brenton's political stance is perhaps not shared by every member of the Jockey Club, but his play takes the notion of Derby Day as a microcosm of English society and produces a ringing evocation of how the occasion has so many different meanings for different people.*

MARGARET. I love The Derby. I always have loved The Derby. But in this queue, with my child yelling, waiting for a common garden pee, I hate The Derby.

She looks up to the sky and closes her eyes.

I hate the fat, happy people on the grass, with their teeth stuck in chicken drums. Jubilee flags coming out of their hairy ears.

Minds red with booze and bets. I hate the little men in pretty colours, who go by on the horses, with their mean, hard little heads and mean, hard little bums. I hate the penguins in the grandstand we gawk at through binoculars. I hate the race officials whizzing along the other side of the rail in their yellow car, chinless wonder masks behind the glass. I hate the jolly boys on the tops of the buses, roaring pissed, stripped to their navels, showing off their lovely tummies in the sun. I hate the coach party lovers. The totties that are pulled. The marriages that are made beneath the great wheel at the fair. Oooooh I begin to hate my fellow men and women, squeezing my insides, keeping my knees together in this queue. Trying to think of something else. If I get a pee, will I join in? Have a good time again? Love my husband and my children again? Love the crowd by the rails again? Not feel choked by the gas, rising over the crowd, the gas of a good time had by all – oooooh, come on Sharon. Let's go and have a piss in the grass.

MARGARET *runs off pushing* SHARON *who, still crying, waves her frog round her head.* MR TILLOTSON *comes on.*

PUBLIC ADDRESS SYSTEM. And the runners are going into the stalls – now.

1ST BOOKMAKER. The Derby comes but once a year!

2ND BOOKMAKER. One minute before they go!

1ST BOOKMAKER. Lester, still five to one!

MR TILLOTSON. Seven bets on. So sweet. Like warm blood. And easy. Like Our Lord, walking on water.

2ND BOOKMAKER. Blushing Groom, gone out to three to one now! Three to one the favourite!

MR TILLOTSON *hunts in his pockets.*

1ST BOOKMAKER. Ten to one, Hot Grove!

2ND BOOKMAKER. Ten to one, Lucky Sovereign!

MR TILLOTSON. Lucky Sovereign? Jubilee year? It can't fail. I got to get it on.

MR TILLOTSON *runs off.* MARGARET *wheels a happy* SHARON *on.* SANDY *comes on from the other side.*

PUBLIC ADDRESS SYSTEM. All the runners are in the stalls now.

MARGARET. The Derby, Sandy.
SANDY. The Derby, Margaret.

SANDY *and* MARGARET *embrace, he lifts her and swings her in an arc.*

SHARON. My want – see The Derby.
SANDY. Come on then!

They run off, MARGARET *pushing* SHARON. *The stage is deserted.*

PUBLIC ADDRESS SYSTEM. The flag is up. They are under starter's orders – now.

The stage deserted. THE DERBY, *played by one actor, comes on over the hill. The actor is festooned with the regalia of the race.*

THE DERBY. I am the Epsom Derby Stakes.
Being –
   Twelve tons of twenty-two horses and twenty-two small men –
   Boots, bridles, crash helmets, weights and whips – silks and light underwear –
   Each horse carrying nine stone –
   The lot worth twelve million pounds sterling plus –
   A race for three-year-old horses, run over one and a half miles –
   Begun over a hill, behind trees, where no one can see a blind thing that's going on.

THE DERBY *strides over the hill out of sight. The* DERBY COURSE *comes on. He smokes a cigarette in a long holder, wears a summer suit with two-toned shoes and carries a cut turf in the palm of a hand.*

THE COURSE. I am the Derby Course. Don't be fooled by lush green curves in the countryside. I am dangerous. I am a bad-tempered bastard. I bite legs. On me the second-rate burst blood vessels and heart valves. Only the fast, the brave and the beautiful get anything out of me. First, I am a killer gallop, up a long hill. Then I sweep down, curving to the left, to the real ball-tearer, a vicious left-hand corner, Tattenham Corner, turned at forty miles an hour. Then the straight run to the finish, but down another hill. And at the last hundred yards – the ground falls away from the Stand into the farside rails. That's me. Switchback. Twisty. Feared by the hardened man and animal. To win

the Derby – out-think me. Then kick my brains in. Or I'll break
you apart.

The actor lays the turf in the centre of the stage. A CROWD, *rushing to
the rails, comes on. Among the crowd is* MR TILLOTSON. *He carries his
'None in Hell' placard. The* DERBY COURSE *actor joins the crowd.*

FIRST CROWD

MAN IN THE CROWD. Get down on the rails now, don't take no for
an answer, woomph!

THE DERBY *out of sight.*

2ND MAN. Where are they?

3RD MAN. Miles away, over behind us.

4TH MAN. Henri Samani, my dreams go with you!

MR TILLOTSON. I've got it. That trembling feeling. They're going to
go, any moment now.

1ST WOMAN. I can't see anything. Just grass.

2ND WOMAN. You'll just see 'em when they go by.

3RD WOMAN. Where's Lester? Annie, where's Lester?

2ND WOMAN. He's not gone by yet! You'll know him, when he
does. He's got an arse like a little cream bun.

4TH MAN. Henri Samani! My life is in your hands.

3RD MAN. How much you put on him then?

4TH MAN. Fifty p.

MR TILLOTSON. My tongue's gone furry! I'm going to be sick, I'm
going to die, no I'm not! Oh Jesus Christ Our Lord forgive me
I've bet on The Derby and I'm in Heaven!

PUBLIC ADDRESS SYSTEM. And they are off.

THE DERBY *actor begins his display of the race.*

THE DERBY. Clang go the gates!

Leap goes twelve tons of horse and men!

AND it's Baudelaire the first to show. Frankie Durr that tough
little walnut on top. Then Lucky Sovereign, the no-hope offspring of the great Nijinsky, the Jubilee mug punters' tipple.
Then Milliondollarman, then Nebbiolo, the Two Thousand
Guineas winner – is this horse a paper tiger?

AND now it's Milliondollarman on the farside, neck and neck
with Baudelaire and Lucky Sovereign going up to join them.

Just in behind comes Nebbiolo, then Caporello, then Be My

Guest.
Who's going to blow it going up the hill? Who's going to take up the running? What the fuck is Lester Piggott doing?

The CROWD *runs to another position, as if six furlongs from the start at the top of Tattenham Hill.* MR TILLOTSON *keeps his position. The* CROWD *leaves litter behind.*

MR TILLOTSON. The action is what a gambler craves for. Two and a half minutes the race lasts, but I'll hold my breath and the action will go on forever.

MR TILLOTSON *takes a deep breath and his cheeks puff out.*

SECOND CROWD
1ST WOMAN. Why we got to stand on the hill?
2ND MAN. Always watched The Derby from here. You see 'em come up and you see 'em go down.
1ST WOMAN. Why can't we watch the finish?
2ND MAN. Cos you got to pay ten quid and dress up like a bloody penguin.
2ND WOMAN. I'm pregnant. I'm pregnant.
3RD WOMAN. Don't tell me, tell your husband.
2ND WOMAN. Ted – I'm pregnant.
3RD MAN. What?
2ND WOMAN. I wanted to tell you. When The Derby goes by.
3RD MAN. Great. If it's a boy we'll call it Lester.
2ND WOMAN. What if it's a girl?
3RD MAN. We'll call it Lesterine.

THE DERBY *coming into sight.*

THE DERBY. And suddenly all the jockeys know. Baudelaire is buggering himself up the hill, giving them all the ride.
AND as they race up to the top of the hill it's still Baudelaire – Gairloch makes a challenge but falls back, broken by the speed. And breaking the hearts of his owners, Mr Paul de Moussac and Miss V. Hermann-Hodge.
Baudelaire continues the ball-breaking gallop on the inside, Royal Plume comes to challenge but being driven hard by Joe Mercer.

AND it's Royal Plume from Valinsky, Milliondollarman, Caporello.

AND to the outside – Blushing Groom, the Aga Khan's horse. Never beaten in its life. The favourite. The wonder horse.

And looking to the back markers it's Sultan's Ruby. Lordelaw. And in among the stragglers – Lester Piggott on The Minstrel.

3RD MAN. Where the hell is Lester?

4TH MAN. At the back. Like a monkey on your spine, waiting to pounce.

THE DERBY And Night Before pulls up. Pat Eddery pulls up Night Before. A blood vessel burst.

THE DERBY *screams.* THE DERBY *actor arranges the* CROWD *into positions of the field.*

They race over the top of the hill. Baudelaire disputing it with Milliondollarman. Valinsky makes ground on the inside. Right up with them – Caporello and Lucky Sovereign and Noble Venture. Just in behind them, Willie Carson on Hot Grove. Behind Hot Grove, Henri Samani on Blushing Groom, well placed on the inside. Behind Blushing Groom, Lester Piggott on The Minstrel.

(*Aside.*) Lester – sneaking up from the back, to sniff the bollocks of the French favourite.

1ST JOCKEY. What the fuck is Lester doing?

2ND JOCKEY. Go down the hill you bugger.

3RD JOCKEY. What's that cunt trying to do to me?

4TH JOCKEY. Keep cool you beauty, you fucker.

5TH JOCKEY. For fucksake, someone bust that frog horse now.

6TH JOCKEY. Mille fois merdes.

7TH JOCKEY. Shit.

The CROWD *runs to another position as if on the inside of Tattenham Corner.* MR TILLOTSON *lets out a big breath and pants. The* CROWD *leaves litter behind.*

MR TILLOTSON. It's got to me again, every bit of my body. Gambling, I'm sorry I walked out on you.

THE DERBY. Milliondollarman from Baudelaire. Caporello. Lucky Sovereign.

In behind them – Be My Guest, Valinsky, Nebbiolo, then Blushing Groom. Losing ground – Royal Plume. The backmarker is – Mr Music Man.
AND at the front Milliondollarman takes over the lead!

THIRD CROWD
1ST MAN. Milliondollarman! Sixty-six to one! I'm going to be rich!
1ST WOMAN. I want my kid to see The Derby!
2ND WOMAN. Hold her up then.

A CHILD, *played by the* 3RD WOMAN, *bursts into tears within the* CROWD.

2ND MAN. Come on little girl. See The Derby. Tell your dollies all about it when you get back home.
THE DERBY. Hot Grove makes progress on the outside, Willie Carson like a pea on a drum.
AND they round Tattenham Corner. Where a jockey can utterly lose his bottle and the race. And a horse on the inside rail can have his hide peeled like a ripe tomato. Milliondollarman. Hot Grove. Caporello third. Baudelaire fourth. And fifth, The Minstrel coming strongly.
(*Aside.*) Lester's brain ticks – like an intercontinental ballistic missile, on trajectory.

The THIRD CROWD *produces Union Jack flags in a tableau – the* CHILD *is held up above crying. At the back of the crowd a* STREAKER *bares his behind.*

THE DERBY. Milliondollarman from Hot Grove, to face the hill down to the finish.
The crucifixion of the horse that won't stay begins.

The CROWD *runs to another position shedding litter to form the* FOURTH CROWD *around* MR TILLOTSON.

GRANDPA *sits at the front of the* CROWD, *on his little canvas stool, impassive and silent.*

Three furlongs to run in The Derby. Milliondollarman is pressed by Hot Grove. The Minstrel in third place. Then Be My Guest.
AND Blushing Groom unleashes a run. Henri Samani asks the question.

(*Aside.*) Will the French favourite stay? Bred by Red God out of Runaway Bride. But Red God never did more than a mile. Genes in the animal's chromosomes grind and shudder.
Two furlongs to run in The Derby.

FOURTH CROWD

| THE DERBY. It is Hot Grove from The Minstrel. Then Blushing Groom still making progress. Monseigneur moves into fourth place. Hot Grove from The Minstrel from Blushing Groom. | *The* FOURTH CROWD *shouts the names of* HENRI, LESTER, WILLIE, THE MINSTREL, HOT GROVE *and* BLUSHING GROOM, *as* THE DERBY *passes them.* GRANDPA *on his stool, silent.* |

THE DERBY *is past the* FOURTH CROWD, *which strains to see the finish.*

The closing stages of the nineteen seventy-seven Epsom Derby Stakes.
Blushing Groom has nothing left.
Willie Carson on Hot Grove thinks the race is his.
Then Lester Piggott – lets the reins slip two inches through the palms of his hands.
The Minstrel responds. A bat out of hell, bullet out of a gun, the lash of a whip.
A hundred yards to run in The Derby. Lester Piggott and Willie Carson. The Minstrel on the near side, Hot Grove on the far side.
AND in the last second, like throwing a knife through a doorway as the door slams – The Minstrel wins.

THE DERBY *walks off.*

PUBLIC ADDRESS SYSTEM. Photofinish. There will be a photograph.
MR TILLOTSON. The Minstrel's Derby. I'd tear my eyes out to bet on a race like that again.

MR TILLOTSON *studies his race-card feverishly. The crowd disperses, stunned, to become the* FIFTH CROWD, MARGARET, SANDY *and* GRANDPA *amongst them.*

FIFTH CROWD

MARGARET. Sandy. We won.

SANDY. Maggy. Aluminium ladders.

1ST WOMAN. First I saw the race – just like a crowd of bees.

2ND WOMAN. What happened?

2ND MAN. They call for a photograph when it's under a length. But the word is definitely Lester.

The 3RD MAN *starts and runs off.*

SANDY. Take a picture of me.

MARGARET. We've not got a camera.

SANDY, *holding the winning ticket to his chest.*

SANDY. Someone take a picture of me. I won The Derby.

MARGARET. Someone take a picture of my husband.

SANDY. For crying out loud what am I doing? Let's get to that bookie.

SANDY *takes* MARGARET'S *hand. They run off.*

1ST WOMAN. Like bees, on the horizon. Then they were dead in front of me. All whips and froth. Then just grass again.

A couple embrace.

PUBLIC ADDRESS SYSTEM. Here is the result of the third race, The Epsom Derby Stakes. First number twenty-three, The Minstrel. Second number six, Hot Grove. Third number three, Blushing Groom.

The couple lie on the grass, embracing.

MR TILLOTSON. The four twenty. Lester's on Golden Libra.

MR TILLOTSON *goes off*

GRANDPA. Lester Piggott? Win The Derby on The Minstrel? What good's that to the working man? Five to one, less tax? No good at all. Bloody conspiracy. That Lester Piggott. That trainer from Tipperary. Got together with that man on the telly with the hat. Done the working man in, yet again. The Minstrel? Drifts to the left. Oh well. Derby done. Heavy boozing starts.

A panic in the stock market, when companies are crumbling, and the funds falling two, three, and four per cent in the hour, and foreign shares are dwindling away to next to nothing, when each haggard messenger brings tidings of a rise in the bank-rate, and the discount houses won't touch legitimate paper and good bills at short dates under an unprecedented price – when every telegram brings fresh reports of monetary convulsions in every capital in Europe, and men look terror-stricken at one another, and blanche with a nameless dread of some unheard-of catastrophe – is as nothing to the race for the Derby.

from *The Derby Day, or Won by a Neck – A Sporting Novel* (1864)

That gossip and superstition are for the majority of mankind the main apparatus of selection is a sad fact: the Derby, alas, has its place in the history of folly. Out of every hundred students who in the early weeks of the season make some pretence at treating the problem of the Derby winner as an intellectual enquiry, about ninety-seven will suffer some last-minute village gossip to upset their rational selection. The cook's young man has a friend in a racing stable in Northumberland, a talkative travelling companion's business associate has a brother in the breeches-making trade, and the vaguely reported opinions of these distant and unknown informants are allowed to determine our choice in the face of reason, experience and commonsense. It would appear that most men are more ready to trust the often ambiguous and always unexplained judgment of some obscure oracle than their own intelligible conclusions. And those who escape the tyranny of gossip fall into the hands of superstition. For some dreams and visions, their own or those of their friends, take the place of any more rational method of determination. In 1934 a family of three brothers and their little sister had a nice win on *Windsor Lad* solely because their maternal grandmother, wholly ignorant even of the names of the runners, dreamed of something of the sort after visiting her nephew at Eton; and there is a record of a man who was unfortunate enough in 1928 to back *Flamingo* on no better authority than a premonition which came to his aunt while she was in church that her favourite parrot had escaped. And those to whom no such supernatural source of information is available will often base their selection upon some coincidence between the name of a horse and an event in their life: *Hot Night* was a favourite selection because on the Tuesday night before the race the temperature in the home counties never fell below 67 degrees, and *Manna* was a 9–1 win for a devoted but shortsighted son who misread the name as *Mamma*.

There is also the person who makes her selection by closing her eyes and pricking the first list of runners that comes to hand with a pin; but, though it is not impossible that a winner has been chosen in this way, it is a boring method of choice, attractive only to rustics or dilettanti. Other common beliefs with regard to the winner of the Derby which must be classed as superstitions although they are not altogether without a basis in experience, are those which make the selection turn upon the name of the horse, the reputation of the jockey, or the past record of the owner or trainer. The Derby being a classic race, it is felt that the winner must have at least a not quite undignified name, and from this feeling arises the doctrine of the winning name. *Sansovino*, *Blenheim* and *Hyperion*, for example, would be given a very good chance on this method of selection, and believers in this doctrine would at once rule out of consideration *Sponge Bun* or *Cabbage Patch* on the ground of the vulgarity of their names. . . .

Preparing for the Derby is an elaborate affair. The lucky tie and the winning suit must be worn; a sharp eye must be kept for black cats and chimney sweeps; and inner significance must be looked for in every incident of the journey. It is scarcely to be wondered at that going to the Derby is about the most tiring holiday a man may take, as well as the pleasantest. We have known people, also, who for weeks before the Derby turn daily to the racing page of their newspaper for information about the home gallops of the runners. And it is not for us to say that such information may not occasionally be informative for some races – for a handicap or a seller. But for the Derby it is best neglected altogether. The racing page should be consulted for the public form of the runners; and if a Derby candidate goes lame, starts coughing or is scratched from the race the news will be on the front page, and we need look no farther. Gallops, for the ordinary man, are the most insidious of all superstitions, because they appear to give valuable information, but as a matter of fact they give no information at all. Winners before now have been backed on the grounds of exclusive stable information, but rarely, if ever, the winner of the Derby.

GUY GRIFFITH and MICHAEL OAKESHOTT, from *A Guide to the Classics*

A BREAD AND BUTTER MISS

'Starling Chatter and Oakhill have both dropped back in the betting', said Bertie van Tahn, throwing the morning paper across the breakfast table.

'That leaves Nursery Tea practically favourite,' said Odo Finsberry.

'Nursery Tea and Pipeclay are at the top of the betting at present,' said Bertie, 'but that French horse, Le Five O'Clock, seems to be fancied as much as anything. Then there is Whitebait, and the Polish horse with a name like some one trying to stifle a sneeze in church; they both seem to have a lot of support.'

'It's the most open Derby there's been for years,' said Odo.

'It's simply no good trying to pick the winner on form,' said Bertie; 'one must just trust to luck and inspiration.'

'The question is whether to trust to one's own inspiration, or somebody else's. *Sporting Swank* gives Count Palatine to win, and Le Five O'Clock for a place.'

'Count Palatine – that adds another to our list of perplexities. Good morning, Sir Lulworth; have you a fancy for the Derby by any chance?'

'I don't usually take much interest in turf matters,' said Sir Lulworth, who had just made his appearance, 'but I always like to have a bet on the Guineas and the Derby. This year, I confess, it's rather difficult to pick out anything that seems markedly better than anything else. What do you think of Snow Bunting?'

'Snow Bunting?' said Odo, with a groan, 'there's another of them. Surely, Snow Bunting has no earthly chance?'

'My housekeeper's nephew, who is a shoeing-smith in the mounted section of the Church Lads' Brigade, and an authority on horseflesh, expects him to be among the first three.'

'The nephews of housekeepers are invariably optimists,' said Bertie; 'it's a kind of natural reaction against the professional pessimism of their aunts.'

'We don't seem to get much further in our search for the probable winner,' said Mrs de Claux; 'the more I listen to you experts the more hopelessly befogged I get.'

'It's all very well to blame us,' said Bertie to his hostess; '*you* haven't produced anything in the way of an inspiration.'

'My inspiration consisted in asking you down for Derby week,' retorted Mrs de Claux; 'I thought you and Odo between you might throw some light on *the* question of the moment.'

Further recriminations were cut short by the arrival of Lola Pevensey, who floated into the room with an air of gracious apology.

'So sorry to be so late,' she observed, making a rapid tour of inspection of the breakfast dishes.

'Did you have a good night?' asked her hostess with perfunctory solicitude.

'Quite, thank you,' said Lola; 'I dreamt a most remarkable dream.'

A flutter, indicative of general boredom, went round the table. Other people's dreams are about as universally interesting as accounts of other people's gardens, or chickens, or children.

'I dreamt about the winner of the Derby,' said Lola.

A swift reaction of attentive interest set in.

'Do tell us what you dreamt,' came in a chorus.

'The really remarkable thing about it is that I've dreamt it two nights running,' said Lola, finally deciding between the allurements of sausages and kedgeree; 'that is why I thought it worth mentioning. You know, when I dream things two or three nights in succession, it always means something; I have special powers in that way. For instance, I once dreamed three times that a winged lion was flying through the sky and one of his wings dropped off, and he came to the ground with a crash; just afterwards the Campanile at Venice fell down. The winged lion is the symbol of Venice, you know,' she added for the enlightenment of those who might not be versed in Italian heraldry. 'Then,' she continued, 'just before the murder of the King and Queen of Servia I had a vivid dream of two crowned figures walking into a slaughter-house by the banks of a big river, which I took to be the Danube; and only the other day – '

'Do tell us what you've dreamt about the Derby,' interrupted Odo impatiently.

'Well, I saw the finish of the race as clearly as anything; and one horse won easily, almost in a canter, and everybody cried out "Bread and Butter wins! Good old Bread and Butter." I heard the name distinctly, and I've had the same dream two nights running.'

'Bread and Butter,' said Mrs de Claux, 'now, whatever horse can that point to? Why – of course; Nursery Tea!'

She looked round with the triumphant smile of a successful unraveller of mystery.

'How about Le Five O'Clock?' interposed Sir Lulworth.

'It would fit either of them equally well,' said Odo; 'can you remember any details about the jockey's colours? That might help us.'

'I seem to remember a glimpse of lemon sleeves or cap, but I can't be sure,' said Lola, after due reflection.

'There isn't a lemon jacket or cap in the race,' said Bertie, referring to a list of starters and jockeys; 'can't you remember anything about the appearance of the horse? If it were a thick-set animal, thick bread and butter would typify Nursery Tea; and if it were thin, of course, it would mean Le Five O'Clock.'

'That seems sound enough,' said Mrs de Claux; 'do think, Lola dear, whether the horse in your dream was thin or stoutly built.'

'I can't remember that it was one or the other,' said Lola; 'one wouldn't notice such a detail in the excitement of a finish.'

'But this was a symbolic animal,' said Sir Lulworth; 'if it were to typify thick or thin bread and butter, surely it ought to have been either as bulky and tubby as a shire cart-horse, or as thin as a heraldic leopard.'

'I'm afraid you are rather a careless dreamer,' said Bertie resentfully.

'Of course, at the moment of dreaming I thought I was witnessing a real race, not the portent of one,' said Lola; 'otherwise I should have particularly noticed all helpful details.'

'The Derby isn't run till tomorrow,' said Mrs de Claux; 'do you think you are likely to have the same dream again tonight? If so you can fix your attention on the important detail of the animal's appearance.'

'I'm afraid I shan't sleep at all tonight,' said Lola pathetically; 'every fifth night I suffer from insomnia, and it's due tonight.'

'It's most provoking,' said Bertie; 'of course, we can back both horses, but it would be much more satisfactory to have all our money on the winner. Can't you take a sleeping-draught, or something?'

'Oakleaves, soaked in warm water and put under the bed, are recommended by some,' said Mrs de Claux.

'A glass of Benedictine, with a drop of eau-de-Cologne – ' said Sir Lulworth.

'I have tried every known remedy,' said Lola, with dignity; 'I've been a martyr to insomnia for years.'

'But now we are being martyrs to it,' said Odo sulkily; 'I particularly want to land a big coup over this race.'

'I don't have insomnia for my own amusement,' snapped Lola.

'Let us hope for the best,' said Mrs de Claux soothingly; 'tonight may prove an exception to the fifth-night rule.'

But when breakfast time came round again Lola reported a blank night as far as visions were concerned.

'I don't suppose I had as much as ten minutes' sleep, and, certainly, no dreams.'

'I'm so sorry, for your sake in the first place, and ours as well,' said her hostess; 'do you think you could induce a short nap after breakfast? It would be so good for you – and you *might* dream something. There would still be time for us to get our bets on.'

'I'll try if you like,' said Lola; 'it sounds rather like a small child being sent to bed in disgrace.'

'I'll come and read the *Encyclopædia Britannica* to you if you think it will make you sleep any sooner,' said Bertie obligingly.

Rain was falling too steadily to permit of outdoor amusement, and the party suffered considerably during the next two hours from the absolute quiet that was enforced all over the house in order to give Lola every chance of achieving slumber. Even the click of billiard balls was considered a possible factor of disturbance, and the canaries were carried down to the gardener's lodge, while the cuckoo clock in the hall was muffled under several layers of rugs. A notice, 'Please do not Knock or Ring,' was posted on the front door at Bertie's suggestion, and guests and servants spoke in tragic whispers as though the dread presence of death or sickness had invaded the house. The precautions proved of no avail: Lola added a sleepless morning to a wakeful night, and the bets of the party had to be impartially divided between Nursery Tea and the French colt.

'So provoking to have to split our bets,' said Mrs de Claux, as her guests gathered in the hall later in the day, waiting for the result of the race.

'I did my best for you,' said Lola, feeling that she was not getting her due share of gratitude; 'I told you what I had seen in my dreams, a brown horse, called Bread and Butter, winning easily from all the rest.'

'What?' screamed Bertie, jumping up from his seat, 'a *brown* horse! Miserable woman, you never said a word about its being a brown horse.'

'Didn't I?' faltered Lola. 'I thought I told you it was a brown horse. It was certainly brown in both dreams. But I don't see what colour has got to do with it. Nursery Tea and Le Five O'Clock are both chestnuts.'

'Merciful Heaven! Doesn't brown bread and butter with a sprinkling of lemon in the colours suggest anything to you?' raged Bertie.

A slow, cumulative groan broke from the assembly as the meaning of his words gradually dawned on his hearers.

For the second time that day Lola retired to the seclusion of her room; she could not face the universal looks of reproach directed at her when Whitebait was announced winner at the comfortable price of fourteen to one.

SAKI (H. H. Munro) (1919)

The heyday of the Derby as unofficial public holiday was the mid-nineteenth century, and the greatest writers of the time were drawn to the event.

Charles Dickens wrote two hefty pieces on the Derby. In 1851 he and his Household Words *collaborator W. H. Wills visited Epsom on the Monday before the race and on Derby Day itself. In the article, Dickens himself wrote the section from the paragraph opening 'On that great occasion' to the end. The rest – including the famous passage in the kitchens, usually attributed to Dickens – is most likely to have been written by Wills. The winner of the Derby that year was Teddington.*

EPSOM

A straggling street, an undue proportion of inns, a large pond, a pump, and a magnificent brick clock case, make up – with a few more touches not necessary to be given here – the picture of the metropolis of English racing, and the fountain of Epsom salts. For three hundred and sixty-four days in the year a cannon-ball might be fired from one end of Epsom to the other without endangering human life. On the three hundred and sixty-fifth, or Derby Day, a population surges and rolls, and scrambles through the place, that may be counted in millions.

Epsom during the races, and Epsom at any other time, are things as unlike as the Desert of Saharah and the interior of the Palace of Glass in Hyde Park. We intend, for the edification of the few who know Epsom races only by name, and for the amusement (we hope) of the many who have sported over its Downs during the races, to give some account of Epsom under both aspects.

Our graver readers need not be alarmed – we know little of horses; and, happily, for ourselves, nothing of sporting; but, believing in the dictum of the Natural History chapters of the Universal Spelling Book that the 'horse is a noble animal,' and that he is nowhere so noble, so well bred, so handsome, so tractable, so intelligent, so well cared for, and so well appreciated, as in this country; and that, in consequence of the national fondness for races his breed has been improved until he has attained his present excellency – believing all this, we think it quite possible to do him justice, without defiling the subject with any allusion to the knavery to which he, sometimes, innocently gives rise. Those who practise it are his vulgar parasites; for the owners of race-horses number among them the highest and most honourable names in the country.

Financially, the subject is not unworthy of notice. Racers give employment to thousands. According to Captain Rous, there are upwards of two hundred thorough-bred stallions, and one thousand one hundred brood mares, which produce about eight hundred and thirty foals annually: of these there are generally three in the first class of race-horses, seven in the second class; and they descend gradually in the scale to the amount of four hundred and eighty, one half of which never catch the judge's eye; the remainder are either not trained, or are found unworthy at an early period.

The number of race-courses is one hundred and eleven; of which three are in Ireland, and six in Scotland.

It is Monday – the Monday before the Derby Day, and a railway takes us, in less than an hour, from London Bridge to the capital of the racing world, close to the abode of its Great Man, who is – need we add! – the Clerk of the Epsom Course. It is, necessarily, one of the best houses in the place; being – honour to literature – a flourishing bookseller's shop. We are presented to the official. He kindly conducts us to the Downs, to show how the horses are temporarily stabled; to initiate us into some of the mysteries of the 'field;' to reveal to us, in fact, the private life of the race-horse.

We arrive at a neat farm-house, with more outbuildings than are usually seen appended to so modest a homestead. A sturdy, well-dressed, well-mannered, purpose-like, sensible-looking man, presents himself. He has a Yorkshire accent. A few words pass between him and the Clerk of the Course, in which we hear the latter asseverate with much emphasis that we are, in a sporting sense, quite artless – we rather think 'green' was the exact expression – that we never bet a shilling, and are quite incapable, if even willing, to take advantage of any information, or of any inspection vouchsafed to us. Mr Filbert (the trainer) hesitates no longer. He moves his hat with honest politeness; bids us follow him, and lays his finger on the latch of a stable.

The trainer opens the door with one hand; and, with a gentle-man-like wave of the other, would give us the precedence. We hesitate. We would rather not go in first. We acknowledge an enthusiastic admiration for the race-horse; but at the very mention of a race-horse, the stumpy animal whose portrait headed our earliest lesson of equine history, in the before-quoted 'Universal Spelling Book,' vanishes from our view, and the animal described in the Book of Job prances into our mind's eye: 'The glory of his nostril is terrible. He mocketh at fear and is not affrighted. He swalloweth the ground with the fierceness of his rage!' To enjoy, therefore, a fine racer – not as one does a work of art – we like the point of sight to be the point of distance. The safest point, in case of accident (say, for instance, a sudden striking-out of the hinder hoofs), we hold to be the vanishing point – a point by no means attainable on the inside of that contracted kind of stable known as a 'loose box'.

The trainer evidently mistakes our fears for modesty. We boldly step forward to the outer edge of the threshold, but uncomfortably close to the hind-quarters of Pollybus, a 'favourite' for the Derby. When we perceive that he has neither bit nor curb; nor bridle, nor halter; that he is being 'rubbed down' by a small boy, after having taken his gallops; that there is nothing on earth – except the small boy – to prevent his kicking, or plunging, or biting, or butting his visitors to death; we breathe rather thickly. When the trainer exclaims, 'Shut the door, Sam!' and the little groom does his master's bidding, and boxes us up, we desire to be breathing the fresh air of the Downs again.

'Bless you, sir!' says our good-tempered informant, when he sees us shrink away from Pollybus, changing sides at a signal from his cleaner; 'these horses' (we look round, and for the first time perceive, with a tremor, the heels of another high-mettled racer protruding from an adjoining stall) 'these horses are as quiet as you are; and – I say it without offence – just as well behaved. It is quite laughable to hear the notions of people who are not used to them. They are the gentlest and most tractable creeturs in creation. Then, as to shape and symmetry, is there anything like them?'

We acknowledge that Pretty Perth – the mare in the adjoining box – could hardly be surpassed for beauty.

'Ah, *can* you wonder at noblemen and gentlemen laying out their twenty and thirty thousand a year on them?'

'So much?'

'Why, my gov'nor's stud costs us five-and-twenty thousand a year, one year with another. – There's an eye, sir!'

The large, prominent, but mild optics of Pretty Perth are at this moment turned full upon us. Nothing, certainly, can be gentler than the expression that beams from them. She is 'taking,' as Mr Filbert is pleased to say, 'measure of us.' She does not stare vulgarly, or peer upon us a half-bred indifference; but, having duly and deliberately satisfied her mind respecting our external appearance, allows her attention to be leisurely diverted to some oats with which the boy had just supplied the manger.

'It is all a mistake,' continues Mr Filbert, commenting on certain vulgar errors respecting race-horses; 'thorough-breds are not nearly so rampagious as mongrels and half-breds. The two horses in this stall are gentlefolks, with as good blood in their veins as the best nobleman in the land. They would be just as back'ard in doing anything unworthy of a lady or gentleman, as any lord or lady in St James's – such as kicking, or rearing, or shying, or biting. The pedigree of every horse that starts in any great race, is to be traced as regularly up to James the First's Arabian, or to Cromwell's White Turk, or to the Darley or Godolphin barbs, as your great English families are to the Conqueror. The worst thing they will do, is running away now and then with their jockeys. And what's that? Why, only the animal's animal-spirit running away with *him*. They are not,' adds Mr Filbert, with a merry twinkle in his eye, 'the only young bloods that are fond of going too fast.'

To our question whether he considers that a race-horse *could* go too fast, Mr Filbert gives a jolly negative, and remarks that it is all owing to high feeding and fine air; 'for, mind you, horses get much better air to breathe than men do, and more of it.'

All this while the two boys are sibillating lustily while rubbing and polishing the coats of their horses; which are as soft as velvet, and much smoother. When the little grooms come to the fetlock and pastern, the chamois-leather they have been using is discarded as too coarse and rough, and they rub away down to the hoofs with their sleek and plump hands. Every wish they express, either in words or by signs, is cheerfully obeyed by the horse. The terms the quadruped seems to be on with the small biped, are those of the most easy and intimate friendship. They thoroughly understand one another. We feel a little ashamed of our mistrust of so much docility, and leave the stable with much less awe of a race-horse than we entered it.

'And now, Mr Filbert, one delicate question – What security is there against these horses being drugged, so that they may lose a race?'

Mr Filbert halts, places his legs apart, and his arms akimbo, and throws into his reply a severe significance, mildly tinged with

201

indignation. He commences with saying, 'I'll tell you where it is: – there is a deal more said about foul play and horses going amiss, than there need be.'

'Then the boys are never heavily bribed?'

'Heavily bribed, Sir!' Mr Filbert contracts his eyes, but sharpens up their expression, to look the suspicion down. 'Bribed! – it may not be hard to bribe a man, but it's not so easy to bribe a boy. What's the use of a hundred-pound note to a child of ten or twelve year old? Try him with a pen'north of apples, or a slice of pudding, and you have a better chance; though I would not give you the price of a sugar-stick for it. Nine out of ten of these lads would not have a hair of their horse's tail ruffled if they could help it; much more any such harm as drugs or downright poison. The boy and the horse are so fond of one another, that a racing stable is a regular happy family of boys and horses. When the foal is first born, it is turned loose into the paddock; and if his mother don't give him enough milk, the cow makes up the deficiency. He scampers about in this way for about a year: then he is "taken up"; that is, bitted, and backed by a "dumb-jockey" – a cross of wood made for the purpose. When he has got a little used to that, we try him with a speaking jockey – a child some seven or eight years old, who has been born, like the colt, in the stables. From that time till the horse retires from the turf, the two are inseparable. They eat, drink, sleep, go out and come in together. Under the directions of the trainer, the boy tells the horse what to do, and he does it; for he knows that he is indebted to the boy for everything he gets. When he is hungry, it is the boy that gives him his corn; when he is thirsty, the boy hands him his water; if he gets a stone in his foot, the boy picks it out. By the time the colt is old enough to run, he and the boy have got to like one another so well that they fret to be away from one another. As for bribing! Why, you may as well try to bribe the horse to poison the boy, as the boy to let the horse be injured.'

'But the thing *has* happened, Mr Filbert?'

'Not so much as is talked about. Sometimes a likely foal is sent to a training stable, and cracked up as something wonderful. He is entered to run. On trial, he turns out to be next to nothing; and the backers, to save their reputation, put it about, that the horse was played tricks with. There is hardly a great race, but you hear something about horses going amiss by foul play.'

'Do many of these boys become jockeys?'

'Mostly. Some of them are jockeys already, and ride "their own" horses, as they call them. Here comes one.'

A miniature man, with a horsewhip neatly twisted round the crop or handle, opens the gate.

'Well, Tommy, how are you, Tommy?'

'Well, Sir, bobbish. Fine day, Mr Filbert.'

Although Mr Filbert tells us in a whisper that Tommy is only twelve next birth-day, Tommy looks as if he had entered far into his teens. His dress is deceptive. Light trousers terminating in buttons, laced shoes, long striped waistcoat, a cut-away coat, a coloured cravat, a collar to which juveniles aspire under the name of 'stick-ups,' and a Paris silk hat, form his equipment.

'Let's see, Tommy; what stakes did you win last?'

Tommy flicks, with the end of his whip-crop, a speck of dirt from the toe of his 'off' shoe, and replies carelessly, 'The Great Northamptonshire upon Valentine. But then, I have won a many smaller stakes, you know, Mr Filbert.'

Are there many jockeys so young as Tommy?

'Not many so young,' says Tommy, tying a knot in his whip thong, 'but a good many smaller.' Tommy then walks across the straw-yard to speak to some stable friend he has come to see. Tommy has not only the appearance, but the manners of a man.

'That boy will be worth money,' says Mr Filbert. 'It is no uncommon thing for a master to give a lad like that a hundred pound when he wins a race. As he can't spend it in hard-bake, or ginger-beer, or marbles, (the young rogue *does*, occasionally, get rid of a pound or two in cigars,) he saves it. I have known a racing-stable lad begin the world at twenty, with from three to four thousand pound.'

Tommy is hopping back over the straw, as if he had forgotten something. 'O, I beg your pardon for not asking before,' he says, 'but – how does Mrs Filbert find herself?'

'Quite well, thank you, Tommy.' Tommy says he is glad to hear it, and walks off like a family-man.

Our interview with Mr Filbert is finished, and we pace towards the race-course with its indefatigable clerk. Presently, he points to a huge white object that rears its leaden roof on the apex of the highest of the 'Downs.' It is the Grand Stand. It is so extensive, so strong, and so complete, that it seems built for eternity, instead of for busy use during one day in the year, and for smaller requisition during three others. Its stability is equal to St Paul's or the Memnonian Temple. Our astonishment, already excited, is increased when our cicerone tells us that he pays as rent, and in subscriptions to stakes to be run for, nearly two thousand pounds per annum for that stand. Expecting an unusually great concourse of visitors this year, he has erected a new wing, extended the betting enclosure, and fitted up two apartments for the exclusive use of ladies.

Here we are! Let us go into the basement. First into the weighing-house, where the jockeys 'come to scale' after each race. We then inspect the offices for the Clerk of the Course himself; wine-cellars, beer-cellars, larders, sculleries, and kitchens, all is gigantically appointed, and as copiously furnished as if they formed part of an Ogre's Castle. To furnish the refreshment-saloon, the Grand Stand has in store two thousand four hundred tumblers, one thousand two hundred wine-glasses, three thousand plates and dishes, and several of the most elegant vases we have seen out of the Glass Palace, decorated with artificial flowers. An exciting odour of cookery meets us in our descent. Rows of spits are turning rows of joints before blazing walls of fire. Cooks are trussing fowls, confectioners are making jellies; kitchen-maids are plucking pigeons; huge crates of boiled tongues are being garnished on dishes. One hundred and thirty legs of lamb, sixty-five saddles of lamb, and one hundred and thirty shoulders of lamb; in short, a whole flock of sixty-five lambs have to be roasted, and dished, and garnished, by the Derby Day. Twenty rounds of beef, four hundred lobsters, one hundred and fifty tongues, twenty fillets of veal, one hundred sirloins of beef, five hundred spring chickens, three hundred and fifty pigeon-pies; a countless number of quartern loaves, and an incredible quantity of ham have to be cut up into sandwiches: eight hundred eggs have got to be boiled for the pigeon-pies and salads. The forests of lettuces, the acres of cress, and beds of radishes, which will have to be chopped up; the gallons of 'dressing' that will have to be poured out and converted into salads for the insatiable Derby Day, will be best understood by a memorandum from the chief of that department to the *chef-de-*

cuisine, which happened, accidentally, to fall under our notice: 'Pray don't forget a large tub and a birch-broom for mixing the salad!'

We are preparing to ascend, when we hear the familiar sound of a printing machine. Are we deceived? O, no! The Grand Stand is like the kingdom of China – self-supporting, self-sustaining. It scorns foreign aid; even to the printing of the Racing Lists. This is the source of the innumerable cards with which hawkers persecute the sporting world on its way to the Derby, from the Elephant and Castle to the Grand Stand. 'Dorling's list! Dorling's correct list! with the names of the horses, and colours of the riders!'

We are now in the hall. On our left, are the parlours, – refreshment-rooms specially devoted to the Jockey Club; on our right, a set of seats, reserved, from the days of Flying Childers, for the members of White's Club-house.

We step out upon the lawn; in the midst is the betting-ring, where sums of money of fabulous amounts change hands. The following salutary notice, respecting too numerous a class of characters, is printed on the admission card:

The Lessee of the Epsom Grand Stand hereby gives notice that no person guilty of any malpractices, or notoriously in default in respect of stakes, forfeits, or bets lost upon horse-racing, will be admitted within the Grand Stand or its enclosure during any race meetings at Epsom; and if any such person should gain admittance therein or thereupon, he will be expelled, upon his presence being pointed out to the Stewards for the time being, or to the Clerk of the Course.

The first floor is entirely occupied with a refreshment-room and a police court. Summary justice is the law of the Grand Stand. Two magistrates sit during the races. Is a pickpocket detected, a thimble-rigger caught, a policeman assaulted? The delinquent is brought round to the Grand Stand, to be convicted, sentenced, and imprisoned in as short a time as it takes to run a mile race.

The sloping roof is covered with lead, in steps; the spectator from that point has a bird's-eye view of the entire proceedings, and of the surrounding country, which is beautifully picturesque. When the foreground of the picture is brightened and broken by the vast multitude that assembles here upon the Derby Day, it presents a whole which has no parallel in the world.

On that great occasion, an unused spectator might imagine that all London turned out. There is little perceptible difference in the bustle of its crowded streets, but all the roads leading to Epsom Downs are so thronged and blocked by every description of carriage that it is marvellous to consider how, when, and where, they were all made – out of what possible wealth they are all maintained – and by what laws the supply of horses is kept equal to the demand. Near the favourite bridges, and at various leading points of the leading roads, clusters of people post themselves by nine o'clock, to see the Derby people pass. Then come flitting by, barouches, phætons, broughams, gigs, four-wheeled chaises, four-in-hands, Hansom cabs, cabs of lesser note, chaise-carts, donkey-carts, tilted vans made arborescent with green boughs and carrying no end of people, and a cask of beer, – equestrians, pedestrians, horse-dealers, gentlemen, notabilities, and swindlers, by tens of thousands – gradually thickening and accumulating, until, at last, a mile short of the turnpike, they become wedged together, and are very slowly filtered through layers of policemen, mounted and a-foot, until, one by one, they pass the gate and skurry down the hill beyond. The most singular combinations occur in these turnpike stoppages and presses. Four-in-hand leaders look affectionately over the shoulders of ladies, in bright shawls, perched in gigs; poles of carriages appear, uninvited, in the midst of social parties in phætons; little, fast, short-stepping ponies run up carriage-wheels before they can be stopped, and hold on behind like footmen. Now, the gentleman who is unaccustomed to public driving, gets into astonishing perplexities. Now, the Hansom cab whisks craftily in and out, and seems occasionally to fly over a waggon or so. Now, the postboy on a jibbing or a shying horse, curses the evil hour of his birth, and is ingloriously assisted by the shabby hostler out of place, who is walking down with seven shabby companions more or less equine, open to the various chances of the road. Now, the air is fresh, and the dust flies thick and fast. Now, the canvas-booths upon the course are seen to glisten and flutter in the distance. Now, the adventurous vehicles make cuts across, and get into ruts and gravel-pits. Now, the heather in bloom is like a field of gold, and the roar of voices is like a wind. Now, we leave the hard road and go smoothly rolling over the soft green turf, attended by an army of unfortunate worshippers in red jackets and stable-jackets, who make a very Juggernaut-car of our equipage, and now breathlessly call us 'My Lord,' and now, 'your Honor.' Now, we pass the outer settlements of tents where pots and kettles are – where gipsy children are – where airy stabling is – where tares for horses may be bought – where water, water, water, is proclaimed – where the Tumbler in an old pea-coat, with a spangled fillet round his head, eats oysters, while his wife takes care of the golden globes, and the knives, and also of the starry little boy, their son, who lives principally upside-down. Now, we pay our one pound at the barrier, and go faster on, still Juggernaut-wise, attended by our devotees, until at last we are drawn, and rounded, and backed, and sidled, and cursed, and complimented, and vociferated into a station on the hill opposite the Grand Stand, where we presently find ourselves on foot, much bewildered, waited on by five respectful persons, who *will* brush us all at once.

Well, to be sure, there never was such a Derby Day, as this present Derby Day! Never, to be sure, were there so many carriages, so many fours, so many twos, so many ones, so many horsemen, so many people who have come down by 'rail,' so many fine ladies in so many broughams, so many of Fortnum and Mason's hampers, so much ice and champagne! If I were on the turf, and had a horse to enter for the Derby, I would call that horse Fortnum and Mason, convinced that with that name he would beat the field. Public opinion would bring him in somehow. Look where I will – in some connexion with the carriages – made fast upon the top, or occupying the box, or tied up behind, or dangling below, or peeping out of window – I see Fortnum and Mason. And now, Heavens! all the hampers fly wide open, and the green Downs burst into a blossom of lobster-salad!

As if the great Trafalgar signal had been suddenly displayed from the top of the Grand Stand, every man proceeds to 'do his duty.' The weaker spirits, who were ashamed to set the great example, follow it instantly, and all around me there are table-cloths, pies, chickens, hams, tongues, rolls, lettuces, radishes, shell-fish, broad-bottomed bottles, clinking glasses, and carriages turned inside out. Amidst the hum of voices a bell rings. What's that? What's the matter? They are clearing the course. Never mind. Try the pigeon-pie. A roar. What's the matter? It's only the dog upon the course. Is that all? Glass of wine. Another roar. What's that? It's only the man who wants to cross the course, and is intercepted, and brought back. Is that all? I wonder whether it is always the same dog and the same man, year after year! A great roar. What's the matter? By Jupiter, they are going to start.

A deeper hum and a louder roar. Everybody standing on Fortnum and Mason. Now they're off! No. *Now* they're off! No. *Now* they're off. No. *Now* they are! Yes!

There they go! Here they come! Where? Keep your eye on Tattenham Corner, and you'll see 'em coming round in half a minute. Good gracious, look at the Grand Stand, piled up with human beings to the top, and at the wonderful effect of changing light as all their faces and uncovered heads turn suddenly this way! Here they are! Who is? The horses! Where? Here they come! Green first. No: Red first. No: Blue first. No: the Favourite first. Who says so? Look! Hurrah! Hurrah! All over. Glorious race. Favourite wins! Two hundred thousand pounds lost and won. You don't say so? Pass the pie!

Now, the pigeons fly away with the news. Now, every one dismounts from the top of Fortnum and Mason, and falls to work with greater earnestness than before, on carriage boxes, sides, tops, wheels, steps, roofs, and rumbles. Now, the living stream upon the course, dammed for a little while at one point, is released, and spreads like parti-colored grain. Now, the roof of the Grand Stand is deserted. Now, rings are formed upon the course, where strong men stand in pyramids on one another's heads; where the Highland lady dances; where the Devonshire Lad sets-to with the Bantam; where the Tumbler throws the golden globes about, with the starry little boy tied round him in a knot.

Now, all the variety of human riddles who propound themselves on race-courses, come about the carriages, to be guessed. Now, the gipsy woman, with the flashing red or yellow handkerchief about her head, and the strange silvery-hoarse voice, appears, 'My pretty gentleman, to tell your fortin, Sir; for you have a merry eye, my gentleman, and surprises is in store; for you're connected with a dark lady as loves you better than you love a kiss in a dark corner when the moon's a-shining; for you have a lively 'art, my gentleman, and you shall know her secret thoughts, and the first and last letters of her name, my pretty gentleman, if you will cross your poor gipsy's hand with a little bit of silver, for the luck of the fortin as the gipsy will read true, from the lines of your hand, my gentleman, both as to what is past, and present, and to come.' Now, the Ethiopians, looking unutterably hideous in the sunlight, play old banjoes and bones, on which no man could perform ten years ago, but which, it seems, any man may play now, if he will only blacken his face, put on a crisp wig, a white waistcoat and wristbands, a large white tie, and give his mind to it. Now, the sickly-looking ventriloquist, with an anxious face (and always with a wife in a shawl) teaches the alphabet to the puppet pupil, whom he takes out of his pocket. Now, my sporting gentlemen, you may ring the Bull, the Bull, the Bull; you may ring the Bull! Now, try your luck at the knock-em-downs, my Noble Swells – twelve heaves for sixpence, and a pincushion in the centre, worth ten times the money! Now the Noble Swells take five shillings' worth of 'heaves,' and carry off a halfpenny wooden pear in triumph. Now, it hails, as it always does hail, formidable wooden truncheons round the heads, bodies, and shins of the proprietors of the said knock-em-downs, whom nothing hurts. Now, inscrutable creatures, in smock frocks, beg for bottles. Now, a coarse vagabond, or idiot, or a compound of the two, never beheld by mortal off a race-course, hurries about, with ample skirts and a tattered parasol, counterfeiting a woman. Now, a shabby man, with an over-hanging forehead, and a slinking eye, produces a small board, and invites your attention to something novel and curious – three thimbles and one little pea – with a one, two, three, – and a two, three, one, – and a one – and a two – in the middle – right hand, left hand – go you any bet from a crown to five sovereigns you don't lift the thimble the pea's under! Now, another gentleman (with a stick) much interested in the experiment, will 'go' two sovereigns that he does lift the thimble, provided strictly, that the shabby man holds his hand still, and don't touch 'em again. Now, the bet's made, and the gentleman with the stick, lifts obviously the wrong thimble, and loses. Now, it is as clear as day to an innocent bystander, that the loser must have won if he had not blindly lifted the wrong thimble – in which he is strongly confirmed by another gentleman with a stick, also much interested, who proposes to 'go him' halves – a friendly sovereign to *his* sovereign – against the bank. Now, the innocent agrees, and loses; – and so the world turns round bringing innocents with it in abundance, though the three confederates are wretched actors, and could live by no other trade if they couldn't do it better.

Now, there is another bell, and another clearing of the course, and another dog, and another man, and another race. Now, there are all these things all over again. Now, down among the carriage-wheels and poles, a scrubby growth of drunken postboys and the like has sprung into existence, like weeds among the many-coloured flowers of fine ladies in broughams, and so forth. Now, the drinking-booths are all full, and tobacco-smoke is abroad, and an extremely civil gentleman confidentially proposes roulette. And now, faces begin to be jaded, and horses are harnessed, and wher-ever the old grey-headed beggarman goes, he gets among traces and splinter-bars, and is roared at.

So now we are on the road again, going home. Now, there are longer stoppages than in the morning; for we are a dense mass of men and women, wheels, horses, and dust. Now, all the houses on the road seem to be turned inside out, like the carriages on the course, and the people belonging to the houses, like the people belonging to the carriages, occupy stations which they never occupy at another time – on leads, on housetops, on out-buildings, at windows, in balconies, in doorways, in gardens. Schools are drawn out to see the company go by. The academies for young gentlemen favour us with dried peas; the Establishments for Young Ladies (into which sanctuaries many wooden pears are pitched), with bright eyes. We become sentimental, and wish we could marry Clapham. The crowd thickens on both sides of the road. All London appears to have come out to see us. It is like a triumphant entry – except that, on the whole, we rather amuse than impress the populace. There are little love-scenes among the chestnut trees by the roadside – young gentlemen in gardens resentful of glances at young ladies from coachtops – other young gentlemen in other gardens, minding young ladies, whose arms seem to be trained like the vines. There are good family pictures – stout fathers and jolly mothers – rosy cheeks squeezed in between the rails – and infinitesimal jockeys winning in canters on walking-sticks. There are smart maid-servants among the grooms at stable-doors, where Cook looms large and glowing. There is plenty of smoking and drinking among the tilted vans and at the public-houses, and some singing, but general order and good-humour. So, we leave the gardens and come into the streets, and if we there encounter a few ruffians throwing flour and chalk about, we know them for the dregs and refuse of a fine, trustworthy people, deserving of all confidence and honour.

And now we are at home again – far from absolutely certain of the name of the winner of the Derby – knowing nothing whatever about any other race of the day – still tenderly affected by the beauty of Clapham – and thoughtful over the ashes of Fortnum and Mason.

Dickens also brought the Derby into his fiction. In Great Expectations *the convict Magwitch tells how he had met the swindler Compeyson:*

'At Epsom races, a matter of over twenty years ago, I got acquainted wi' a man whose skull I'd crack wi' this poker, like the claw of a lobster, if I'd got it on this hob.'

In The Old Curiosity Shop *Little Nell comes across a Punch and Judy Show at an unidentified race meeting which is clearly based on Derby Day:*

The child, sitting down with the old man close behind it, had been thinking how strange it was that horses who were such fine honest creatures should seem to make vagabonds of all the men they drew about them.

Dickens's second great Derby Day set piece, 'The Dirty Derby' in the journal All the Year Round, *covered the 1863 running won by Macaroni – and concerned the weather as much as the race. The conditions were so bad that Dickens went only to avoid disappointing his Irish visitor Mr O'Hone.*

For O'Hone to miss seeing the race would have been wretched, though even then he would not have been worse off than an American gentleman who crossed the Atlantic expressly to attend the Epsom festival, and who, being seized with the pangs of hunger at about half-past two on the Derby Day, entered Mr Careless's booth and began amusing himself with some edible 'fixings' in the way of lunch, in which pleasant task he was still engaged when shouts rent the air, and the American gentleman rushing hatless out of the booth, and finding that the race had been run and was over, burst into the piercing lamentation: 'Oh, Je—rusalem! To come three thousand miles to eat cold lamb and salad!'

That year's Derby – the first to be attended by the Prince of Wales, later Edward VII – was delayed by no fewer than thirty-four false starts.

For one mortal hour do we stand on the soaked turf in the pouring rain, with that horrid occasional shiver which always accompanies wet feet, waiting for a start to be effected. Every ten minutes, rises a subdued murmur of hope, followed by a growl of disappointment. At last they are really 'off,' and for two minutes we forget our misery. But it comes upon us with redoubled force when the race is over, and there is nothing more to look forward to.

The Pre-Raphaelite painter John Everett Millais visited the Derby in 1853 (when the race went to West Australian, who was to become the first winner of the Triple Crown), and reported to his friend Charles Collins.

We presently dived into the alleys of the racing ground, and I speedily came to the conclusion that the audience attend principally for the sake of gorging themselves with pigeon pie and lobster salad . . . Such tragic scenes I saw on the course! One moustached guardsman was hanging over the side of a carriage in a state of abject intoxication . . . In the same carriage, seated beside him, endeavouring to look as though she were not cognisant of the disgusting reality, his mistress was offering a bottle of champagne to some other swells who sat in the box. In another carriage I saw a woman crying bitterly, evidently a paramour of the man who was languidly lolling back in the cushions flushed with drink and trying to look unconcerned at the woman's grief. This was probably caused by a notice that his losses that day obliged him to do without her society for the future . . .

You perceive that you are 'in' for the vulgar on an unsurpassable scale, something blatantly, unimaginably, heroically shocking to timid 'taste'; all that is necessary is to accept this situation and look out for illustrations. Beside you, before you, behind you, is the mighty London populace taking its *ébats*. You get for the first time a notion of the London population at large. It has piled itself into carts, into omnibuses, into every possible and impossible species of 'trap'. A large proportion of it is of course on foot, trudging along the perilous margin of the middle way in such comfort as may be gathered from fifteen miles' dodging of broken shins. The smaller the vehicle, the more rat-like the animal that drags it, the more numerous and ponderous its human freight; and as every one is nursing in his lap a parcel of provender as big as himself, wrapped in ragged newspaper, it is not surprising that roadside halts are frequent and that the taverns all the way to Epsom (it is wonderful how many there are) are encompassed by dense groups of dusty pilgrims, indulging liberally in refreshment for man and beast. And when I say man I must by no means be understood to exclude woman. The female contingent on the Derby day is not the least remarkable part of the London outpouring. Every one is prepared for 'larks', but the women are even more brilliantly and resolutely prepared than the men; there is no better chance to follow the range of type – not that it is to be called large – of the British female of the lower orders. The lady in question is usually not ornamental. She is useful, robust, prolific, excellently fitted to play the somewhat arduous part allotted to her in the great scheme of English civilisation, but she has not those graces which enable her to lend herself easily to the decoration of life. On smaller holidays – or on simple working days – in London crowds, I have often thought she had points to contribute to the primary fine drawing, as to head and shoulders, of the Briton of the two sexes as the race at large sketches them. But at Epsom she is too stout, too hot, too thirsty, too boisterous, too strangely accoutred. And yet I wish to do her justice; so I must add that if there is something to which an American cannot refuse a tribute of admiration in the gross plebeian jollity of the Derby day, it is not evident why these dowdy Bacchantes should not get part of the credit of it. The striking thing, the interesting thing, both on the outward drive and on the return, was that the holiday was so frankly, heartily, good-humouredly taken. The people that of all peoples is habitually the most governed by decencies, proprieties, rigidities of conduct, was for one happy day unbuttoning its respectable straight-jacket and affirming its large and simple sense of the joy of life. In such a spectacle there was inevitably much that was unlucky and unprofitable; these things came uppermost chiefly on the return, when demoralisation was supreme, when the temperament of the people had begun really to take the air. For the rest, to be dressed with a kind of brutal gaudiness, to be very thirsty and violently flushed, to laugh perpetually at everything and at nothing, thoroughly to enjoy, in short, a momentous occasion – all this is not, in simple persons of the more susceptible sex, an unpardonable crime.

The course at Epsom is in itself very pretty, and disposed by nature herself in sympathetic provision of the sporting passion. It is something like the crater of a volcano without the mountain. The outer rim is the course proper; the space within it is a vast, hollow, grassy concavity in which vehicles are drawn up and beasts tethered and in which the greater part of the multitude – the mountebanks, the betting men and the myriad hangers-on of the scene – are congregated. The outer margin of the uplifted rim in question is occupied by the grand stand, the small stands, the paddock. The day was exceptionally beautiful; the charming sky was spotted over with little idle looking, loafing, irresponsible clouds; the Epsom Downs went swelling away as greenly as in a coloured sporting-print, and the wooded uplands, in the middle distance, looked as innocent and pastoral as if they had never seen a policewoman or a rowdy. The crowd that spread itself over this immense expanse was as rich a representation of human life off its guard as one need see. One's first fate after arriving, if one is perched upon a coach, is to see the coach guided, by means best known to the coachman himself, through the tremendous press of vehicles and pedestrians, introduced into a precinct roped off and guarded from intrusion save under payment of a fee, and then drawn up alongside of the course, as nearly as possible opposite the grand stand and the winning post. Here you have only to stand up in your place – on tiptoe, it is true, and with a good deal of stretching – to see the race fairly well. But I hasten to add that seeing the race is indifferent entertainment. In the first place you *don't* see it, and in the second – to be Irish on the occasion of a frolic – you perceive it to be not much worth the seeing. It may be fine in quality, but in quantity it is inappreciable. The horses and their jockeys first go dandling and cantering along the course to the starting-point, looking as insubstantial as sifted sunbeams. Then there is a long wait, during which, of the sixty thousand people present (my figures are imaginary), thirty thousand declare positively that they have started, and thirty thousand as positively deny it. Then the whole sixty thousand are suddenly resolved into unanimity by the sight of a dozen small jockey heads whizzing along a very distant sky-line. In a shorter space of time than it takes me to write it, the whole thing is before you, and for the instant it is anything but beautiful. A dozen furiously revolving arms – pink, green, orange, scarlet, white – whacking the flanks of as many straining steeds; a glimpse of this, and the spectacle is over. The spectacle, however, is of course an infinitesimally small part of the purpose of Epsom and the interest of the Derby. The finer vibration resides presumably in having money on the affair.

When the Derby Stakes had been carried off by a horse of which I confess I am barbarous enough to have forgotten the name, I turned my back to the running, for all the world as if I too were largely 'interested', and sought entertainment in looking at the crowd. The crowd was very animated; that is the most succinct description I can give it. The horses of course had been removed from the vehicles, so that the pedestrians were free to surge against the wheels and even to a certain extent to scale and overrun the carriages. This tendency became most pronounced when, as the mid-period of the day was reached, the process of lunching began to unfold itself and every coach top to become the scene of a picnic. From this moment, at the Derby, demoralisation begins. I was in a position to observe it, all around me, in the most characteristic forms. The whole affair, as regards the conventional rigidities I spoke of a while since, becomes a real *dégringolade*. The shabbier pedestrians bustle about the vehicles, staring up at the lucky mortals who are perched in a kind of tormentingly near empyrean – a region in which dishes of lobster-salad are passed about and champagne-corks cleave the air like celestial meteors.

There are nigger-minstrels and beggars and mountebanks and spangled persons on stilts and gipsy matrons, as genuine as possible, with glowing Oriental eyes and dropping their *h*'s; these last offer you for sixpence the promise of everything genteel in life except the aspirate. On a coach drawn up beside the one on which I had a place, a party of opulent young men were passing from stage to stage of the higher beatitude with a zeal which excited my admiration. They were accompanied by two or three young ladies of the kind that usually shares the choicest pleasures of youthful British opulence – young ladies in whom nothing has been neglected that can make a complexion superlative. The whole party had been drinking deep, and one of the young men, a pretty lad of twenty, had in an indiscreet moment staggered down as best he could to the ground. Here his cups proved too many for him, and he collapsed and rolled over. In plain English he was beastly drunk. It was the scene that followed that arrested my observation. His companions on the top of the coach called down to the people herding under the wheels to pick him up and put him away inside. These people were the grimiest of the rabble, and a couple of men who looked like coal-heavers out of work undertook to handle this hapless youth. But their task was difficult; it was impossible to imagine a young man more drunk. He was a mere bag of liquor – at once too ponderous and too flaccid to be lifted. He lay in a helpless heap under the feet of the crowd – the best intoxicated young man in England. His extemporised chamberlains took him first in one way and then in another; but he was like water in a sieve. The crowd hustled over him; every one wanted to see; he was pulled and shoved and fumbled. The spectacle had a grotesque side, and this it was that seemed to strike the fancy of the young man's comrades. They had not done lunching, so they were unable to bestow upon the incident the whole of that consideration which its high comicality deserved. But they did what they could. They looked down very often, glass in hand, during the half-hour that it went on, and they stinted neither their generous, joyous laughter not their appreciative comments. Women are said to have no sense of humour; but the young ladies with the complexions did liberal justice to the pleasantry of the scene. Toward the last indeed their attention rather flagged; for even the best joke suffers by reiteration, and when you have seen a stupefied young man, infinitely bedusted, slip out of the embrace of a couple of clumsy roughs for the twentieth time, you may very properly suppose that you have arrived at the furthest limits of the ludicrous.

HENRY JAMES, from *English Hours* (1877)

How that race was run, and how both Prime Minister and Quousque were beaten by an outsider named Fishknife, Prime Minister, however, coming in a good second, the present writer having no aptitude in that way, cannot describe. Such, however, were the facts, and then Dolly Longstaff and Lord Silverbridge drove the coach back to London. The coming back was not so triumphant, though the young fellows bore their failure well. Dolly Longstaff had lost a 'pot of money', Silverbridge would have to draw upon that inexhaustible Mr Morton for something over two thousand pounds, – in regard to which he had no doubt as to the certainty with which the money would be forthcoming, but he feared that it would give rise to special notice from his father. Even the poor younger brother had lost a couple of hundred pounds, for which he would have to make his own special application to Mr Morton.

But Tifto felt it more than anyone. The horse ought to have won. Fishknife had been favoured by such a series of accidents that the whole affair had been a miracle. Tifto had these circumstances at his fingers' ends, and in the course of the afternoon and evening explained them accurately to all who would listen to him. He had this to say on his own behalf, – that before the party had left the course their horse stood first favourite for the Leger. But Tifto was unhappy as he came back to town, and in spite of the lunch, which had been very glorious, sat moody and sometimes even silent within his gay apparel.

'It was the unfairest start I ever saw,' said Tifto, almost getting up from his seat on the coach so as to address Dolly and Silverbridge on the box.

'What the — is the good of that?' said Dolly from the coachbox. 'Take your licking and don't squeal.'

'That's all very well. I can take my licking as well as another man. But one has to look to the causes of these things. I never saw Peppermint ride so badly. Before he got round the Corner I wished I'd been on the horse myself.'

'I don't believe it was Peppermint's fault a bit,' said Silverbridge.

'Well; – perhaps not. Only I did think that I was a pretty good judge of riding.'

Then Tifto again settled down into silence.

SANTHONY TROLLOPE, from *The Duke's Children* (1880)

An hour previous to this time, and at a different part of the course, there might have been seen an old stage-coach, on the battered roof of which a crowd of shabby raffs were stamping and hallooing, as the great event of the day – the Derby race – rushed over the greensward, and by the shouting millions of people assembled to view that magnificent scene. This was Wheeler's (the 'Harlequin's Head') drag, which had brought down a company of choice spirits from Bow Street, with a slap-up luncheon in the 'boot.' As the whirling race flashed by, each of the choice spirits bellowed out the name of the horse or the colours which he thought or he hoped might be foremost. 'The Cornet!' 'It's Muffineer!' 'It's blue sleeves!' 'Yellow Cap! yellow cap! yellow cap!' and so forth, yelled the gentlemen sportsmen during that delicious and thrilling minute before the contest was decided; and as the fluttering signal blew out, showing the number of the famous horse Podasokus as winner of the race, one of the gentlemen on the 'Harlequin's Head' drag sprang up off the roof, as if he was a pigeon and about to fly away to London or York with the news.

But his elation did not lift him many inches from his standing-place, to which he came down again on the instant, causing the boards of the crazy old coach-roof to crack with the weight of his joy. 'Hurray, hurray!' he bawled out, 'Podasokus is the horse! Supper for ten, Wheeler, my boy. Ask you all round of course, and damn the expense.'

And the gentlemen on the carriage, the shabby swaggerers, the dubious bucks said, 'Thank you – congratulate you, colonel: sup with you with pleasure!' and whispered to one another. 'The colonel stands to win fifteen hundred, and he got the odds from a good man, too.'

And each of the shabby bucks and dusky dandies began to

eye his neighbour with suspicion, lest that neighbour, taking his advantage, should get the colonel into a lonely place and borrow money of him. And the winner on Podasokus could not be alone during the whole of that afternoon, so closely did his friends watch him and each other.

WILLIAM MAKEPEACE THACKERAY, from *Pendennis* (1850)

Benjamin Disraeli's novel Sybil, *published in 1845, is subtitled 'The Two Nations' – the two nations being the rich and the poor, a distinction all too familiar to followers of racing. The story opens at Crockford's gaming-house on the night before the 1837 Derby: of the gentlemen arranging their betting books on the race, only Cockie Graves would profit from a victory by the outsider Phosphorus. The action then moves to Epsom on Derby Day itself.*

'Will any one do anything about Hybiscus?' sang out a gentleman in the ring at Epsom. It was full of eager groups; round the betting post a swarming cluster, while the magic circle itself was surrounded by a host of horsemen shouting from their saddles the odds they were ready to receive or give, and the names of the horses they were prepared to back or to oppose.

'Will any one do anything about Hybiscus?'

'I'll bet you five to one,' said a tall, stiff Saxon peer, in a white great-coat.

'No; I'll take six.'

The tall, stiff peer in the white great-coat mused for a moment with his pencil at his lip, and then said, 'Well, I'll bet you six. What do you say about Mango?'

'Eleven to two against Mango,' called out a little hump-backed man in a shrill voice, but with the air of one who was master of his work.

'I should like to do a little business with you, Mr Chippendale,' said Lord Milford, in a coaxing tone, 'but I must have six to one.'

'Eleven to two, and no mistake,' said this keeper of a second-rate gaming-house, who, known by the flattering appellation of Hump Chippendale, now turned with malignant abruptness from the heir-apparent of an English earldom.

'You shall have six to one, my Lord,' said Captain Spruce, a debonair personage, with a well-turned silk hat arranged a little aside, his coloured cravat tied with precision, his whiskers trimmed like a quickset hedge. Spruce, who had earned his title of Captain on the plains of Newmarket, which had witnessed for many a year his successful exploits, had a weakness for the aristocracy, who, knowing his graceful infirmity, patronized him with condescending dexterity, acknowledged his existence in Pall-Mall as well as at Tattersall's, and thus occasionally got a point more than the betting out of him. Hump Chippendale had none of these gentle failings; he was a democratic leg, who loved to fleece a noble, and thought all men were born equal; a consoling creed that was a hedge for his hump.

'Seven to four against the favourite; seven to two against Caravan; eleven to two against Mango. What about Benedict? Will any one do anything about Pocket Hercules? Thirty to one against Dardanelles.'

'Done.'

'Five-and-thirty ponies to one against Phosphorus,' shouted a little man vociferously and repeatedly.

'I will bet forty,' said Lord Milford. No answer; nothing done.

'Forty to one!' murmured Egremont, who stood against Phosphorus. A little nervous, he said to the peer in the white greatcoat, 'Don't you think that Phosphorus may, after all, have some chance?'

'I should be cursed sorry to be deep against him,' said the peer.

Egremont with a quivering lip walked away. He consulted his book; he meditated anxiously. Should he hedge? It was scarcely worth while to mar the symmetry of his winnings; he stood 'so well' by all the favourites; and for a horse at forty to one. No; he would trust his star, he would not hedge.

'Mr Chippendale,' whispered the peer in the white great-coat, 'go and press Mr Egremont about Phosphorus. I should not be surprised if you got a good thing.'

At this moment, a huge, broad-faced, rosy-gilled fellow, with one of those good-humoured yet cunning countenances that we meet occasionally north of the Trent, rode up to the ring on a square cob, and, dismounting, entered the circle. He was a carcase-butcher famous in Carnaby-market, and the prime counsellor of a distinguished nobleman, for whom privately he betted on commission. His secret service to-day was to bet against his noble employer's own horse, and so he at once sung out, 'Twenty to one against Man-trap.'

A young gentleman just launched into the world, and who, proud of his ancient and spreading acres, was now making his first book, seeing Man-trap marked eighteen to one on the cards, jumped eagerly at this bargain, while Lord Fitzheron and Mr Berners, who were at hand, and who in their days had found their names in the book of the carcase-butcher, and grown wise by it, interchanged a smile.

'Mr Egremont will not take,' said Hump Chippendale to the peer in the white great-coat.

'You must have been too eager,' said his noble friend.

The ring is up; the last odds declared; all gallop away to the Warren. A few minutes, only a few minutes, and the event that for twelve months has been the pivot of so much calculation, of such subtle combinations, of such deep conspiracies, round which the thought and passion of the sporting world have hung like eagles, will be recorded in the fleeting tablets of the past. But what minutes! Count them by sensation, and not by calendars, and each moment is a day and the race a life. Hogarth, in a coarse and yet animated sketch, has painted 'Before' and 'After'. A creative spirit of a higher vein might develop the simplicity of the idea with sublimer accessories. Pompeius before Pharsalia, Harold before Hastings, Napoleon before Waterloo, might afford some striking contrasts to the immediate catastrophe of their fortunes. Finer still, the inspired mariner who has just discovered a new world; the sage who has revealed a new planet; and yet the 'Before' and 'After' of a first-rate English race, in the degree of its excitement, and sometimes in the tragic emotions of its close, may vie even with these.

They are saddling horses; Caravan looks in great condition; and a scornful smile seems to play upon the handsome features of Pavis, as, in the becoming colours of his employer, he gracefully gallops his horse before his admiring supporters. Egremont, in the delight of an English patrician, scarcely saw Mango, and never even thought of Phosphorus; Phosphorus, who, by-the-by, was the first horse that showed, with both his forelegs bandaged.

They are off!

As soon as they are well away, Chifney makes the running with Pocket Hercules. Up to the Rubbing House he is leading; this is the only point the eye can select. Higher up the hill, Caravan, Hybiscus, Benedict, Mahometan, Phosphorus, Michel Fell, and Rat-trap are with the grey, forming a front rank, and at the new ground the pace has told its fate, for half a dozen are already out of the race.

The summit is gained; the tactics alter; here Pavis brings up Caravan, with extraordinary severity; the pace round Tattenham corner terrific; Caravan leading, then Phosphorus a little above him, Mahometan, next, Hybiscus fourth, Rat-trap looking badly. Wisdom, Benedict, and another handy. By this time Pocket Hercules has enough, and at the road the tailing grows at every stride. Here the favourite himself is hors de combat, as well as Dardanelles, and a crowd of lesser celebrities.

There are now but four left in the race, and of these, two, Hybiscus and Mahometan, are some lengths behind. Now it is neck and neck between Caravan and Phosphorus. At the stand, Caravan has decidedly the best; but just at the post, Edwards, on Phosphorus, lifts the gallant little horse, and with an extraordinary effort contrives to shove him in by half a length.

'You look a little low, Charley,' said Lord Fitzheron, as, taking their lunch in their drag, he poured the champagne into the glass of Egremont.

'By Jove!' said Lord Milford, 'only think of Cockie Graves having gone and done it!'

Another who had gone and done it with 40–1 outsider Phosphorus was a versifier who under the pseudonym 'Vates' previewed the 1837 Derby in verse in Bell's Life *on the Sunday before the race. At the end of a lengthy poem Vates reveals how he thinks the Derby will finish:*

> See Benedict fails, making desperate play
> Victoria shows in the front with John Day;
> Whilst Phosphorus, Mickle Fell, live at the bat,
> And Mango looks easy, directed by Nat;
> Sir Frederick running so gallant before

Gives up, and the contest now lies with the four;
Mickle Fell is in trouble, and spite of Bill Scott,
Of the whipcord and steel he has 'sufficit' got!
'Mango, Wintonian, and Phosphorus do it –
Oh! moments of agony – go it then – go it!'
'Tis over – the trick for the thousands is done –
George Edwards, on Phosphorus, the Derby has won!
With Victoria next him, a neck beat away,
And Mango a pickle will prove some odd day;
So those who have found out their error too late,
And the victor opposed of the Rowley-Mile Plate,
Their fingers must burn in the Phosphoric flame
Whilst the Lamplighter runs up the ladder of fame.

The Derby is one of the events which has undergone a distinct metamorphosis of recent years. Until comparatively a short time since, it was essentially a man's race. No one who was anyone amongst women went at all. The legacy of this is seen still in the dinner party given by the King to men only on the evening of the great race. For a good many years, however, the character of the event has been changing. More and more women went with their husbands and brothers – more and more men wanted the companionship of their sisters and their cousins and their aunts – and now for several years the seal has been set upon fashion by the presence of the Queen. So that the Derby has its own place in social life for men and women alike. It still remains, however, a race meeting above all things, and not the combination of race and garden party which distinguishes Ascot in particular and Goodwood up to a point. The dresses chosen, therefore, are just those which would come naturally into use at any outdoor meeting at the end of May; and, indeed, so great a variety is seen that anything suitable passes muster.

The other meetings are frankly races, pure and simple. Tailor-mades hold the field, and coats and skirts or overcoats, according to the season, provide the correct garb for womenkind, with undress kit, again regulated by the time of year, for men.

MRS MASSEY LYON, from *Etiquette* (1927)

And a characteristially sane appraisal of the importance of the Derby from Griffith and Oakeshott:

It is for many who have never made a habit of following the horses a matter of the greatest interest, providing them yearly with the opportunity of applying their minds to something really worth while. For one reason or another, business or pleasure, a large part of the inhabitants of the civilized world is accustomed to spend some of the leisure hours of the spring of the year picking the Derby winner. It is a blameless pleasure, which has kept more men out of trouble than it has led astray.

GUY GRIFFITH and MICHAEL OAKESHOTT, from *A Guide to the Classics*

7

'You won't get far on this one'

The Grand National

Like the Derby, the Grand National has an atmosphere and feel all its own, and the race has inspired some memorable accounts by those who have taken part. John Hislop's Steeplechasing *was published in 1951, when National day provided a mixed bill of Flat and jump racing.*

On 'National day there is an electric atmosphere of anticipation that pervades the whole course. It spreads through the people on the stands, in the paddock, the crowds along the railway embankment and the Canal, and even through the officials, whom one tends to regard as emotionless. In the jockey's room, too, it is evident – perhaps more markedly than anywhere else, since here are to be found those most directly concerned in the event itself, the actors in the play.

To start with, there are many more jockeys crowded into the changing-rooms than usual. Besides all those riding in the race, and there may be forty or fifty, there are a great many who are not: hurdle race jockeys who are riding at the meeting, flat race riders who are doing likewise, old-timers who have come to revive memories of the past and renew acquaintance with the valets who used to 'do' them in their riding days, travelling lads coming in and out leaving their little leather satchels containing the racing colours, and trainers in search of their riders, or wishing to leave some instruction with the valet concerning equipment.

It is a scene and an atmosphere which will always be clear in my mind – possibly because I have not experienced it often enough to lose the illusion, but, even so, I cannot think that the hardiest veteran of the profession can remain quite unmoved by the environment.

Almost the sole topic of conversation is the 'National: what will win it (and what will not), how it will be run, whether or not there will be many falls, anecdotes of horses and jockeys past and present, and personal views about one's own and other riders' probable fate in the race. Jockeys who have never ridden in the race before will be seeking advice from the experienced, some of those who have taken part in it (perhaps only once, getting no further than the first or second fence) will, like a second-termer holding forth to a new boy, address the inexperienced with the patronizing assurance of one who has ridden over the course many times.

In the weighing-room is to be seen the unusual sight of movie cameras perched up in various corners, aimed at the scales and ready to take the jockeys as they weigh out, a scene that comprises part of the news film of the race. In odd places arc-lamps are being set by to provide light for the photographers, and technicians and cameramen, strangely out of place in this environment, flit about among members of the racing world making adjustments to their equipment.

On this day the weighing-room board is almost completely covered with telegrams: messages of good wishes to jockeys riding, from friends, relations and fans, with a few letters among them from those wishing to express their sentiments more fully or solicit information about a jockey's chances in the race.

Outside, the approaches to the weighing-room, too, are crowded, and a jockey on his way into this building will find many well-wishers – as likely as not complete strangers – among the bystanders, who will give them a word of encouragement, and perhaps a pat on the back as they pass through. The 'National crowd is distinctive. In the Members' Enclosure and Paddock are to be seen a preponderance of bowler hats, a great proportion of their wearers being hunting men, who, except for the National Hunt meeting at Cheltenham and the 'National and possibly their local meeting, never go racing at all.

It also comprises many non-racing people who have come to see it, as one would go to see the Aldershot Tattoo, the Tower of London, or any other of our national scenes or spectacles. Most of these are tourists from abroad, which comprise quite a number of Americans, many of whom are keen followers of English steeplechasing, possibly because the scope of the sport in their own country is rather limited, except for hunt-racing.

The 'National is the third race of the day, being due to start at 3.15 p.m. Owing to a large number of runners and to the fact that there is a parade for the race it is necessary to weigh out in good time, and most riders begin to get ready before the first race.

The sense of excitement and anticipation increases – it always makes me think of the time of preparation before doing a parachute jump: the procedure of adjusting attire, drawing parachutes from the store, checking that they have been correctly put on, and then the tension of waiting until the time comes to emplane, having a sharp similarity to the procedure in the jockeys' room, where in a like manner racing clothes are put on, saddles are got down and given to the appropriate jockeys, and all the procedure of preparing and checking equipment is gone through.

There is the same feeling of comradeship that arises among those who share a common danger, however remote and slight that risk may be: the same feeling of thrill, and the vague apprehension that is born of awaiting the fulfilment of fate which, whether or not it is predestined, cannot be foreseen. In an hour or so's time, someone's fortune will be made, someone's reputation enhanced or created; there will be disappointments, surprises, shocks; comedy and perhaps tragedy, but how – and to whom – such things may happen no one can tell.

The atmosphere affects individuals in different ways. Some become garrulous, others silent; some unusually cheerful, others morose. The face of one will be pale and set, of another flushed and animated. Some will appear unaffected, except perhaps for some mannerism such as a tendency to yawn; others will be unable to stop their muscles quivering as if stricken with ague – I have seen jockeys of iron nerve and brilliant dash in a race so affected, and have noticed in my own case – though I lay no claim to the latter qualities – that I have often ridden best when particularly nervous and jittery in the dressing-room.

Some of the most amiable of characters, in the ordinary course of events, will snap their valets' heads off for no apparent reason, others will become unusually hearty and sociable. One man's

229

speech will become pedantic, another's blasphemous. Whatever the nature of the individual, and no matter how calm or undisturbed he may be, he will almost certainly betray the effect of the nervous tension within him by some expression or action to which he is not usually prone.

As time passes there is a tendency for conversation to veer away from the subject of the race – even from steeplechasing itself – and to circle round such more distant topics as the cinema, women, domestic affairs, clothes and so on, and in spite of its ever-nearing presence the race itself seems to become something remote and unreal, almost a dream to which one does not belong, and, as one sometimes finds in dreams, there arises the wish to awake in order to discover whether or not it is a phantasy.

When a jockey is ready he moves along to the weighing-room and joins the queue leading to the scales, which stretches the whole length of the room, its tail winding into one of the changing rooms, so many riders does it comprise.

Here the unreality does not cease, for by now the arc-lamps will be blazing, with a white, slightly violet-tinted glare, lighting up the racing colours with a brilliancy foreign to them, glinting from stirrup-irons, and turning the scene from an ordinary part of race-course procedure to one that might be taken from some theatrical production as *Ali Baba and the Forty Thieves*.

The line gradually moves forward, stopping while each jockey steps on to the weighing-machine for his weight to be passed as correct. During this respite the others will lean against the wall, their saddles under their arm, every now and then shifting the load from one arm to the other, their skull-caps stuck carelessly on their heads, the strings of their racing cap dangling down like a pair of pigtails, the small squares of paper given them at the trial scales and bearing their number on the race-card and the weight they should carry, stuck into a fold of the girths, wound round the saddle and transformed to a starchy whiteness by the glare; or they will stand in their place in the closely-packed line, their saddles balanced on their hips, or rested momentarily on anything within reach, to ease the burden of the weight.

Every now and then the cameras will whirr and click in action as the rider of a fancied horse steps on to the scales, and then return to silence as less publicized contemporaries take their place.

Soon the jockeys who have been riding in the second race, one on the flat, come in. Those who have finished in the first four holding up the line as they pause to weigh-in, the others breaking through the queue on their way back to the dressing-room, exchanging a quip or letting fall a word of encouragement on the way: 'Hope you haven't forgotten the glue; good luck and get round safely,' or some such remark.

Most trainers like to get their jockeys weighed out in good time, even if they do not actually put the saddle on the horse till the last possible minute. It allows time for changing the girths, going back for a pad to put under the front of the saddle, or any similar contingency, so that, after he has passed the scales, a jockey will probably have at least half an hour on his hands before being called out for the race.

This spell is, I think, the most unpleasant of all. There is nothing to do; one is dressed and ready, except for tying up the cap ribbons, which is a matter of seconds, and the only occupation is sitting aimlessly on the bench and talking – or just sitting. Some adjust and readjust their boots, wristlets, or some part of their equipment; others sit on the table swinging their legs, or tapping their boot with their whip; some smoke, suck sweets or chew gum, others stretch themselves out when and where there is room, relaxing until the last moment.

For all, the time drags on as if the hour of the race would never come.

There will probably be a cluster of jockeys round the fire, availing themselves of all the warmth and comfort they can before going out into the cold, and perhaps one will go over to the wash-basin and rinse out his mouth with cold water to remove that unpleasant dryness that sometimes seems to accrue.

Jockeys who are not riding, and others, come into the room to tender their good wishes and pass the time of day – 'Wish I was coming with you' is a remark often passed by those for whom retirement or circumstances have made its fulfilment an impossibility – and the valets sort out and distribute whips to those who have not already got them.

So the minutes gradually slip away, until at last the official assigned for the purpose enters the room and announces the 'Jockeys out, please,' which is the call to move to the paddock.

A cat pitched into a dovecot could hardly cause more disturbance than these words. There is an immediate scuffling to find
and put on coats – if they have not already been donned – one
man has suddenly lost his whip, a second is asking the valet to let
him have a last puff from the latter's cigarette, and a third has
broken his cap-string in his eagerness to get it tied securely, and
is bawling at the valet's assistant to give him an elastic band to
take its place.

Finally, the last man has been attended to, and the jockeys are
streaming out of the weighing-room into the paddock, leaving the
valets hastily putting on their jackets and diving under the
benches, or into the hampers, for race-glasses, preparatory to jos-
tling for a place on the stand to see the race, as eager for one of
the jockeys they look after to win the race as are their patrons
themselves.

After the stuffiness of the changing-room, the cool air of the
paddock is a refreshing tonic – I always like to take two or three
deep breaths of it to get rid of all the smoke and fustiness of the
last half hour – and it seems to bring one back to reality, and
the task on hand.

In the paddock the density of the crowd increases as one nears
the parade-ring, and walking up the slope of the bank which
surrounds the latter enclosure, it is necessary to elbow one's way
through a tightly packed throng, which, however, opens up to
allow one through with cheerful readiness, as soon as those in the
way are aware of the riders' approach. Friends, acquaintances and
even strangers will be free with their good wishes and greetings,
which are a heartening pleasantry to those at whom they are
directed, however commonplace and meaningless they may be as
regards the speaker.

There is something rather impressive about large numbers of
people, especially when one can view their massed formation from
a position of comparative isolation, and though, containing as it
does many groups of owners, trainers and jockeys, the centre of
the parade ring could hardly be termed isolated, in comparison
to the mass of people ringing its perimeter, and packing the bank
in solid tiers of humanity, its oval of grass with the beautifully
laid-out bed of scarlet flowers in the centre – I am no gardener so
will not attempt to name them – is a veritable oasis. To one who

is little accustomed to such circumstances, the sight and experience is remarkable and not a little awe-inspiring.

The runners for the race are being led round the inside of the perimeter, each with a white sheet bearing his name over his stable clothing, and on the way towards the owner and trainer for whom one is riding, the inclination is to search for the horse one will soon be mounting. Sometimes it is a minute or two before one can pick him out, in 1947 there were so many runners that the horses were walking round two deep, but soon a familiar feature or trait catches the eye: perhaps a white blaze or star, a particular way of walking, the set of his ears, or merely the name on his sheet, but I would say that most racing men instinctively look for natural means of identification before they fall back upon this last, simplest, and most accurate clue.

When speaking of my own feelings I by no means impute that other riders experience the same, and even at this stage of the proceedings I cannot say that I have ever felt anything but rather ill-at-ease – one owner who was gracious (and courageous) enough to avail himself of my services in the 'National, on my appearance in the parade-ring enquired most feelingly after my health, admitting to me afterwards that, from the colour of my face, he feared that I was suffering from a bilious attack.

However, by paying strict attention to the advice and instruction of whoever is responsible for delivering the same, and a well-regulated stable will always see that either the owner or the trainer, never both, do this; otherwise their directions are apt to be confusing, occasionally contradictory – and concentrating upon forming a clear conception of the plan of campaign in one's mind, this feeling gradually passes, and when one is finally in the saddle it has gone, and one is, as it were, in a new atmosphere, with no time for apprehension and superstition, and no thoughts beyond the actions of the moment.

While it is important enough to see to one's equipment in an ordinary race, it is doubly essential to do so in the 'National, and though the trainer will take pains in such matters, it is as well to cast a quick eye over everything; it is not the trainer that is going to be the direct sufferer as the result of any carelessness, and it is possible that one may be riding the least-fancied of several runners, in which case it is unlikely that the horse in question will be given quite the same careful scrutiny as will be the case with the more fancied candidates; in fact, it is more than probable that the saddling of it has been assigned to an assistant, or one of the many free-lances who follow round the meetings in order to hire out their services in this respect, and it will be little consolation to the rider of a horse whose saddle finished up round its belly owing to carelessness or lack of adjustment in saddling, that the accident was not really his fault.

On leaving the paddock, the horses assemble just by the gate leading on to the course and sort themselves out into the order in which they appear on the race-card. On such occasions, when there are a considerable number of horses milling around in close proximity to one another, it is not difficult to get a horse kicked, and it is therefore advisable to avoid taking up a position that might enable such an occurrence to come about, and to keep clear of any horse that shows signs of letting drive.

Whether the day was clear or misty, I have never failed to be moved at the vista offered from the back of a horse in the 'National parade. Straight down is the long, green avenue of the course, neatly and strikingly hemmed by the white rails; on the one side the tightly-packed stands soar up towards the sky – in contrast to the empty stretches of the track, they seem bigger and more densely thronged than when seen from among the crowd itself or from any part of them; on the other, a thinner gathering, spread out along the far rails, and the trim, formidable outlines of the water-jump and the 'Chair'.

On a clear day every detail stands out as if viewed through a telescope; when it is misty the course vanishes into nothingness and the stands become indistinct dark masses against a background of grey, the horses themselves an endless snake, whose head, or tail (according to one's position in the line) disappears into the greyness.

When about level with the end of Tattersall's enclosure, the horses turn round and canter back past the stands. As each arrives at the point of departure, the lad leading him slips off the rein, gives his horse a pat, the rider a word of encouragement or exhortation, sometimes of warning – 'You won't get far on this one,' was the somewhat dampening farewell offered to me on one occasion – and he is swinging down to the post.

MY AINTREE NIGHTMARE

Every life has a waking dream that turns into nightmare. Mine happened exactly 20 years ago next Saturday. It was called the Grand National.

Distance is supposed to lend enchantment. Aintree memories are meant to be of heroic days and joshing nights, and when tackled about any pre-race nerves our hero gives a B-movie laugh and says: 'Well there were a few butterflies in the changing room, but once we were out for the race everything was great.' Not here it wasn't.

Mind you, everybody was very nice to the still pretty innocent Mr B. Scott – the other jockeys, the tough but kindly 'Frenchy' Nicholson as he legged me up, stable lad Barry Davies as he led us out on to the track and even big, thundering Time as he plodded beneath me during the parade.

But the problems now were quite appallingly obvious. All those runners (there were no fewer than 47 that year) over those all-too-famous Grand National fences (the obligatory on-foot inspection had been no comfort); and on this horse. Time was a huge, tough old sod, and we'd been through a fairly encouraging run at Cheltenham a fortnight earlier. But the year before, when National favourite, he had kept landing too heavily in the drops, and the idea today was to go more gently, to let him 'fiddle' round to (oh happy phrase!) 'keep out of trouble'.

Well, Julius Caesar might have liked having fat men around him for reassurance, but the trick at the start of the National is to get beside someone lean and hungry who looks as if they know what they are doing. But just as we got jammed in next to crack jockeys Bill Rees and David Nicholson, old Time contrarily backed out of line, the space was taken and when we finally got back in it was between two nervous looking amateurs, one of whom, Chris Collins, had wasted so deathly white that I remember giving him last words of unneeded support. He eventually finished third, I ended up in Walton hospital.

Maybe I had read too much Siegfried Sassoon about war in the trenches but the parallel here had just about everything save the Flanders mud. The long, stamping, cursing line was the 'stand to'. The starter's shout and the tapes flying up was 'over the top'. The grit of the Melling Road was 'through the wire into no man's land'. The long row of fences up ahead were the enemy lines.

And we were straightaway in trouble. Off his legs and at the back of the field, Time landed deep in the drop at the first, and all the way down to Becher's it was a horrible, scrambling struggle to stay in one piece.

We could never get any rhythm, find any passage. There were loose horses everywhere, and even the mounted cavalry were all over the place. A grey horse kept coming leftwards into me. At the fifth fence I'd seemed to have escaped him. The next was Becher's; you could hear the commentary and see the crowds on the far side. Two strides off it, the grey horse came slap across us. For a dreadful doomed moment we blundered completely blind into the fence of fences.

Even in hell you can have moments of love. I loved Time then. For somehow he got over Becher's, survived the steep, steep landing, bulldozed past two fallers and suddenly the first smoke of horror had cleared. Chesterton's donkey might have had his hour, 'one far, fierce hour and sweet'. Time and I only had about four minutes. But as the fences began to flick by below us, and we began actually to make contact with this race, this Grand National, we had our moment, everything except the palms beneath our feet.

But nightmare, albeit of a simpler kind, was waiting. Going out for the second circuit, Time was steaming along so strongly that the 30 lengths we were off the leaders seemed no great gap. Confidence was growing, but carelessness was close. At the big ditch, I sat still, indecisive. Time galloped slap into it, somersaulted high and heavy, and then I was in the ambulance with the Duke of Alburquerque.

The pay-off put things into perspective. The ambulance went from fence to fence, and stretcher parties brought across the wounded. Eventually we headed back to the racecourse doctor, on to hospital and presumably to anxious orderlies all ready to greet and tend their heroes.

Well, poor Jimmy Morrissey was rushed in to have his smashed head treated. The old duke was put behind a curtain, where he mystified the assembled medics by moaning, 'Mon genou, mon genou.' But the other two of us, still in breeches, boots and grass-stained jockey sweaters, just sat on the bench next to the granny who had tripped over on the pavement, and the little boy who had cut his hand on a milk bottle.

Eventually a polite little doctor called us forward. The broken collarbone was not difficult to diagnose, but the cause of the accident appeared to be beyond him. 'What have you been doing?' he asked. 'At what races? How long ago?' Maybe it was a dream after all.

BROUGH SCOTT in the Sunday Times, 24 March 1985

John Oaksey's account of his narrow defeat on Carrickbeg in the 1963 race remains unsurpassed as a description of 'so near yet so far' in the National.

There are 494 yards between the last fence and the winning post in the Grand National at Aintree – and, for about 480 of them, I was, last Saturday afternoon, the happiest man in the world. But the last battle is the only one to count – and for that, for those final, ghastly 14 yards, Carrickbeg and I had nothing left. So there, in a split second, the dream of glory became a nightmare and Pat Buckley swept past on Mr P. B. Raymond's Ayala to win the great steeplechase.

The pair of them won it fair and square because, together, with certain defeat staring them between the eyes, they had the courage and endurance to go on fighting what was an apparently hopeless battle.

A horse with slightly less bottomless stamina than Ayala, or a man slightly less strong, fit and determined than Buckley, would never have been able to seize the chance when it came.

At the time – at that bitter moment when Ayala's head appeared at my knee – I wished them both at the bottom of the deep, blue sea. Now, with admiration and only a little envy, I salute them for winning, deservedly, a truly wonderful race – a race, I think, as thrilling and spectacular as any Grand National since the war.

But besides the winner there was another hero. At the age of seven, in only his second season as a 'chaser, Carrickbeg had outjumped and outgalloped 46 older, more experienced horses for nearly 4½ miles.

Steady as the rock of Gibraltar from the first fence to the last, he was never for one single moment in danger of falling and, until his last reserves gave out ten strides before the end, he had answered my every call with cheerful, unhesitating obedience.

Unless he gives it me, I never expect to have a better ride at Aintree or anywhere else, and for those 9½ unforgettable minutes I offer him my heartfelt thanks.

They had begun as, with the long, nerve-racking preliminaries over at last, Mr Alec Marsh got the huge field off to a perfect start.

A bitter, biting wind had greeted us as we left the weighing-room and, by the time we turned in front of the stands to canter down, my spirits for one were at their lowest ebb.

Carrickbeg restored them slightly – striding out like a lion on the way to the post – but the last moments before a National will never be anything but a dreadful, goldfish-bowl ordeal and only when the first few fences are safely crossed can you begin to forget how much is at stake and settle down to enjoy the greatest thrill the sport of steeplechasing has to offer.

After our dismal experience together at Cheltenham, those first few fences were, for Carrickbeg and me, especially important. But if he felt the same misgivings as his rider, Carrickbeg concealed them well. He measured the first to an inch and, even more encouraging, hit the top of the open ditch quite hard – and somehow made it feel no stiffer than a soft French hurdle.

As expected, Out And About (10st 7lb) had led from the start, but Josh Gifford held him well and the pace they set was nothing extraordinary. As the red and white flag fluttered its awe-inspiring warning over Becher's Brook, Jonjo (10st 6lb), French Lawyer (10st 6lb), Forty Secrets (10st 7lb), Chavara (10st 2lb) and Dandy Tim (10st 6lb) were in the leading group – and Carrickbeg (10st 3lb) sailed over like a bird not far behind to land far out beyond the ditch and gallop on without a check.

Good Gracious (10st 7lb) fell at Becher's, Magic Tricks (10st) had gone at the first, Look Happy (10st) at the second, Merganser (10st 4lb) and Wingless (10st 3lb) at the third and Solonace (10st) somewhere thereabouts. But for most, as we swung round the Canal Turn, the fences were setting no great problems.

I personally had not seen one faller until Connie II (10st) ploughed through the tenth beside me, but the sickening crash she made was a violent reminder that this is still Aintree, where to take one liberty too many can mean a sudden end to all your hopes.

Ayala (10st), never far from the leaders, had, in fact, taken one at the Canal – carving a huge chunk from the fence, but failing completely to disturb either his own or Pat Buckley's equilibrium. I watched, with admiration, their recovery – and little knew how dear it was to cost me by and by.

On the long run back towards the stands, loose horses began to be a problem. Merganser, riderless, was a serious thorn in Josh Gifford's flesh, constantly unsettling Out And About and making him pull harder than ever, and, as we galloped towards the Chair – never an enjoyable moment – Wingless, dodging gaily about in front of Carrickbeg, made the towering cliff of the great fence an even less welcoming prospect than usual.

But all was well and now, with the water safely crossed, I found myself, for the first time ever, in a position from which the National had to be considered *as a race* – not merely as a struggle for survival. And the next 100 yards – swinging out into the country – were, in a way, more exciting than any in the whole 4½ miles.

There, deciding that the moment had come to get a bit closer, I picked Carrickbeg up for the first time – and the effortless power with which he surged up towards the leaders suddenly brought home the unbelievable truth that we were in the race with a real chance.

At Becher's the second time, in nine Grand Nationals out of ten, the shape of the finish can already be seen. And so it was now, for although Out And About was still in front together with Loyal Tan, French Lawyer and Dandy Tim, Ayala was close behind them, Springbok (10st 12lb) was improving steadily and, as Carrickbeg landed over the Brook, the leaders were not ten lengths ahead of us.

At the fence after Becher's, Loyal Tan and Dandy Tim dropped out exhausted and by the Canal there were (although I certainly did not realise it at the time) only six left in the race with a real chance. They were Out And About, now disputing the lead with

239

French Lawyer, Hawa's Song (10st), Springbok, Ayala and Carrickbeg.

This list may be wronging some who were, in fact, still close enough to win at the Canal, but the fact is that from Valentine's on I saw only five horses.

And now it was a race in deadly earnest – no longer time to look about or manoeuvre for a clear run, but kick and push and get ground where you can.

The four fences from Valentine's to Anchor Bridge were as exciting as any I ever jumped – and at one of them, the fourth from home, the dice rolled fractionally against Carrickbeg for the first time and only time in the whole race.

Understandably, having led almost all the way, Out And About was tiring now and, as French Lawyer went on, he crashed low through the fence and fell.

Perhaps three lengths behind, confronted with a gaping hole and a cloud of flying twigs, Carrickbeg hesitated for a split second, failed to take off when I asked, scrambled through the gap – and had then to swerve past his fallen rival.

These things happen so fast – and are so quickly driven from one's mind by what comes after – that is all too easy to exaggerate their importance.

The newsreel film does not, unfortunately, show the incident in full, but it does, I think, prove that whereas Carrickbeg was bang with the leaders five from home, one fence later, after Out And About's fall, he had definitely lost at least a couple of lengths. Whatever the truth I do not offer it as an excuse. Such things happen in all Grand Nationals and the winner is the one who best overcomes them.

Probably, in any case, I should have given Carrickbeg a better chance to recover before asking him to go and win. But, passing Anchor Bridge, with the second last in sight, I saw Gerry Scott go for his whip on Springbok, saw the favourite stagger sideways, beaten – and, with Carrickbeg strong under me, it seemed that the time had come.

Until you have tried to ride a finish up it no one, I think, can fully appreciate just how long and wearisome the run-in at Aintree can be after 4 miles and 30 fences.

In the back of my mind now, as I sent Carrickbeg past Ayala

and Springbok to join Hawa's Song at the second last, there was the foolish fear that something with a better turn of speed – Owen's Sedge, for instance – would come from behind and beat us all.

In fact, of course, what I *should* have feared was the dreadful strain put upon any horse who, after jumping for 4 miles, finds himself in front with neither fence nor company to help him up that final desperate, staring straight.

Next time, perhaps, I shall know better, but now, as Carrickbeg swept gallantly over the last with Ayala at his quarters, it still seemed possible. His stride had still not faltered and, straightening round the elbow half-way home with the roar of the crowd rising to a crescendo in our ears, the only feeling I remember was one of wild, incredulous hope that the dream first dreamt on a nursery rocking horse long ago was really coming true.

Until this moment, sustained by my horse's strength and by the heat of battle, I had felt no real physical strain, but now, all at once, the cold, clammy hand of exhaustion closed its grip on my thighs and arms.

Even to swing the whip had become an effort and the only thing that kept me going was the unbroken rhythm of Carrickbeg's heroic head, nodding in time with his stride. And suddenly, even that was gone.

With a hundred yards to go and still no sound of pursuit, the prize seemed within our grasp. Eighty, seventy, sixty perhaps – and then it happened. In the space of a single stride I felt the last ounce of Carrickbeg's energy drain away and my own with it. One moment we were a living, working combination, the next, a struggling, beaten pair. There was still hope – but not for long.

As we passed Ayala before the second last, Carrickbeg had, to Pat Buckley himself, looked the winner bar a fall. 'Go on John,' he found the breath and good nature to say, but saying it, did not for one second relax his efforts. He had been riding hard for longer than I but, with the strength and determination of youth, managed to keep Ayala in the race.

Half-way up the run-in, still two lengths behind, it must have looked as hopeless to him as it did, I believe, from the stands. But he never gave up and, as Carrickbeg began to falter, pulled Ayala out for a final desperate effort.

The gallant chestnut cannot, I think, have quickened much if at all, but the depths of *his* stamina were as yet unplumbed, and so abrupt and complete was Carrickbeg's collapse that in half-a-dozen strides the gap was closed and the race over.

To my dying day I shall never forget the sight of Ayala's head beside my knee. Two heartbeats later he was half a length in front and, although I dropped my hands before the post, I can honestly promise any aggrieved supporter that it made not one yard of difference.

A wonderful race had been gallantly won and, though perhaps it is not for me to say it, almost equally gallantly lost.

Five lengths away, third, came Hawa's Song who, I believe, had made a bad mistake at the second last. Whether or how much this affected his chance I cannot say, but his running had, in any case, brilliantly justified Willie Stephenson's judgment in buying the horse from his cousin Arthur only a few days before the race.

Springbok, whose supposedly limitless stamina had, oddly enough, let him down three-quarters of a mile from home, tired on the flat and was beaten inches for fourth place by Team Spirit (10st 3lb). Mr R. B Woodard's game little horse had, according to Willie Robinson, always been jumping too big, spending too much time and effort in the air.

From a hopeless position at the Canal, however, he ran on doggedly all the way home and there were no more delighted spectators on the course than his sporting American owners.

An even braver – and far sadder – story is that of old Kilmore, who landed on a fallen horse at Becher's the second time and, almost certainly, broke down in the effort of recovery. Even so, according to Fred Winter, he never once put a foot wrong and although never within striking distance of the leaders, struggled gallantly round to be sixth.

The old horse finished very lame and having, as his rider said, 'run the best and bravest race of his life', will never be asked to run again.

Behind Kilmore in seventh place came Owen's Sedge who, watched by his owner, Mr Gregory Peck, had jumped safely all the way. Going to the Canal Turn, Pat Taaffe thought he had a chance of being placed, but Owen's Sedge was baulked there by loose horses and could never thereafter get into the race.

French Lawyer, who, for a comparatively inexperienced 'chaser, had run a truly marvellous race – he was, remember, in front four fences from home – finished eighth, just ahead of Dark Venetian (10st 2lb) and Nicolaus Silver (11st).

The 1961 winner, despite going softer than he likes, had jumped as well as ever but never gave Bobby Beasley the slightest hope of success. Twelve more finished – 22 in all – and only 16 of the 47 runners fell or were brought down.

Among them was Jonjo who, until he over-jumped at Becher's second time round, had given his owner, the Duke of Alburquerque, a wonderful ride. Watching the newsreel, I noticed the Duke sitting up his horse's neck like a hero over the first eight fences, and Spain can be proud of its representative in the greatest steeplechase of all.

Frenchman's Cove (12st) made a hash of the first Canal Turn and, despite Dave Dick's vigorous efforts, would take no interest thereafter. Of the other well-backed horses, the worst disappointments were Dagmar Gittell (10st 5lb) and Loving Record (10st 12lb), both of whom were pulled up when hopelessly tailed off.

Mr Jones (10st 10lb), the sort of dour stayer who might have taken a hand in the finish, was unlucky enough to fall at the water and Forty Secrets (10st 7lb) lost any chance he had with a desperate blunder at the second last first time round.

No jockey was seriously injured, but Avenue Neuilly, alas, broke a foreleg and had to be destroyed after falling when already riderless at Becher's second time.

And that, I think, is the story of the 1963 Grand National, a race as fine and spectacular as any ever seen at Aintree.

As has been the case for the past two years, the modified fences presented no insurmountable problems to any reasonably competent jumper, and despite the huge field there was, so far as I could tell, practically no crowding or interference even in the first hectic mile.

The story of Ayala, like that of so many past Grand National winners, is studded with good and bad luck.

Now a nine-year-old chestnut gelding, he was bred by Mr J. P. Phillips at Dalham Hall and is by Supertello out of Admiral's Bliss by Admiral's Walk.

Ironically enough, Mr Phillips, when he has jumpers, now sends them to Don Butchers – so if things had gone differently Ayala could conceivably have become a stable companion of Carrickbeg's.

In fact, however, he was an extremely unpromising yearling with moderate forelegs who, as Mr Phillips's stud-groom C. Palmer recalls, was 'a real headache from the time he was foaled'.

Sent up, with his dam, to Newmarket sales (he was scouring so badly until the day before that Palmer despaired of getting him ready), Ayala was sold for 400 guineas to Mr G. Mostyn Owen – and, in the many transactions in which he has figured since, has never reached so high a price again!

Nor was poor Mr Mostyn Owen's money well spent, for when sent to Henri Jelliss at Newmarket, Ayala proved, in the words of the trainer, 'too slow to win a donkey race and too big even to get on a racecourse'. At the end of his second season he was, therefore, sold again, this time for only 40 guineas, to Mr N. Smith, who lives in Epping Forest.

It was then that Mr John Chapman, a tremendously keen and sporting enthusiast, heard of a potential hunter for sale and his wife, seeing Ayala one day on her way back from Newmarket, bought him 'for a song'.

Ayala was in fact a pretty bad hunter – as Mr Chapman's daughter soon discovered – so his owner decided to send him to Keith Piggott to be tried as a hurdler.

This venture, too, met with little success and, since he had another horse in training with Piggott of apparently greater promise, Mr Chapman told the trainer to send him to Epsom sales.

It was a tragic decision, for Mr Chapman, like most jumping owners, has dreamed all his life of getting a Grand National horse – and had he only held on a little longer, Ayala's true milieu would have become clear.

In fact, with Mr Chapman's full permission, Piggott bought the horse for 250 guineas and sold a half-share in him to Mr P. B. Raymond, the celebrated ladies' hairdresser.

In 1960–61, Ayala won three steeplechases and, although he had to be pin-fired last season, Piggott told Mr Raymond long ago that what they had was a potential winner of the Grand National.

That hope did not look very realistic when Ayala turned over at the open ditch on his reappearance at Cheltenham, but, next time out, he won well at Worcester and as Stan Mellor dismounted Mr Raymond told him 'you have just ridden the winner of the 1963 Grand National'.

Mellor, however, was already engaged for Frenchman's Cove and after asking at least one other jockey (Gene Kelly) Piggott approached Pat Buckley.

Only 19 years old, Buckley was born in Kildare and got his early riding experience there out hunting and as a member of the Pony Club. He joined Neville Crump's stable three years ago and quickly showed himself a tough, able horseman.

Last year, taking Gerry Scott's place on Springbok in the Grand National, he had the appalling luck to fall at the very first fence; but the fates did not wait long to give him ample repayment.

No one could have ridden a better or stronger race than Buckley did on Saturday – and who knows what further triumphs may be waiting in the long, bright future that stretches ahead of him?

I hope I shall be forgiven for holding over description of other events last week to our next issue. Perhaps I am prejudiced, but it seems to me that the 1963 Grand National was big enough to fill these pages on its own!

Horse and Hound, 6 April 1963

At least Velvet Brown was first past the post, before being disqualified on a technicality of the 1930s rules: no lady jockeys in those days. National Velvet, *Enid Bagnold's tale (published in 1935) of how a young girl rides the winner of the Grand National on the piebald horse she has won in a raffle, is a perennial favourite, and the description of the race itself – in effect a non-description – is cleverly achieved by being experienced through the character of the stable-hand Mi Taylor.*

At the post the twenty horses were swaying like the sea. Forward . . . No good! Back again. Forward . . . No good! Back again.

The line formed . . . and rebroke. Waves of the sea. Drawing a breath . . . breaking. Velvet fifth from the rail, between a bay and a brown. The Starter had long finished his instructions. Nothing more was said aloud, but low oaths flew, the cursing and grumbling flashed like a storm. An eye glanced at her with a look of hate. The breaking of movement was too close to movement to be borne. It was like water clinging to the tilted rim of the glass, like the sound of the dreaded explosion after the great shell has fallen. The will to surge forward overlaid by something delicate and terrible and strong, human obedience at bursting point, but not broken. Horses' eyes gleamed openly, men's eyes set like chips of steel. Rough man, checked in violence, barely master of himself, barely master of his horse. The Piebald ominously quiet, and nothing coming from him . . . up went the tape.

The green Course poured in a river before her as she lay forward, and with the plunge of movement sat in the stream.

'Black slugs' . . . said Mi, cursing under his breath, running, dodging, suffocated with the crowd. It was the one thing he had overlooked, that the crowd was too dense ever to allow him to reach Becher's in the time. Away up above him was the truckline, his once-glorious free seat, separated from him by a fence. 'God's liver . . .' he mumbled, his throat gone cold, and stumbled into an old fool in a mackintosh. 'Are they off?' he yelled at the heavy crowd as he ran, but no one bothered with him.

He was cursed if he was heeded at all. He ran, gauging his position by the cranes on the embankment. Velvet coming over Becher's in a minute and he not there to see her. 'They're off.' All around him a sea of throats offered up the gasp.

He was opposite Becher's but could see nothing: the crowd thirty deep between him and the Course. All around fell the terrible silence of expectancy. Mi stood like a rock. If he could not see then he must use his ears, hear. Enclosed in the dense, silent, dripping pack he heard the thunder coming. It roared up on the wet turf like the single approach of a multiple-footed animal. There were stifled exclamations, grunts, thuds. Something in the air flashed and descended. The first over Becher's! A roar went up from the crowd, then silence. The things flashing in the air were indistinguishable. The tip of a cap exposed for the briefest of seconds. The race went by like an express train, and was gone. Could Velvet be alive in that?

Sweat ran off Mi's forehead and into his eyes. But it was not sweat that turned the air grey and blotted out the faces before him. The ground on all sides seemed to be smoking. An extra-ordinary mist, like a low prairie fire, was formed in the air. It had dwelt heavily all day behind the Canal, but the whole of the Course had remained clear till now. And now, before you could turn to look at your neighbour, his face was gone. The mist blew in shreds, drifted, left the crowd clear again but hid the whole of the Canal Corner, fences, stand and horses.

There was a struggle going on at Becher's; a horse had fallen and was being got out with ropes. Mi's legs turned to water and he asked his neighbour gruffly 'who's fallen?' But the neighbour, straining to the tip of his toes, and glued to his glasses, was deaf as lead.

Suddenly Mi lashed round him in a frenzy. 'Who's fallen, I say? Who's hurt!'

'Steady on,' said a little man whom he had prodded in the stomach.

'Who's fallen?' said Mi desperately. 'I gotta brother in this . . .'

'It's his brother!' said the crowd all around him. 'Let him through.'

Mi was pushed and pummelled to the front and remained embedded two from the front line. The horse that had fallen was a black horse, its neck unnaturally stretched by the ropes that were hauling it from the ditch.

There was a shout and a horse, not riderless, but ridden by a tugging, cursing man, came galloping back through the curling fumes of the mist, rolled its wild eye at the wrong side of Becher's and disappeared away out of the Course. An uproar began along the fringes of the crowd and rolled back to where Mi stood. Two more horses came back out of the mist, one riderless. The shades of others could be discerned in the fog. Curses rapped out from unseen mouths.

'What's happened at the Canal Turn? What's wrong down at the Turn?'

'The whole field!' shouted a man. The crowd took it up.

'The field's out. The whole field's come back. There's no race!'

It was unearthly. Something a hundred yards down there in the fog had risen up and destroyed the greatest steeplechase in the world.

Nineteen horses had streamed down to the Canal Turn, and

suddenly, there across the Course, at the boundary of the fog, four horses appeared beyond Valentine's, and among them, fourth, was The Piebald.

'Yer little lovely, yer little lovely!' yelled Mi, wringing his hands and hitting his knees. 'It's her, it's him, it's me brother!'

No one took any notice. The scene immediately before them occupied all the attention. Horses that had fallen galloped by riderless, stirrups flying from their saddles, jockeys returned on foot, covered with mud, limping, holding their sides, some running slowly and miserably over the soggy course, trying to catch and sort the horses.

'It's "Yellow Messenger",' said a jockey savagely, who had just seized his horse. 'Stuck on the fence down there and kicking hell.' And he mounted.

'And wouldn't they jump over him?' called a girl shrilly.

'They didn't wanter hurt the poor thing, lady,' said the jockey, grinning through his mud, and rode off.

'Whole lot piled up and refused,' said a man who came up the line. 'Get the Course clear now, quick!'

'They're coming again!' yelled Mi, watching the galloping four. 'Get the Course clear! They'll be coming!'

They were out of his vision now, stuck down under Becher's high fence as he was. Once past Becher's on the second round would he have time to extricate himself and get back to the post before they were home? He stood indecisively and a minute went by. The Course in front of him was clear. Horses and men had melted. The hush of anticipation began to fall. 'They're on the tan again,' said a single voice. Mi flashed to a decision. He could not afford the minutes to be at Becher's. He must get back for the finish and it would take him all his time. He backed and plunged and ducked, got cursed afresh. The thunder was coming again as he reached the road and turned to face the far-off Stands. This time he could see nothing at all, not even a cap in the air. 'What's leading? What's leading?'

'Big brown. Tantibus, Tantibus. Tantibus leading.'

'Where's The Piebald?'

'See that! Leonora coming up . . .'

They were deaf to his frantic questions. He could not wait, but ran. The mist was ahead of him again, driving in frills and wafting sedgily about. Could Velvet have survived Becher's twice? In any case no good wondering. He couldn't get at her to help her. If she fell he would find her more quickly at the hospital door. Better that than struggle through the crowd and be forbidden the now empty Course.

Then a yell. 'There's one down!'

'It's the Yank mare!'

The horse ambulance was trundling back with Yellow Messenger from the Canal Turn. Mi leapt for a second on to the turning hub of the wheel, and saw in a flash, across the momentarily mist-clear course, the pride of Baltimore in the mud underneath Valentine's. The Piebald was lying third. The wheel turned and he could see no more. Five fences from the finish; he would not allow himself to hope, but ran and ran. How far away the Stands in the gaps of the mist as he pushed, gasping, through the people. Would she fall now? What had he done, bringing her up here? But would she fall now? He ran and ran.

'They're coming on to the Racecourse . . . coming on to the Racecourse . . .'

'How many?'

'Rain, rain, can't see a thing.'

'How many?'

Down sank the fog again, as a puff of wind blew and gathered it together. There was a steady roaring from the Stands, then silence, then a hubbub. No one could see the telegraph.

Mi, running, gasped, 'Who's won?'

But everyone was asking the same question. Men were running, pushing, running, just as he. He came up to the gates of Melling Road, crossed the road on the fringe of the tan, and suddenly, out of the mist The Piebald galloped riderless, lolloping unsteadily along, reins hanging, stirrups dangling. Mi burst through on to the Course, his heart wrung.

'Get back there!' shouted a policeman. 'Loose horse!'

'Hullo Old Pie there!' shouted Mi. The animal, soaked, panting, spent, staggered and slipped and drew up.

'What've you done with 'er?' said Mi weeping, and bent down to lift the hoof back through the rein. 'You let 'er down, Pie? What in God's sake?' He led the horse down the Course, running, his breath catching, his heart thumping, tears and rain on his face.

Two men came towards him out of the mist.

'You got him?' shouted one. 'Good fer you. Gimme!'

'You want him?' said Mi, in a stupor, giving up the rein.

'Raised an objection. Want him for the enclosure. Chap come queer.'

'Chap did? What chap?'

'This here's the winner! Where you bin all day, Percy?'

'Foggy,' said Mi. 'Very foggy. Oh my God!'

Like Velvet, John White rode first past the post in a National, but the horses who eventually set off in the 1993 running had scarcely reached first Becher's before the event was being labelled 'The Race That Never Was'. One of the most extraordinary aspects of the shenanigans at the start of the race was the way they triggered any number of articles seeing the fiasco as a metaphor of The Decline of Britain. The Economist *of 10 April 1993 pooh-poohed that interpretation:*

Saturday's fiasco is not a true cameo of modern Britain. Neanderthals no longer occupy the commanding heights of industry. The City is run by professionals who lunch off sandwiches at their desks. The 'yes, minister' types are on the retreat in Whitehall. Now, the old guard is being evicted from its last bastions, including the Jockey Club. The events at Aintree were a disaster for the National, but not a national disaster: they displayed the Britain of yesterday, not that of today.

For a detached account of what actually happened, you could not do better than Matthew Engel in The Guardian *on the Monday following the race.*

AN OFFICER, AN ERK AND A HORSE LAUGH

For the past few years the race has seemed a little mundane: with Red Rum retired, Aintree no longer facing imminent closure and the fences safer too, the old spice has been missing.

It is hard to remember most of the recent winners. There was a growing feeling before Saturday that the Grand National was turning into something ordinary, a handicap steeplechase only a little more exciting than anything at Kelso or Catterick.

Well, what piffle that all was. The race that produced Devon Loch and Foinavon has not lost its supernatural ability to hit the sporting world between the eyes with something truly astonishing. This year it produced a cock-up on a heroic scale, a sequence of events so absurd that it could have been fashioned in Downing Street.

It was announced yesterday that the greatest non-event in sporting history will have to do as the 1993 Grand National. Peter Greenall, the chairman of Aintree, said the race would not be rerun. The decisive factor was that the vast majority of trainers were against it.

Undoubtedly, the practical problems could have been overcome had everyone been determined. Had the course been waterlogged or frozen, a new date would have been found. In that case it could have been a triumph: there would have been no trouble securing public interest as the race has never had more publicity.

But though all the humans now know the National never happened, most of the horses ran all or part of the 4$^1/_2$ miles and are appropriately knackered. No one has explained to them that the race was declared void because most of the jockeys failed to realise there had been a second false start.

In contrast, there was no trouble at all finding a scapegoat. Ken Evans, the £28-a-day flagman, was singled out. He was supposed to wave his flag in front of the horses in response to the starter's red flag. At 3.50 pm on Saturday the flagman's duties would have been as obscure as those of a saggermaker's bottom-knocker to 99.9 per cent of the nation; by 4.30 everyone was lucidly expert on his technical failings.

To recap: there were two false starts. The first was handled smoothly. One or two runners were caught in the elasticised tape but they shook it off quickly; as it happens the race could have been run well enough with no one at a significant disadvantage. But at that stage the rules were still rules. The starter, Capt. Keith Brown, waved his red flag; Evans, 100 yards or so down the course, responded with his and the riders pulled their mounts up.

The second time was far more serious. The tape was caught between the legs of one horse, Travel Over, and round the neck of Richard Dunwoody on Wont Be Gone Long, who actually was not going anywhere at all. That was the one potentially horrific moment, because if another horse had got caught up as well, Dunwoody might have been Isadora Duncan-ed.

That time, no one saw Evans's flag. But the video shows that Capt. Brown did not unfurl his flag properly: all he did, in effect, was to shake a stick in the air. It is not surprising if it could not be seen. But the issue was confused further yesterday when Evans was quoted saying he did see the starter's flag and did wave his own. If true, that makes it all even more mysterious. Whatever the answer, it would not be in racing's nature to blame an officer if a convenient erk can be found.

Before both starts there were invasions of the course by a few animal-rights activists, 30 according to some reports, though there were never that many visible from the stands and none at all were visible to television viewers because the BBC self-righteously declined to show them. The leaflets the demonstrators handed out were riddled with inaccuracies and quarter-truths. There are easy answers to them; censorship is not one of them.

The protesters did not directly cause the problems but they added to uncertainty at the start. Once the alleged race began, horses and humans did as they were programmed. Normally there is nattering between riders. If there is something wrong, word gets round. But as one jockey put it: 'There's not too much chatter in the National. You don't come to the first asking someone what he did the night before.'

Furthermore, it had been raining hard for almost two hours; there was a howling wind; the crowd was making a lot of noise too, though the jockeys might have noticed that the cheers had turned to boos. It is also remotely possible that they might have taken note of the PA system had the course commentators not carried on blithely as though things were normal, except for the bizarre comment: 'This race is not actually taking place.'

Then came the incident at the Chair when a lone figure with a red flag and one motorway cone did appear to try to stop the horses. Reasonably, most riders ignored that too. The cone is supposed to denote some kind of obstruction and is not a recall signal. And if you see someone with a red flag in Liverpool, it is normal to assume it is a member of Militant and not a Jockey Club employee.

And so John White and Esha Ness 'won'. Afterwards Capt. Brown was immediately surrounded by aggrieved parties, over-reacting. John Upson, trainer of the hot fancy Zeta's Lad, said to him: 'See you in the courts. I've never heard anything so stupid in my life.'

Brown was then given police protection, though once he had removed his bowler and put on a flat cap, people only recognised him because of the phalanx of policemen.

Then came the perfectly normal announcement 'Stewards' Inquiry' for a very abnormal situation. Under the Rules of Racing the race should have been run again with the nine runners left at the start, but common sense at least prevented that.

Jenny Pitman, Esha Ness's trainer and the nearest thing British sport has produced to a Margaret Thatcher, was variously reported to be in floods of tears and fighting all comers in the weighing room. She strode back to the stables calmly but grim-faced. She spoke only of her horse that won 10 years ago: 'Corbiere didn't deserve this,' she said enigmatically.

Carol Morgan, whose husband Ken trained the Slovak entry Quirinus, summed up the prevailing mood: 'I'm just so embarrassed for racing. This is 1993. What are we doing with a red flag for Christ's sake?'

Toby Balding, trainer of Romany King, was one of the few people maintaining any perspective. 'Jolly bad luck,' he said. 'That's what racing's all about.'

The Stewards of the Jockey Club meet in London today to investigate how to conduct the investigation. In the British way, there will be endless recommendations and technological safe-guards to prevent a recurrence: as a nation we always have 20–20 hindsight. If there is a red flag in 1994 it will probably be controlled or backed up by a computer.

It is clear that the starting gate, a product of 19th-century tech-nology, was unsatisfactory for such a race. The tapes at normal National Hunt courses now go across rather than up but Aintree is too wide for that. There is no need for modernisation. There would have been no difficulty had Brown used the 18th-century technology of starting by flag. All the electronics in the world cannot produce a system more efficient than two men with flags – if they do their job right.

Esha Ness was brought into the winners' enclosure, as though he had really won. Most people wandered through the rain shocked, as though a real disaster had taken place, until they recovered their wits and realised they could get their money back. The course bookmakers tried to chalk up the odds for the next race but no one cared about that.

Momentarily, one could even feel sorry for the bookies. It was raining so hard that the clerks, at the back of the umbrellas, could hardly read the smudged figures in the ledgers.

It might have got nasty, though. In front of the weighing room Merseyside police were beginning to get a little free with their American-style nightsticks. 'I just thank God for the rain,' said one senior officer. 'I don't know what would have happened had it been a sunny day. There are a lot of irate punters out there.'

But most were only moaning. 'I've come all the way from Stoke for this pigging crap,' shouted one irate punter to a complete stranger. He picked the wrong audience. 'I flew especially from Holland,' said the other man, slowly.

Meanwhile, behind the County Stand, the band played on. And people did begin to see the funny side. No one had been killed, no horse had been killed, the stakes had been returned and they had seen something they would never forget.

Greenall, a member of the brewing family, said he expected no damage to the race any more than there was to the Boat Race when Oxford sank. There were some remarks as to whether or not he could organise a piss-up in his own brewery. But that was quite unfair: Aintree is a very impressively run racecourse these days; in the late 1970s it was a disgrace. Far from damaging the race, this ridiculous business will create a marvellous sense of anticipation for 1994.

Peter O'Sullevan was using the word tragic after the first false start. But the weekend of FA Cup semi-finals is no occasion to bandy the word tragic around. The biggest losers are the bookmakers, who miss their anticipated profits – William Hill is muttering about suing Aintree – and the Treasury, which loses £6 million in betting tax, so you have to laugh. A horse laugh.

The Guardian, 5 April 1993

8

'Collecting injustices'

The world of betting

I didn't have a bet in the next race but then at the very last moment, as they were going into the stalls for the sixth, I got hit over the head by a hunch and, running like Last Tycoon himself towards the bookies, I got a fiver on Bicoque. As they raced past us inside the final furlong it seemed like a mess of a blanket finish. Then they announced that Bicoque had won by a head. There was more agony to come in the form of a stewards' enquiry which went on for fifteen minutes and then they gave the all clear. Bicoque the winner at 33–1. But you know what really kills me about betting on the horses? You're never happy. I'm not, anyway. I sat there under the trees sipping the last dregs of the Bollinger, cursing myself for not having put a tenner on. It was pathetic, really, and got me to thinking that a psychiatrist I know probably hit the nail on the head when he described punting as 'collecting injustices'.

JEFFREY BERNARD, from *Talking Horses*

And being a betting man involves not just backing winners or losers; it also involves the annoyance of others expecting tips, as Jeffrey Bernard so acutely describes:

THE FALSE MESSIAH

To see a newcomer to racing getting hooked, then stumbling, then crashing, is like watching a man falling off the top of a building in slow motion. Take Antonio. Antonio was the Portuguese barman who served in the Soho pub I used to frequent. He gave the impression of being carefree, but really he was manic. His addiction to matters concerning the Turf began one day when he put fifty pence on a horse of Scobie Breasley's called Hittite Glory. The animal trotted up at 100–1 and Antonio got the idea that he could repeat the performance every day for the rest of his life. The fact that he didn't know one end of a horse from the other made things awkward for him and watching him study the midday *Evening Standard* (as it then was) was sadly like watching a junkie who can't remember how a hypodermic's put together.

Anyway, someone told him I knew the odd trainer and horses, and he started asking me to mark his card for him every day. As far as Antonio went, looking back on it, it was already too late to shout a warning. I simply tried to cushion the inevitable sickening thud by giving him a few winners on the way down, but I think the results may have speeded up his descent. I started off by giving him a couple of good things each day and then astounded myself by giving him four out of four which he did in a yankee. The very next day I gave him a nourishing 32–1 double, followed by another winner the day after which cruised in at 9–1.

I then began to fear for his sanity although I had always thought he was suspect in the head. In two lousy weeks only, he suddenly knew it all, and one night I nearly killed him when he, like a baby trying to walk by himself for the first time, actually had the nerve to venture an opinion. 'That horse Wollow, he's no good,' he said. So crass was the remark that I can very nearly savour it now, but at the time I was tremendously tempted to jump over the counter and hit him over the head with a bottle of his own revolting Mateus Rosé. I know a teacher at St Martin's School of Art who felt much the same when one of his students told him that Rembrandt couldn't paint, and there was Antonio, only one and a half flat seasons, a yankee and a couple of doubles old, telling me that Wollow was no good. They really make me want to weep, do newcomers to racing.

I debated whether or not I should intentionally give Antonio a couple of pigs to back in the hope that it would put him off and shut him up for good, but even that harsh measure isn't as easy as it sounds. In the fifties and in the same pub I used to have a pound bet with a friend every day in which we'd try to go through the card naming a horse in every race that would *not* get placed.

Time after time I thought, and we both thought, we'd done it and then some hack would get its nose in the frame at 20–1.

But if only Antonio's lunacy had stopped there. It didn't. He acquired an irritating habit of telling me that the Portuguese discovered the world. Surely, I asked him the first time he said it, you mean a part of it? No. Apparently not. Before Mr Ferdinand Magellan's trip there was nothing. Worse was to come. Antonio then began falling under the spell of one 'Irish' Des, a man who claimed that Lester Piggott couldn't ride racehorses. God preserve us from people like that. Perhaps it's a bit like what Stevenson said about marriage. Betting on a horse is a step so grave and decisive that·it attracts light-headed, variable men by its very awfulness. It could even be simpler. Maybe I just happened to use a pub frequented by two lunatics.

Impersonating God, giving tips in other words, is a tricky business. Many tips are simply flushed away. I sometimes think, when the game is really bad that is, that the easiest way out would be to get up in the morning, just shove fifty quid in the loo and then pull the chain. What fascinates me is the way that people react to losing tips.

Inured as I am to personal disaster, I have come to regard losing bets over the past few years as losses of bits of paper. I don't mean to sound flash by that. I just mean that I don't expect miracles but don't mind them when they come to pass. On the other hand, when I do get what I think is a genuine bit of information, then I feel bound and obliged to pass it on.

I once lumbered a friend of mine, a painter of some repute, with two complete stinkers. He is a fearless gambler and I guessed he must have lost a thousand pounds on the two. I met him on the next Monday morning over coffee and he uttered not a single word of reproach. Lovely and as it should be. I ran across him once in a betting shop. I was moaning because I was down a little. 'How's it going?' he asked. 'Awful. I've just lost twenty-five quid and I'm really fed up. How about you?' 'Not so good either,' he replied. 'I've just lost two thousand seven hundred, including the tax.' It was only two-thirty. There had only been two races. (Another painter of my acquaintance used to owe a mad Irish bookmaker so much money that he had to keep painting his portrait for nothing. If you see a show of his, look out for pictures of 'The Pink Man'.)

But others accept losing tips with less equanimity than my painter friend. What I'm getting at is the fact that there are those who mistakenly accept the hunch as gospel. They're not Christians, just punters and I wish to God that they'd get it right. A tip is an opinion. It might be a strong opinion – one stated with some conviction – but it's still just an opinion and if all of them were bang on target then there wouldn't be such things as horse races. Worse than tipping losers to bad losers is tipping winners to idiots and then not backing them yourself.

I was having a shave in a barber's shop in Old Compton Street one Monday morning and the man operating the cut-throat asked me what I fancied. For a moment I couldn't answer him since I'd noticed the most extraordinary thing. Instead of using tissue paper to wipe the razor on after every clean sweep of the chin, he was using betting slips nicked from the local betting shop. Having digested that, I went on to say that a certain horse of Fred Winter's might oblige at a long price. Gastronomic and alcoholic events that followed prevented me from having a wager that afternoon. In the evening, when I read that the horse had won at 12–1, I choked.

At one time in my life, I found myself being followed and I didn't like it. Almost every time I stuck a bet with my unlicensed bookmaker in the local pub the wager was duplicated by a woman called Eva. She had a sort of faith in me that was more dumb than blind. It had started in the spring. I had called round to her flat – it was more of a 'salon' than a flat actually – to discuss the previous day's appalling behaviour and to borrow some money from her. She asked me if there was, by any chance, a particular nag that I fancied that day. I told her that I'd been waiting for a certain hurdler which was running that afternoon and she gave me a tenner to put on for her. That evening, I presented her with a hundred pounds and it was that evening that she got the idea that winning a hundred on a horse was as easy as falling out of a taxi.

In fact, I suspect that she got the idea that winning a hundred was something that could be done on every race, never mind once a day. Well, we had our ups and downs, did Eva and I, and that was the beginning of the best run of luck I'd had for a very long time. We took to having snacks in the Connaught and I went on making inspired guesses and, d'you know, we just couldn't go wrong.

Then came the inevitable period when I couldn't pick anything that even made the frame, never mind won. Well, nearly. But the plucky little woman still followed me. It put me in something of a quandary. In the first place the said Eva, hereinafter referred to as the PLW (for plucky little woman), had the extraordinary idea that money is pieces of paper. In view of that you might think it odd of me to have a conscience about tipping her losers, but it doesn't work like that.

It's something that you just can't help feeling bad about. The nitty gritty of the business is the fact that I can't bear putting money on for someone else even when it's their wretched choice. If you're betting on credit and sticking on for other people you can do your money by the time they send out the cheques or the bills and you've still got to find the readies for your friends. Is that quite clear? I thought it was a terrible sentence. Another thing that's unbearable about getting involved with others is the person who has a go at you when they lose. It's unforgivable in fact. The PLW didn't do that; she was as good as gold, or in her case platinum. What she did do when she lost was bathe me in one of those looks that labradors give you after you've kicked them and which mean, 'I hope you didn't hurt your foot.'

No, what then began troubling my conscience was the fact that my luck turned again and I had two very nourishing touches on horses trained by J. Webber. On both occasions I snuck off round the corner to put the money on, having told the PLW that I wasn't betting that day. I was almost in her boots because I was tipped both animals and the man that gave them to me was furious that I didn't put more on. Megalomania had reared its ugly head. Winning tipsters want to play God a little.

Can you imagine it? That man was actually angry that his tips hadn't made me rich. I can understand it in a way because I can remember feeling slightly irritated with the PLW when I'd given her a winner and she'd said I'm wonderful but hadn't gone on and on saying it. Then, of course, there's superstition and the more you try and despise that the more superstitious you get. On the quiet, I began thinking that the PLW might have been a jinx on me. I knew logically that what she happened to be doing at closing time couldn't possibly affect the performance of a horse in tomorrow's three o'clock at Ripon, but I *felt* it. Mind you, there wasn't much I could do about it. She was hell-bent on throwing pieces of paper at the bookmaking fraternity and if one is doomed to make that kamikaze trip to Carey Street then one might as well have company.

That reminds me. Just about the most honest thing that could ever have been uttered in a bankruptcy court was the classic remark made by the actor Valentine Dyall, radio's 'The Man in Black'. The Recorder asked him, 'To what do you attribute your downfall?' Mr Dyall replied, 'Two-and-a-half-mile handicap hurdles.' What I'd like to know is what about the bloody summer sprint handicaps? Come to that, what about the Bollinger in the Members' Bar, and the novice chases, and the hunter-chasers? It's one hell of a struggle, isn't it?

THE DEAN: What weak creatures we are!

BLORE: We are, sir – we are – 'specially when we've got a tip, sir. Think of the temptation of a tip, sir.

ARTHUR WING PINERO, from *Dandy Dick* (1887)

In At Swim-Two-Birds, *Flann O'Brien's anarchic first novel published in 1939, the student narrator regularly receives information from a New-market tipster. His friend Brinsley has also heard about a good thing.*

Gob I see that horse of Peacock's is going today, he said.

I folded my manuscript without a word and replaced it in my clothing.

Eight stone four, he said.

Listen here, he continued looking up, we'd be bloody fools if we didn't have something on this.

He stopped and peeled the paper from the floor, reading it intently.

What horse is this? I asked.

What horse? Grandchild. Peacock's horse.

Here I uttered an exclamation.

Nature of exclamation: Inarticulate, of surprise, recollection.

Wait till I show you something, I said groping in my pocket. Wait till you read this. I got this yesterday. I am in the hands of a man from Newmarket.

I handed him a letter.

Mail from V. Wright, Wyvern Cottage, Newmarket, Suffolk: V. Wright, the Backer's Friend. Dear friend and member. Many thanks for yours to hand. As promised I send you my promised 'good thing' which is GRANDCHILD in the 4.30 at Gatwick on Friday. Do not hesitate to plunge and put on an extra shilling for me towards my heavy expenses. This animal has been saved *for this race only* for the past two months and is a certain starter, ignore newspaper probabilities and GO IN FOR THE WIN OF YOUR LIFE. This horse is my treble nap CAST-IRON PLUNGER for the week – no other selection given – and I know all there is to be known about it. Old friends will know that I do not send 'guessworks' but only STRICTLY OCCASIONAL advices over animals already as good as past the post. Of course I have to pay heavily for my information, each winner costs me a packet so do not fail to remit the odds to a 'bob' promptly so as to make sure to not miss my next CAST-IRON PLUNGER and remain permanently on my books. Those not clear on my books by Tuesday next will be in danger of missing the *cream of racing information* which I expect to have available next week. So do not hesitate to plunge to your limit on GRANDCHILD on Friday and remit immediately after the race, on the same evening if possible. Excuses over winners will be ignored. If going away please do not fail to send me your new address so as not to miss my good things. Please have a good bet on Grandchild. Yours and best of luck together, V. Wright. Remittance Form. To V. Wright, Wyvern Cottage, Newmarket, Suffolk. Herewith please find P.O. for £   s.   d. being the odds to 1/- over Grandchild (thus 4 to 1, 4/-), and hoping to receive further winners of the same kind. Name, address.

Do you know this man? asked Brinsley.

I do not, I said.

Do you intend to back the horse?

I have no money, I answered.

Nothing at all? I have two shillings.

In the interior of my pocket I fingered the smooth disks of my book-money.

I have to buy a book today, I said. I got five shillings for it this morning.

The price given here, said Brinsley from the paper, is ten to one and say that's seven to one at a half-a-crown each way that's twenty-one bob. Buy your book and you have sixteen shillings change.

More by accident than by mastery of the body, I have expressed my doubts on the proposal by the means of a noise.

Title of noise, the Greek version : πορδή

That same afternoon I was sitting on a stool in an intoxicated condition in Grogan's licensed premises. Adjacent stools bore the forms of Brinsley and Kelly, my two true friends. The three of us were occupied in putting glasses of stout into the interior of our bodies and expressing by fine disputation the resulting sense of physical and mental well-being. In my thigh pocket I had eleven and eightpence in a weighty pendulum of mixed coins. Each of the arranged bottles on the shelves before me, narrow or squat-bellied, bore a dull picture of the gas bracket. Who can tell the stock of a public-house? Many no doubt are dummies, those especially within an arm-reach of the snug. The stout was of superior quality, soft against the tongue but sharp upon the orifice of the throat, softly efficient in its magical circulation through the conduits of the body.

THE ROCKING-HORSE WINNER

There was a woman who was beautiful, who started with all the advantages, yet she had no luck. She married for love, and the love turned to dust. She had bonny children, yet she felt they had been thrust upon her, and she could not love them. They looked at her coldly, as if they were finding fault with her. And hurriedly she felt she must cover up some fault in herself. Yet what it was that she must cover up she never knew. Nevertheless, when her children were present, she always felt the centre of her heart go mad. This troubled her, and in her manner she was all the more gentle and anxious for her children, as if she loved them very much. Only she herself knew that at the centre of her heart was a hard little place that could not feel love, no, not for anybody. Everybody else said of her: 'She is such a good mother. She adores her children.' Only she herself, and her children themselves, knew it was not so. They read it in each other's eyes.

There were a boy and two little girls. They lived in a pleasant house, with a garden, and they had discreet servants, and felt themselves superior to anyone in the neighbourhood.

Although they lived in style, they felt always an anxiety in the house. There was never enough money. The mother had a small income, and the father had a small income, but not nearly enough for the social position which they had to keep up. The father went into town to some office. But though he had good prospects, these prospects never materialized. There was always the grinding sense of the shortage of money, though the style was always kept up.

At last the mother said: 'I will see if I can't make something.' But she did not know where to begin. She racked her brains, and tried this thing and the other, but could not find anything successful. The failure made deep lines come into her face. Her children were growing up, they would have to go to school. There must be more money, there must be more money. The father, who was always very handsome and expensive in his tastes, seemed as if he never *would* be able to do anything worth doing. And the mother, who had a great belief in herself, did not succeed any better, and her tastes were just as expensive.

And so the house came to be haunted by the unspoken phrase: *There must be more money! There must be more money!* The children could hear it all the time, though nobody said it aloud. They heard it at Christmas when the expensive and splendid toys filled the nursery. Behind the shining modern rocking-horse, behind the smart doll's house, a voice would start whispering: 'There *must* be more money! There *must* be more money!' And the children would stop playing, to listen for a moment. They would look into each other's eyes, to see if they had all heard. And each one saw in the eyes of the other two that they too had heard. 'There *must* be more money! There *must* be more money!'

It came whispering from the springs of the still-swaying rocking-horse, and even the horse, bending his wooden champing head, heard it. The big doll, sitting so pink and smirking in her new pram, could hear it quite plainly, and seemed to be smirking all the more self-consciously because of it. The foolish puppy, too, that took the place of the teddy bear, he was looking so extraordinarily foolish for no other reason but that he heard the secret whisper all over the house: 'There *must* be more money!'

Yet nobody ever said it aloud. The whisper was everywhere, and therefore no one spoke it. Just as no one ever says: 'We are breathing!' in spite of the fact that breath is coming and going all the time.

'Mother,' said the boy Paul one day, 'why don't we keep a car of our own? Why do we always use uncle's, or else a taxi?'

'Because we're the poor members of the family,' said the mother.

'But why *are* we, mother?'

'Well – I suppose,' she said slowly and bitterly, 'it's because your father had no luck.'

The boy was silent for some time.

'Is luck money, mother?' he asked, rather timidly.

'No, Paul. Not quite. It's what causes you to have money.'

'Oh!' said Paul vaguely. 'I thought when Uncle Oscar said *filthy lucker*, it meant money.'

'*Filthy lucre* does mean money,' said the mother. 'But it's lucre not luck.'

'Oh!' said the boy. 'Then what is luck, mother?'

'It's what causes you to have money. If you're lucky you have money. That's why it's better to be born lucky than rich. If you're rich, you may lose your money. But if you're lucky, you will always get more money.'

'Oh! Will you? And is father not lucky?'

'Very unlucky, I should say,' she said bitterly.

The boy watched her with unsure eyes.

'Why?' he asked.

'I don't know. Nobody ever knows why one person is lucky and another unlucky.'

'Don't they? Nobody at all. Does *nobody* know?'

'Perhaps God. But He never tells.'

'He ought to, then. And aren't you lucky either, mother?'

'I can't be, if I married an unlucky husband.'

'But by yourself, aren't you?'

'I used to think I was, before I married. Now I think I am very unlucky indeed.'

'Why?'

'Well – never mind! Perhaps I'm not really,' she said.

The child looked at her to see if she meant it. But he saw, by the lines of her mouth, that she was only trying to hide something from him.

'Well, anyhow,' he said stoutly, 'I'm a lucky person.'

'Why?' said his mother, with a sudden laugh.

He stared at her. He didn't even know why he had said it.

'God told me,' he asserted, brazening it out.

'I hope He did, dear!' she said, again with a laugh, but rather bitter.

'He did, mother!'

'Excellent!' said the mother, using one of her husband's exclamations.

The boy saw she did not believe him; or rather, that she paid no attention to his assertion. This angered him somewhere, and made him want to compel her attention.

He went off by himself, vaguely, in a childish way, seeking for the clue to 'luck'. Absorbed, taking no heed of other people, he went about with a sort of stealth, seeking inwardly for luck. He wanted luck, he wanted it. When the two girls were playing dolls in the nursery, he would sit on his big rocking-horse, charging madly into space, with a frenzy that made the little girls peer at him uneasily. Wildly the horse careered, the waving dark hair of the boy tossed, his eyes had a strange glare in them. The little girls dared not to speak to him.

When he had ridden to the end of his mad little journey, he climbed down and stood in front of his rocking-horse, staring fixedly into its lowered face. Its red mouth was slightly open, its big eye was wide and glassy-bright.

'Now!' he would silently command the snorting steed. 'Now, take me to where there is luck! Now take me!'

And he would slash the horse on the neck with the little whip he had asked Uncle Oscar for. He *knew* the horse could take him to where there was luck, if only he forced it. So he would mount

267

again and start on his furious ride, hoping at last to get there. He knew he could get there.

'You'll break your horse, Paul!' said the nurse.

'He's always riding like that! I wish he'd leave off!' said his elder sister Joan.

But he only glared down on them in silence. Nurse gave him up. She could make nothing of him. Anyhow, he was growing beyond her.

One day his mother and his Uncle Oscar came in when he was on one of his furious rides. He did not speak to them.

'Hallo, you young jockey! Riding a winner?' said his uncle.

'Aren't you growing too big for a rocking-horse? You're not a very little boy any longer, you know,' said his mother.

But Paul only gave a blue glare from his big, rather close set eyes. He would speak to nobody when he was in full tilt. His mother watched him with an anxious expression on her face.

At last he suddenly stopped forcing his horse into the mechanical gallop and slid down.

'Well, I got there!' he announced fiercely, his blue eyes still flaring, and his sturdy long legs straddling apart.

'Where did you get to?' asked his mother.

'Where I wanted to go,' he flared back at her.

'That's right, son!' said Uncle Oscar. 'Don't you stop till you get there. What's the horse's name?'

'He doesn't have a name,' said the boy.

'Gets on without all right?' asked the uncle.

'Well he has different names. He was called Sansovino last week.'

'Sansovino, eh? Won the Ascot. How did you know this name?'

'He always talks about horse-races with Bassett,' said Joan.

The uncle was delighted to find that his small nephew was posted with all the racing news. Bassett, the young gardener, who had been wounded in the left foot in the war and had got his present job though Oscar Cresswell, whose batman he had been, was a perfect blade of the 'turf'. He lived in the racing events, and the small boy lived with him.

Oscar Cresswell got it all from Bassett.

'Master Paul comes and asks me, so I can't do more than tell him, sir,' said Bassett, his face terribly serious, as if he were speaking of religious matters.

'And does he ever put anything on a horse he fancies?'

'Well – I don't want to give him away – he's a young sport, a fine sport, sir. Would you mind asking him yourself? He sort of takes a pleasure in it, and perhaps he'd feel I was giving him away, sir, if you don't mind.'

Bassett was serious as a church.

The uncle went back to his nephew and took him off for a ride in the car.

'Say, Paul, old man, do you ever put anything on a horse?' the uncle asked.

The boy watched the handsome man closely.

'Why, do you think I oughtn't to?' he parried.

'Not a bit of it! I thought perhaps you might give me a tip for the Lincoln.'

The car sped on into the country, going down to Uncle Oscar's place in Hampshire.

'Honour bright?' said the nephew.

'Honour bright, son!' said the uncle.

'Well then, Daffodil.'

'Daffodil! I doubt it, sonny. What about Mirza?'

'I only know the winner,' said the boy. 'That's Daffodil.'

'Daffodil, eh?'

There was a pause. Daffodil was an obscure horse comparatively.

'Uncle.'

'Yes, son?'

'You won't let it go any further, will you? I promised Bassett.'

'Bassett be damned, old man! What's he got to do with it?'

'We're partners. We've been partners from the first. Uncle, he lent me my first five shillings, which I lost. I promised him, honour bright, it was only between me and him; only you gave me that ten-shilling note I started winning with, so I thought you were lucky. You won't let it go any further, will you?'

The boy gazed at his uncle from those big, hot, blue eyes, set rather close together. The uncle stirred and laughed uneasily.

'Right you are, son! I'll keep your tip private. Daffodil, eh? How much are you putting on him?'

'All except twenty pounds,' said the boy. 'I keep that in reserve.'

The uncle thought it a good joke.

'You keep twenty pounds in reserve, do you, you young romancer? What are you betting then?'

'I'm betting three hundred,' said the boy gravely. 'But it's between you and me, Uncle Oscar! Honour bright?'

The uncle burst into a roar of laughter.

'It's between you and me all right, you young Nat Gould,' he said, laughing. 'But where's your three hundred?'

'Bassett keeps it for me. We're partners.'

'You are, are you! And what is Bassett putting on Daffodil?'

'He won't go as high as I do, I expect. Perhaps he'll go a hundred and fifty.'

'What, pennies?' laughed the uncle.

'Pounds,' said the child, with a surprised look at his uncle. 'Bassett keeps a bigger reserve than I do.'

Between wonder and amusement Uncle Oscar was silent. He pursued the matter no further, but he determined to take his nephew with him to the Lincoln races.

'Now, son,' he said, 'I'm putting twenty on Mirza, and I'll put five on for you on any horse you fancy. What's your pick?'

'Daffodil, uncle.'

'No, not the fiver on Daffodil!'

'I should if it was my own fiver,' said the child.

'Good! Good! Right you are! A fiver for me and a fiver for you on Daffodil.'

The child had never been to a race-meeting before, and his eyes were blue fire. He pursed his mouth tight and watched. A Frenchman just in front had put his money on Lancelot. Wild with excitement, he flayed his arms up and down, yelling *Lancelot! Lancelot!* in his French accent.

Daffodil came in first, Lancelot second, Mirza third. The child, flushed and with eyes blazing, was curiously serene. His uncle brought him four five-pound notes, four to one.

'What am I to do with these?' he cried, waving them before the boy's eyes.

'I suppose we'll talk to Bassett,' said the boy. 'I expect I have fifteen hundred now; and twenty in reserve; and this twenty.'

His uncle studied him for some moments.

'Look here, son!' he said. 'You're not serious about Bassett and that fifteen hundred, are you?'

'Yes, I am. But it's between you and me, uncle. Honour bright?'

'Honour bright all right, son! But I must talk to Bassett.'

'If you'd like to be a partner, uncle, with Bassett and me, we could all be partners. Only, you'd have to promise, honour bright, uncle, not to let it go beyond us three. Bassett and I are lucky, and you must be lucky, because it was your ten shillings I started winning with . . .'

Uncle Oscar took both Bassett and Paul into Richmond Park for an afternoon, and there they talked.

'It's like this, you see, sir,' Bassett said. 'Master Paul would get me talking about racing events, spinning yarns, you know, sir. And he was always keen on knowing if I'd made or if I'd lost. It's about a year since, now, that I put five shillings on Blush of Dawn for him: and we lost. Then the luck changed with that ten shillings he had from you: that we put on Singhalese. And since that time, it's been pretty steady, all things considering. What do you say, Master Paul?'

'We're all right when we're sure,' said Paul. 'It's when we're not quite sure that we go down.'

'Oh, but we're careful then,' said Bassett.

'But when are you *sure*?' smiled Uncle Oscar.

'It's Master Paul, sir,' said Bassett in a secret, religious voice. It's as if he had it from heaven. Like Daffodil, now, for the Lincoln. That was as sure as eggs.'

'Did you put anything on Daffodil?' asked Oscar Cresswell.

'Yes, sir, I made a bit.'

'And my nephew?'

Bassett was obstinately silent, looking at Paul.

'I made twelve hundred, didn't I, Bassett? I told uncle I was putting three hundred on Daffodil.'

'That's right,' said Bassett nodding.

'But where's the money?' asked the uncle.

'I keep it safe locked up, sir. Master Paul he can have it any minute he likes to ask for it.'

'What, fifteen hundred pounds?'

'And twenty! And *forty*, that is, with the twenty he made on the course.'

'It's amazing!' said the uncle.

'If Master Paul offers you to be partners, sir, I would, if I were you: if you'll excuse me,' said Bassett.

Oscar Cresswell thought about it.

'I'll see the money,' he said.

They drove home again, and sure enough, Bassett came round to the garden-house with fifteen hundred pounds in notes. The twenty pounds in reserve was left with Joe Glee, in the Turf Commission deposit.

'You see it's all right, uncle, when I'm *sure*! Then we go strong, for all we're worth. Don't we, Bassett?'

'We do that, Master Paul.'

'And when are you sure?' said the uncle, laughing.

'Oh, well, sometimes, I'm *absolutely* sure, like about Daffodil,' said the boy; 'and sometimes I have an idea; and sometimes I haven't an idea, have I, Bassett? Then we're careful, because we mostly go down.'

'You do, do you! And when you're sure, like about Daffodil, what makes you sure, sonny?'

'Oh, well, I don't know,' said the boy uneasily. 'I'm sure, you know, uncle; that's all.'

'It's as if he had it from heaven, sir,' Bassett reiterated.

'I should say so!' said the uncle.

But he became a partner. And when the Leger was coming on Paul was 'sure' about Lively Spark, which was a quite inconsider-able horse, Bassett went for five hundred, and Oscar Cresswell two hundred. Lively Spark came in first, and the betting had been ten to one against him. Paul had made ten thousand.

'You see,' he said, 'I was absolutely sure of him.'

Even Oscar Cresswell had cleared two thousand.

'Look here, son,' he said, 'this sort of thing makes me nervous.'

'It needn't, uncle! Perhaps I shan't be sure again for a long time.'

'But what are you going to do with your money?' asked the uncle.

'Of course,' said the boy, 'I started it for mother. She said she had no luck, because father is unlucky, so I thought if I was lucky, it might stop whispering.'

'What might stop whispering?'

'Our house. I *hate* our house for whispering.'

'What does it whisper?'

'Why – why' – the boy fidgeted – 'why, I don't know. But it's always short of money, you know, uncle.'

'I know it, son, I know it.'

'You know people send mother writs, don't you, uncle?'

'I'm afraid I do,' said the uncle.

'And then the house whispers, like people laughing at you behind your back. It's awful, that is! I thought if I was lucky – '

'You might stop it,' added the uncle.

The boy watched him with big blue eyes, that had an uncanny cold fire in them, and he said never a word.

'Well, then!' said the uncle. 'What are we doing?'

'I shouldn't like mother to know I was lucky,' said the boy.

'Why not, son?'

'She'd stop me.'

'I don't think she would.'

'Oh!' – and the boy writhed in an odd way – 'I *don't* want her to know, uncle.'

'All right, son! We'll manage it without her knowing.'

They managed it very easily. Paul, at the other's suggestion, handed over five thousand pounds to his uncle, who deposited it with the family lawyer, who was then to inform Paul's mother that a relative had put five thousand pounds into his hands, which sum was to be paid out a thousand pounds at a time, on the mother's birthday, for the next five years.

'So she'll have a birthday present of a thousand pounds for five successive years,' said Uncle Oscar. 'I hope it won't make it all the harder for her later.'

Paul's mother had her birthday in November. The house had been 'whispering' worse than ever lately, and, even in spite of his luck, Paul could not bear up against it. He was very anxious to see the effect of the birthday letter, telling his mother about the thousand pounds.

When there were no visitors, Paul now took his meals with his parents, as he was beyond the nursery control. His mother went into town nearly every day. She had discovered that she had an odd knack of sketching furs and dress material, so she worked secretly in the studio of a friend who was the chief 'artist' for the leading drapers. She drew the figures of ladies in furs and ladies in silk and sequins for the newspaper advertisements. This young woman artist earned several thousand pounds a year, but Paul's mother only made several hundreds, and she was again dissatisfied. She so wanted to be first in something, and she did not succeed, even in making sketches for drapery advertisements.

She was down to breakfast on the morning of her birthday. Paul watched her face as she read her letters. He knew the lawyer's letter. As his mother read it, her face hardened and became more expressionless. Then a cold determined look came on her mouth. She hid the letter under the pile of others, and said not a word about it.

'Didn't you have anything nice in the post for your birthday, mother?' said Paul.

'Quite moderately nice,' she said, her voice cold and absent.

She went away to town without saying more.

But in the afternoon Uncle Oscar appeared. He said Paul's mother had had a long interview with the lawyer, asking if the whole five thousand could not be advanced at once, as she was in debt.

'What do you think, uncle?' said the boy.

'I leave it to you, son.'

'Oh, let her have, then! We can get some more with the other,' said the boy.

'A bird in the hand is worth two in the bush, laddie!' said Uncle Oscar.

'But I'm sure to *know* for the Grand National; or the Lincolnshire; or else the Derby. I'm sure to know for *one* of them,' said Paul.

So Uncle Oscar signed the agreement, and Paul's mother touched the whole five thousand. Then something very curious happened. The voices in the house suddenly went mad, like a chorus of frogs on a spring evening. There were certain new furnishings, and Paul had a tutor. He was *really* going to Eton, his father's school, in the following autumn. There were flowers in the winter, and a blossoming of the luxury Paul's mother had been used to. And yet the voices in the house, behind the sprays of mimosa and almond-blossom, and from under the piles of iridescent cushions, simply trilled and screamed in a sort of ecstasy:

'There *must* be more money! Oh-h-h; there *must* be more money. Oh, now, now-w! Now-w-w – there *must* be more money! – More than ever! More than ever!'

It frightened Paul terribly. He studied away at his Latin and Greek with his tutor. But his intense hours were spent with Bassett. The Grand National had gone by; he had not 'known', and had lost a hundred pounds. Summer was at hand. He was in agony for the Lincoln. But even for the Lincoln he didn't 'know', and he lost fifty pounds. He became wild-eyed and strange, as if something were going to explode in him.

'Let it alone, son! Don't bother about it!' urged Uncle Oscar. But it was as if the boy couldn't really hear what his uncle was saying.

'I've got to know for the Derby. I've got to know for the Derby!' the child reiterated, his big blue eyes blazing with a sort of madness.

His mother noticed how overwrought he was.

'You'd better go to the seaside. Wouldn't you like to go now to the seaside, instead of waiting? I think you'd better,' she said, looking down at him anxiously, her heart curiously heavy because of him.

But the child lifted his uncanny blue eyes.

'I couldn't possibly go before the Derby, mother!' he said. 'I couldn't possibly!'

'Why not?' she said, her voice becoming heavy when she was opposed. 'Why not? You can still go from the seaside to see the Derby with your Uncle Oscar, if that's what you wish. No need for you to wait here. Besides, I think you care too much about these races. It's a bad sign. My family has been a gambling family, and you won't know till you grow up how much damage it has done. But it has done damage. I shall have to send Bassett away, and ask Uncle Oscar not to talk racing to you, unless you promise to be reasonable about it: go away to the seaside and forget it. You're all nerves!'

'I'll do what you like, mother, so long as you don't send me away till after the Derby,' the boy said.

'Send you away from where? Just from this house?'

'Yes,' he said, gazing at her.

'Why, you curious child, what makes you care about this house so much suddenly? I never knew you loved it.'

He gazed at her without speaking. He had a secret within a secret, something he had not divulged, even to Bassett or to his Uncle Oscar.

But his mother, after standing undecided and a little bit sullen for some moments, said:

'Very well, then! Don't go to the seaside till after the Derby, if you don't wish it. But promise me you won't think so much about horse-racing, and *events*, as you call them!'

'Oh, no,' said the boy casually. 'I won't think much about them, mother. You needn't worry. I wouldn't worry, mother, if I were you.'

'If you were me and I were you,' said his mother, 'I wonder what we *should* do!'

'But you know you needn't worry mother, don't you?' the boy repeated.

'I should be awfully glad to know it,' she said wearily.

'Oh, well, you *can*, you know. I mean, you *ought* to know you needn't worry,' he insisted.

'Ought I? Then I'll see about it,' she said.

Paul's secret of secrets was his wooden horse, that which had no name. Since he was emancipated from a nurse and a nursery-governess, he had had his rocking-horse removed to his own bedroom at the top of the house.

'Surely you're too big for a rocking-horse!' his mother had remonstrated.

'Well, you see, mother, till I can have a *real* horse, I like to have *some* sort of animal about,' had been his quaint answer.

'Do you feel he keeps you company?' she laughed.

'Oh yes! He's very good, he always keeps me company, when I'm there,' said Paul.

So the horse, rather shabby, stood in an arrested prance in the boy's bedroom.

The Derby was drawing near, and the boy grew more and more tense. He hardly heard what was spoken to him, he was very frail, and his eyes were really uncanny. His mother had sudden strange seizures of uneasiness about him. Sometimes, for half an hour, she would feel a sudden anxiety about him that was almost anguish. She wanted to rush to him at once, and know that he was safe.

Two nights before the Derby, she was at a big party in town, when one of her rushes of anxiety about her boy, her first-born, gripped her heart till she could hardly speak. She fought with the feeling, might and main, for she believed in common sense. But it was too strong. She had to leave the dance and go downstairs to telephone to the country. The children's nursery-governess was terribly surprised and startled at being rung up in the night.

'Are the children all right, Miss Wilmot?'

'Oh yes, they are quite all right.'

'Master Paul? Is he all right?'

'He went to bed as right as a trivet. Shall I run up and look at him?'

'No,' said Paul's mother reluctantly. 'No! Don't trouble. It's all right. Don't sit up. We shall be home fairly soon.' She did not want her son's privacy intruded upon.

'Very good,' said the governess.

It was about one o'clock when Paul's mother and father drove up to their house. All was still. Paul's mother went to her room and slipped off her white fur cloak. She had told her maid not to wait up for her. She heard her husband downstairs, mixing a whisky and soda.

And then, because of the strange anxiety at her heart, she stole upstairs to her son's bedroom. Noiselessly she went along the upper corridor. Was there a faint noise? What was it?

She stood, with arrested muscles, outside his door listening. There was a strange, heavy, and yet not loud noise. Her heart stood still. It was a soundless noise, yet rushing and powerful. Something huge, in violent, hushed motion. What was it? What in God's name was it? She ought to know. She felt that she knew the noise. She knew what it was.

Yet she could not place it. She couldn't say what it was. And on and on it went, like a madness.

Softly, frozen with anxiety and fear, she turned the door-handle.

The room was dark. Yet in the space near the window, she heard and saw something plunging to and fro. She gazed in fear and amazement.

Then suddenly she switched on the light, and saw her son, in his green pyjamas, madly surging on the rocking horse. The blaze of light suddenly lit him up, as he urged the wooden horse, and lit her up, as she stood, blonde, in her dress of pale green and crystal, in the doorway.

'Paul!' she cried. 'Whatever are you doing?'

'It's Malabar!' he screamed in a powerful, strange voice. 'It's Malabar!'

His eyes blazed at her for one strange and senseless second, as he ceased urging his wooden horse. Then he fell with a crash to the ground, and she, all her tormented motherhood flooding upon her, rushed to gather him up.

But he was unconscious, and unconscious he remained, with some brain-fever. He talked and tossed, and his mother sat stonily by his side.

'Malabar! It's Malabar! Bassett, Bassett, I *know*! It's Malabar!'

So the child cried, trying to get up and urge the rocking-horse that gave him inspiration.

'What does he mean by Malabar?' asked the heart-frozen mother.

'I don't know,' said the father stonily.

'What does he mean by Malabar?' she asked her brother Oscar.

'It's one of the horses running for the Derby,' was the answer.

And, in spite of himself, Oscar Cresswell spoke to Bassett, and himself put a thousand on Malabar: at fourteen to one.

The third day of the illness was critical: they were waiting for a change. The boy, with his rather long, curly hair, was tossing ceaselessly on the pillow. He neither slept nor regained consciousness, and his eyes were like blue stones. His mother sat, feeling her heart had gone, turned actually into a stone.

In the evening, Oscar Cresswell did not come, but Bassett sent a message saying could he come up for one moment, just one moment? Paul's mother was very angry at the intrusion, but on second thoughts she agreed. The boy was the same. Perhaps Bassett might bring him to consciousness.

The gardener, a shortish fellow with a little brown moustache and sharp little brown eyes, tiptoed into the room, touched his imaginary cap to Paul's mother, and stole to the bedside, staring with glittering, smallish eyes at the tossing dying child.

'Master Paul!' he whispered. 'Master Paul! Malabar came in first all right, a clean win. I did as you told me. You've made over seventy thousand pounds, you have; you've got over eighty thousand. Malabar came in all right, Master Paul.'

'Malabar! Malabar! Did I say Malabar, mother? Did I say Malabar? Do you think I'm lucky, mother? I knew Malabar, didn't I? Over eighty thousand pounds! I knew, didn't I know I knew? Malabar came in all right. If I ride my horse till I'm sure, then I tell you, Bassett, you can go as high as you like. Did you go for all you were worth, Bassett?'

'I went a thousand on it, Master Paul.'

'I never told you, mother, that if I can ride my horse, and *get there*, then I'm absolutely sure – oh, absolutely! Mother, did I ever tell you? I *am* lucky!'

'No you never did,' said his mother.

But the boy died in the night.

And even as he lay dead, his mother heard her brother's voice saying to her: 'My God, Hester, you're eighty-odd thousand to the good, and a poor devil of a son to the bad. But, poor devil, poor devil, he's best gone out of a life where he rides his rocking-horse to find a winner.'

D. H. LAWRENCE (1934)

A NOTE LEFT ON THE MANTELPIECE
(for his wife)

Attracted by their winning names I chose
Little Yid and *Welsh Bard*; years later backed
the swanky jockeys, and still thought I lacked
inspiration, the uncommon touch, not
mere expertise. Each way, I paid in prose.

Always the colours and stadiums beckoned
till, on the nose, at Goodwood, the high gods
jinxed the favourite despite the odds.
Addict that I was, live fool and dead cert.
His velvet nostrils lagged a useless second.

A poet should have studied style not form
(sweet, I regret the scarcity of roses)
but by Moses and by the nine Muses

I'll no more. Each cruising nag is a beast
so other shirts can keep the centaur warm.

Adieu, you fading furlongs of boozing,
hoarse voices at Brighton, white rails, green course.
Conclusion? Why, not only the damned horse
but whom it's running against matters.
By the way, apologies for losing.

DANNIE ABSE

The most satisfying way to make your selection is simply to work it out for yourself, but the conditions must be right.

Picking the Derby winner is a ticklish business, and if the reader takes our advice he will make his selection in good time, at least a day or two before the race. It is true that Derby Day itself brings with it certain considerations which might influence our choice – the weather, the draw for places at the start, the appearance of the horses in the paddock – but it is, on the whole, unwise and unnecessary to take these into account. What is essential is absolute quiet and freedom from distraction. We have known men make a winning selection while travelling in an omnibus, but the ordinary human being is advised to attempt no such *tour de force*. He will find himself better able to deal with the situation in solitude, or in the presence of a single tried and sympathetic friend. The position of the body is a matter of personal taste; whether we walk, sit, lounge or lie down each must decide for himself. But what must be avoided at all costs is a hasty decision, due to panic or impatience, and the best way of avoiding it is to be beforehand with our selection. Perhaps the hours between five and seven p.m. are the most favourable for the enterprise of making the Final Selection. The brain is at its best and the nerve is steadiest between these hours. Stimulants should be resorted to sparingly; the feet should be kept warm, and an even supply of blood to the head assured. And if anything approaching a condition of trance makes its appearance the attempt to reach a decision should be abandoned at once; the winner of the Derby was never picked in a trance. And when once the Final Selection has been made, nothing should be allowed to disturb our resolution – except, of course, the last-minute scratching of our choice.

GUY GRIFFITH and MICHAEL OAKESHOTT, from *A Guide to the Classics*

PUNTING ON THE HORSE

'After all, at the Day of Judgement, what will be the odds?'

Lord Clincham

'Tishy, Tishy, all fall down!'

Old Manton Nursery Rhyme

Sometimes when there aren't many people at table and everyone has told everyone else the same story about how they watched Hounds working the Fox to death while the old mare leapt the 'Flying Scotsman', one can for a change start joking in a boastful sort of way about all the 'fivers', 'ponies', 'monkeys', and 'cool thous' one has been losing lately on the Turf.

(The best people understand at once that one didn't let all this money drop out of one's trouser-pocket while lolling around on the Downs or one of the few other places in England where one is definitely warned off the Grass, but lost it in the noblest possible way by punting it on to the wrong horse.)

Very well, then: you had better make your position in society absolutely secure by losing a few millions; and you will no doubt be relieved to know that as opposed to riding on the Horse everything is made as easy as possible for beginners who want to try losing on the 'osses. For instance, unlike the Huntsman, the Puntsman does not need to have a good pair of hands or a grand seat: all he needs is a Grand Stand and a good pair of field-glasses.

Indeed, he does not even need to go to race-courses at all: anyone can learn all he wants to about betting from one of the correspondence-courses conducted by well-known Commission Agents.

You, however, will wish to do the thing in style; so to begin with you will have to go in a Racing Special train full of card-sharpeners who will cheat you frightfully at 'Racing-Demon' and 'Beggar-my-neighbour' and won't allow you to go nap for a minute.

When you reach the course you will purchase a race-card (1s. outside the gate, second-hand; 6d. inside, new) which will tell the age, weight, colour and pedigree of the Clerk of the Scales, the First Lord of the Totalisator (or To'sun) and other officials; and your first impression of the Meeting will be that you have strolled into a vast race-paper basket littered knee-deep with midday editions, race-cards, cigarette cards, betting slips and all the scrum of the earth, not to mention the scurf of humanity – tipsters and tapsters, bookies and crookies, tick-tackers and pick-pocketeers ...

Clutch your monkeys tightly to your breast-pocket and hurry past into the betting ring. Here the game is evidently one of racing pandemonium: bookies are roaring 'Six-to-four-the-Field', orange vendors are howling 'Four-p'nce'ha'p'ny-the-bag', ice-cream merchants are ice-screaming nineteen-to-the-dozen, and everyone seems to have so much to say to no one in particular that you hardly dare interrupt Mr Ike Williams to ask him what time the 2.30 starts, or whether 'backing both-ways' is the same as 'heads-I-win-tails-you-lose', or which horse would be the best to bet on, or even which race he expects to welsh on ...

In the end you decide to punt your money into the Tote, because it never welshes, but whichever horse you back you are almost certain to lose because there is such a lot of white-tape and back-scratching, and objecting about a horse-race; so even if your horse 'arrives' officially on the course it may get its back officially scratched and refuse to start, and even if it starts it may go off the rails and arrive unofficially in the Grand Stand, which doesn't count, and even if it comes in first your jockey may object that he was bored by the whole thing from start to finish and refuse to weigh-in, and your monkey will die after all.

Yes, it hardly matters really which horse you back. An enormous majority of them will lose the race anyway, so if you want to boast of your losses afterwards you have a pretty large choice. But make up your mind beforehand *which way* you want to bet – whether to *win* or to *lose*. Some people (especially when backing the favourite) *back it both ways* i.e., to win *and* to lose: which is pretty safe because the odds are usually *on* the favourite instead of against it, so that you stand to lose more if the horse loses than you stand to win if it wins, and thus, if it wins, you win less than you would have lost if it had been the other way round and had run backwards, or both-ways, while if the horse loses, then you lose too because you betted the bookie you would (unless the horse won). You do follow that, don't you?

But on the whole it is not advisable to back the favourite: *it carries too much weight*. What with the jockey, and all the stones they hang on its saddle, and the thousands of shirts of the male backers and the millions of skirts of the female backers and all the bloomers made by wire and mail on it, the favourite usually gets left behind at the start, or 'lost in the Post', as the saying is.

By far the most sporting thing to do is to put your shirt on an Outsider – and here again you should put it on *both ways* i.e., outside-in *and* inside-out; though it will probably scratch either way . . .

But the bells are already ringing in the bar for you to take your seat. Horses are beginning to canter past from paddock to post. They are pulling their jockeys and trying to get 'off'. (Later some of the jockeys will be getting off and trying to pull their horses). And there goes your Outsider! Pirouetting sideways down the course! He is wearing White, with Scarlet cross-belts (2nd class), Cerise breeches, hooped, with tassels, and boots reversed; cap, Tangerine halved and gutted with White pips, etc., etc.

The race is a Maiden Selling Plate (5 forelocks) for graylings (5lb and upwards), and ghillies (50 years and downwards), the winner to be sold by auction (50 guelders upwards), the losers to be drowned by suction (50 fathoms downwards).

And now they're off! The great moment has come; you have almost lost your first monkey. What a sight! The man in front of you is wearing a Moss-green overcoat with Yellow seams, and Moth-bitten trousers with Black checks, Chocolate collar and cuffs, Amber diamonds, Puce boots, and Orange cap reversed. That is all you can see of the race; but what a sight!

And now everyone is waving umbrellas in the air and shouting. Bookies are beginning to welsh wholesale: Tipsters, as they promised, are beginning to eat their hats piecemeal: suddenly the ghillies flash past and are gone; and the race is over; and everyone is boasting and laughing and chaffing about the monkeys and donkeys and sea-elephants they lost on the favourite . . .

But enough. It is unnecessary for you to describe all these picturesque details over the Port: all you need do is to mention casually that you have been punting heavily and losing handsomely, and to hint darkly that you propose to push the old grey mare 'over the sticks' at Elstree next month. And you might perhaps slip in an occasional mention of the great classic races in the Calendar, such as 'The Oats' or 'The Thousand Pities', and tell them how you hired a tank last August to go to the Derby and saw the best of the race from the corner of Tottenham Court Road, or what horse you fancy for 'The Cezarewitch'.

But bewarewitch! Don't go on too long, or your host will raise the red flag over the decanter and 'object' to you on the ground that you are an Outsider and doped, anyway, now; and that it is time you romped home in a taxi and went to the ground in the bolster.

Finally, if you are sufficiently mean and unsportsmanlike to try deliberately to *make* money by Punting on the Horse, don't imagine that you can do it by 'studying form' or any nonsense of that sort – much less by studying the Noble Animal, which has *nothing to do with betting at all*. What you want is a 'system'.

And the truth is that there is only one 'system' which *works invariably*: it is world-wide, and globe-ridden, and is recommended by all the most reliable swindlers, thimble-riggers and pecksniffs: and it works like this:

Suppose the race in question is at 2.30, say at Doncaster; the Swindler, say at Birmingham, rings up a bookie at Doncaster, say at 2.35, and asks him which horse has won the 2.30. And the bookie says 'Bellerophon', or something like that. Then the Trickster says, keeping quite calm, 'O, thanks – well, I'll lay a cool thou' on Bellerophon for the 2.30', and the bookie says 'Bellerophon!' (or something like that) 'It's too late: your bet doesn't count.' Then the Cheatster, who *always keeps his watch six minutes slow*, says 'On the contrary, my good bookie: it's only 2.29 at Birmingham, so it's OK.' And so it counts, and the Backster makes a lot of money, say about 33 cool thous, and he can't be found out because he gets *lots of witnesses* (who are all picaroons and artful dodgers like himself) to look at his watch while he is telephoning, Bellerophoning, etc., and this establishes an *alibi* (American: *attaboy*; Yiddish: *ichabod*) and the Law can't make head or tail of it and he gets away with it and does it again and again and again, and if you ask him about it he just says 'Well, that's my system, and I stick to it'.

And so now you know.

W. C. SELLAR and R. J. YEATMAN, from *Horse Nonsense* (1933)

That the Turf does not figure as prominently as golf in the work of P. G. Wodehouse is racing's as well as literature's loss. But the sport is often featured in Wodehouse's novels, as well as providing the model for non-racing episodes, most famously The Great Sermon Handicap *in* The Inimitable Jeeves, *with its moral so applicable to betting on racehorses:*

What I have always said, and what I always shall say is, that this ante-post betting is a mistake, an error, and a mug's game. You never can tell what's going to happen. If fellows would only stick to the good old SP, there would be fewer young men go wrong.

A few more choice pieces of Wodehouse wisdom on racing:

'If you were a married man, Bertie, you would be aware that the best of wives is apt to cut up rough if she finds that her husband has dropped six weeks' housekeeping money on a single race. Isn't that so, Jeeves?'

'Yes, sir. Women are odd in that respect.'

from *Very Good, Jeeves*

'Would you mind very much missing the last race, Mr Wooster?' she asked.

'I am all for it', I replied cordially. 'The last race means little or nothing in my life. Besides, I am a shilling and sixpence ahead of the game, and the time to leave off is when you're winning.'

from *Very Good, Jeeves*

Bingo Little stakes a tenner on Spotted Dog:

The Prix Honoré Sauvan was the three o'clock. A horse called

Lilium won it. Kerry second, Maubourget third, Ironside fourth, Irresistible fifth, Sweet and Lovely sixth, Spotted Dog seventh. Seven ran. So there was Bingo owing ten quid to this bookie and not a chance of a happy ending unless the fellow would consent to let the settlement stand over for a bit.

So he buttonholed the bookie and suggested this, and the bookie said 'Certainly.'

'Certainly,' said the bookie. He put his hand on Bingo's shoulder and patted it. 'I like you, Mr Little,' he said.

'Do you?' said Bingo, putting his hand on the bookie's and patting that. 'Do you, old pal?'

'I do indeed,' said the bookie. 'You remind me of my little boy Percy, who took the knock the year Worcester Sauce won the Jubilee Handicap. Bronchial trouble. So when you ask me to wait for my money, I say of course I'll wait for my money. Suppose we say till next Friday?'

Bingo blenched a bit. The period he had had in mind had been something more along the lines of a year or eighteen months.

'Well,' he said. 'I'll try to brass up then . . . but you know how it is . . . you mustn't be disappointed if . . . this world-wide money shortage . . . circumstances over which I have no control . . .'

'You think you may not be able to settle?'

'I'm a bit doubtful.'

The bookie pursed his lips.

'I do hope you will,' he said, 'and I'll tell you why. It's silly to be superstitious, I know, but I can't help remembering that every single bloke that's ever done me down for money has had a nasty accident occur to him. Time after time, I've seen it happen.'

'Have you?' said Bingo, beginning to exhibit symptoms of bronchial trouble, like the late Percy.

'I have, indeed,' said the bookie. 'Time after time after time. It almost seems like some kind of fate. Only the other day there was a fellow with a ginger moustache named Watherspoon. Owed me fifty for Plumpton and pleaded the Gaming Act. And would you believe it, less than a week later he was found unconscious in the street – must have got into some unpleasantness of some kind – and had to have six stitches.'

'Six!'

'Seven. I was forgetting the one over his left eye. Makes you think, that sort of thing does. Hoy, Erbut,' he called.

A frightful plugugly appeared from nowhere, as if he had been a Djinn and the bookie had rubbed a lamp.

'Erbut,' said the bookie, 'I want you to meet Mr Little, Erbut. Take a good look at him. You'll remember him again?'

Herbert drank Bingo in. His eye was cold and grey, like a parrot's.

'Yus,' he said, 'Yus, I won't forget him.'

'Good,' said the bookie. 'That will be all, Erbut. Then about that money, Mr Little, we'll say Friday without fail, shall we?'

from 'All's Well with Bingo', in *Eggs, Beans and Crumpets*

'How's the weather, Jeeves?'

'Exceptionally clement, sir.'

'Anything in the papers?'

'Some slight friction threatening in the Balkans, sir. Otherwise, nothing.'

'I say, Jeeves, a man I met at the club last night told me to put my shirt on Privateer for the two o'clock race this afternoon. How about it?'

'I should not advocate it, sir. The stable is not sanguine.'

That was enough for me. Jeeves knows. How, I couldn't say, but he knows. There was a time when I would laugh lightly, and go ahead, and lose my little all against his advice, but not now.

from *The Inimitable Jeeves*

The waiter, who had slipped out to make a quick telephone call, came back into the coffee room of the Goose and Gherkin wearing the starry-eyed look of a man who has just learned that he has backed a long-priced winner. He yearned to share his happiness with someone, and the only possible confidant was the woman at the table near the door, who was having a small gin and tonic and whiling away the time by reading a book of spiritualistic interest. He decided to tell her the good news.

'I don't know if you would care to know, madam,' he said, in a voice that throbbed with emotion, 'but Whistler's Mother won the Oaks.'

The woman looked up, regarding him with large, dark, soulful eyes as if he had been something recently assembled from ectoplasm.

'The what?'

'The Oaks, madam.'

'And what are the Oaks?'

It seemed incredible to the waiter that there should be anyone in England who could ask such a question, but he had already gathered that the lady was an American lady, and American ladies, he knew, are often ignorant of the fundamental facts of life. He had once met one who had wanted to know what a football pool was.

'It's an annual horse race, madam, reserved for fillies. By which I mean that it comes off once a year and the male sex isn't allowed to compete. It's run at Epsom Downs the day before the Derby, of which you have no doubt heard.'

'Yes, I have heard of the Derby. It is your big race over here, is it not?'

'Yes, madam. What is sometimes termed a classic. The Oaks is run the day before it, though in previous years the day after. By which I mean,' said the waiter, hoping he was not being too abstruse, 'it used to be run the day following the Derby, but now they've changed it.'

'And Whistler's Mother won this race you call the Oaks?'

'Yes, madam. By a couple of lengths. I was on five bob.'

'I see. Well, that's fine, isn't it? Will you bring me another gin and tonic?'

'Certainly, madam. Whistler's Mother!' said the waiter, in a sort of ecstasy. 'What a beauty!'

He went out. The woman resumed her reading. Quiet descended on the coffee room. . . .

The waiter returned with the elixir, and went on where he had left off.

'Thirty-three to one the price was, madam.'

Mrs Spottsworth raised her lustrous eyes.

'I beg your pardon?'

'That's what she started at.'

'To whom do you refer?'

288

'This filly I was speaking of that's won the Oaks.'

'Back to her, are we?' said Mrs Spottsworth with a sigh. She had been reading about some interesting manifestations from the spirit world, and this earthy stuff jarred upon her.

The waiter sensed the lack of enthusiasm. It hurt him a little. On this day of days he would have preferred to have to do only with those in whose veins sporting blood ran.

'You're not fond of racing, madam?'

Mrs Spottsworth considered.

'Not particularly. My first husband used to be crazy about it, but it always seemed to me so unspiritual. All that stuff about booting them home and goats and beetles and fast tracks and mudders and something he referred to as a boat race. Not at all the sort of thing to develop a person's higher self. I'd bet a grand now and then, just for the fun of it, but that's as far as I would go. It never touched the deeps in me.'

'A grand, madam?'

'A thousand dollars.'

'Coo!' said the waiter, awed. 'That's what I'd call putting your shirt on. Though for me it'd be not only my shirt but my stockings and pantie-girdle as well. Lucky for the bookies you weren't at Epsom today, backing Whistler's Mother.'

He moved off, and Mrs Spottsworth resumed her book.

from *Ring for Jeeves*

Betting can be a force for good. George Orwell in The Road to Wigan Pier *called gambling*

the cheapest of all luxuries. Even people on the verge of starvation can buy a few days' hope ('something to live for', as they call it) by having a penny on a sweepstake.

That phrase 'something to live for' echoes George Moore in Esther Waters:

Henceforth something to live for. Each morning bringing news of the horse, and the hours of the afternoon passing pleasantly, full of thoughts of the evening paper and the gossip of the bar. A bet on a race brings hope into lives which otherwise would be hopeless.

The theme was taken up by Lord Wyatt of Weeford, Chairman of the Tote, in a speech in the House of Lords on 11 May 1987.

Statistically, over a year a punter loses on average about 22 per cent of what he stakes. Let us suppose he lays out £15 a week. He may expect to lose only £3.30 a week over a period. He could well have spent that money on demon drink or hiring a salacious video. Instead, he prefers an intellectual entertainment to exercise his mind. He has to work out the form, consider the jockey, the nature of the course and the going, study the habits of owners and of trainers and decide which horses are tuned up to do their best and then make his selection. For millions that is the only satisfying, individual, truly democratic decision they ever make. Otherwise they are in thrall to their superiors at work or to a union official.

When a punter makes a mistake he examines the reasons and he is better armed next time. Sometimes the punter sees that a horse he has followed is likely to start at reasonably good value, at 10–1 or more. He puts on the heroic sum of £3 and pulls off a coup. That makes him very happy, and the glow lasts for weeks. It is almost impossible to be more harmlessly employed than in putting bets on horses. Only a few overdo it, as some overdo drink. It is very rare for anyone to take punting on horses more seriously than as an intellectual, mildly exciting pastime for a very modest cost.

Far from scorning this harmless fun, the Churches should praise it as an extension of liberty of the spirit and individual will.

The moral position of betting is an important theme in Esther Waters. *Esther, whose husband William runs a pub from where he acts as a bookmaker, is uneasy:*

'I've never said nothing about it. I don't believe in a wife interfering with her husband; and business was that bad, and your

'ealth 'asn't been the same since them colds you caught standing
about in them betting rings, so I don't see how you could help it.
But now that business is beginning to come back to us, it might
be as well to give up the betting.'

'It is the betting that brings the business; we shouldn't take five
pounds a week was it not for the betting. What's the difference
between betting on the course and betting in the bar? No-one says
nothing against it on the course; the police is there, and they goes
after the welshers and persecutes them. Then the betting that's
done at Tattersall's and the Albert Club, what is the difference?
The Stock Exchange, too, where thousands and thousands is
betted every day. It is the old story – one law for the rich and
another for the poor. Why shouldn't the poor man 'ave his 'alf-
crown's worth of excitement? The rich man can have his thousand
pounds' worth whenever he pleases. The same with the public-
'ouses – there's a lot of hypocritical folk that is for docking the
poor man of his beer, but there's no one that's for interfering with
them that drink champagne in the clubs. It's all bloody rot, and it
makes me sick when I think of it. Them hypocritical folk. Betting!
Isn't everything betting? How can they put down betting? Hasn't
it been going on since the world began? Rot, says I! They can just
ruin a poor devil like me, and that's about all. We are ruined, and
the rich goes scot-free. Hypocritical, mealy-mouthed lot. "Let's say
our prayers and sand the sugar"; that's about it. I hate them that
is always prating about religion. When I hears too much religion
going about I says now's the time to look into their accounts.'

William leaned out of bed to light his pipe from the candle on
the night-table.

'There's good people in the world, people that never thinks but
of doing good, and do not live for pleasure.'

' "All work and no play makes Jack a dull boy," Esther. Their
only pleasure is a bet. When they've one on they've something to
look forward to; whether they win or lose they 'as their money's
worth. You know what I say is true; you've seen them, how they
look forward to the evening paper to see how the 'oss is going on
in betting. Man can't live without hope. It is their only hope, and
I says no one has a right to take it from them.'

'What about their poor wives? Very little good their betting is
to them. It's all very well to talk like that, William, but you know

that a great deal of mischief comes of betting; you know that once they think of it and nothing else, they neglect their work. Stack 'as lost his place as porter; and there's Journeyman, too, he's out of work.'

'And a good thing for them; they've done a great deal better since they chucked it.'

'For the time, maybe; but who says it will go on? Look at old John; he's going about in rags; and his poor wife, she was in here the other night, a terrible life she's 'ad of it. You says that no 'arm comes of it. What about that boy that was 'ad up the other day, and said that it was all through betting? He began by pawning his father's watch. It was here that he made the first bet. You won't tell me that it is right to bet with bits of boys like that.'

'The horse he backed with me won.'

'So much the worse. The boy'll never do another honest day's work as long as he lives. When they win, they 'as a drink for luck; when they loses, they 'as a drink to cheer them up.'

'I'm afraid, Esther, you ought to have married the other chap. He'd have given you the life that you'd have been happy in. This public-'ouse ain't suited to you.'

When they loses, they 'as a drink to cheer them up. But for some losers a drink is not nearly enough, as the great nineteenth-century Turf writer 'The Druid' – Henry Hall Dixon – knew well.

A suicide in consequence of Ring-losses is seldom heard of now, but the stricken deer generally levants without coming near the rooms, or else arrives with a forehead of brass, receives all he can, 'retires' with his gains without offering to pay, and nods gaily to his creditors when he next meets them. A pan of charcoal or the Serpentine is about the last thing he would dream of; and even Scrope Davis, who cut his throat regularly after every Newmarket Meeting, till the doctors knew exactly when to expect a sewing-up summons, can find no imitators. . . .

As regards the *morale* of the Ring, it must be allowed that speculation is a normal vice in man, and that the world, with its usual unfairness, will persist in frowning on it when it is applied to horses and dogs, and smiles complacently when it views it in connexion with 'bulls' and 'bears.' The very men who gamble without scruple in time bargains and lives, would think their credit as fathers of families compromised if they were known to bet on a horse-race. Still, while we point out this inconsistency, and believe that the turf would sicken and droop without betting, as completely as commerce and business without speculation, we cannot but deeply deplore that men with ample means will not consider such a noble sport quite amusement enough of itself, without the extra stimulant of 'the jingle of the guinea.' We do so more especially, because, as long as those who ought to be con-sidered its leaders will make a business of the odds, instead of occasionally backing their fancy, it is impossible that they can exercise that healthy influence which the turf so much requires to raise its tone, or speak with any real weight in a crisis. Looking at the system of betting generally, not five men in twenty can afford to lose, and certainly not one in twenty can afford to win. This may seem a paradox; but few men, unless they have a very large fortune indeed, can take betting quietly. It can't be done. A young man drawing his first winnings is like a tiger tasting his first blood; he seldom stops again till he is brought to a dead-lock as a defaulter: the finer the fleece, the more the rooks (who began their career as pigeons) come about him; his visits are extended from a few afternoons to weeks after weeks of race-meetings, and the mind becomes untuned for everything else. The Legislature knew this when they stepped in and smashed the deposit system in the list houses. It may be a very Arcadian notion, but still we hold that, to really enjoy sport, a man should never go on to a race-course more than thirteen or fourteen picked afternoons in the course of the year, and never bet a penny.

from 'The Betting Ring', in *The Post and the Paddock* (1856)

LORD HIPPO

Lord Hippo suffered fearful loss
By putting money on a horse
Which he believed, if it were pressed,
Would run far faster than the rest:
For someone who was in the know

Had confidently told him so.
But on the morning of the race
It only took the *seventh* place!

Picture the Viscount's great surprise!
He scarcely could believe his eyes!
He sought the Individual who
Had laid him odds at 9 to 2,
Suggesting as a useful tip
That they should enter Partnership
And put to joint account the debt
Arising from his foolish bet.

But when the Bookie – oh! my word,
I only wish you could have heard
The way he roared he did not think,
And hope that they might strike him pink!
Lord Hippo simply turned and ran
From this infuriated man.

Despairing, maddened and distraught,
He utterly collapsed and sought
His sire, the Earl of Potamus,
And brokenly addressed him thus:
'Dread Sire – today – at Ascot – I . . .'
His genial parent made reply:
'Come! Come! Come! Come! Don't look so glum!
Trust your Papa and name the sum. . . .
WHAT? . . . *Fifteen hundred thousand?* . . . Hum!
However . . . stiffen up, you wreck;
Boys will be boys – so here's the cheque!'

Lord Hippo, feeling deeply – well,
More grateful than he cared to tell –
Punted the lot on Little Nell: –
And got a telegram at dinner
To say that he had backed the Winner!

HILAIRE BELLOC

'Good afternoon, ladies and gentlemen, and welcome to Redcar,' declared a public-address announcement continuing the same consumer-friendly approach. 'I'd particularly like to welcome Mr Mal Bridges, commercial director of Gosforth Engineering who are sponsoring our principal race here today.' The principal race. Which was also our race. The 3.45. Fourth on the card. The six-furlong handicap. The coup. The gamble.

For once none of us felt really able to concentrate on the first few events and we mainly watched them out of the window of the bar while keeping an eye on the first two at Ascot on satellite TV. Just before half past three, Kincaid, Moynahan and myself each went into a separate cubicle in the men's room to count out our betting money for the umpteenth time and to check once again which pitches we were supposed to stake it with.

When we walked outside into the ring a ray of sunshine lit up the racecourse for the first time all afternoon. This, surely, was to be our day. The Tattersalls' crowd must have amounted to barely half the number of punters that had been down at Brighton on Monday but it is only a small ring at Redcar and with no more than eighteen or twenty boards bookies present and all the action compressed into a space about thirty feet by twenty-five the atmosphere seemed pressurised enough.

We saw Major Tom in his distinctive cream felt fedora with the brown hatband. He was standing over by the rails, conferring with Ladbrokes' northern representative, Tom Munt. We later discovered that the Major placed two credit wagers on the Malton 'good thing' – one of five thousand to two with rails layer Francis Habbershawe and another of two and a half thousand to one with Ladbrokes themselves. The 'good thing' – all the real names must be secret so let's just call him Shack – opened up at 9–4 first show on the boards and just after 3.35 p.m. we saw the Major going down the front line to back him again with cash. Moynahan and myself had each been allotted six pitches in two different rows and at 3.37 p.m. after a final, quick, nervous look at one another we moved in. It takes little more than a minute to rid yourself of a wallet full of money at a racetrack and by 3.38 p.m. and thirty seconds the business was done. Our target had been the Lancastrian sprinter, let's call him Glenside Delaware, who had opened up at 7–2 and 4–1 in places first show. Our bets of £50, £100 and in one case £200 a time appeared to strike no fear in the hearts and faces of Ralph Harris, Tom Webster, Morry Peter, Cyril Lynch and others but by 3.41 p.m. they had trimmed Glenside to 5–2 while Shack had dropped to 2–1 and 11–8 in places.

During these two or three minutes of earnest trading we had lost sight of A. J. Kincaid. I was certain that the Major was right and that Kincaid would have been briefed to back the intended winner and not the decoys. Standing at the back of the crowd on the bottom tier of the terracing I suddenly picked out his crumpled suit, his glasses and his distinctive heavyweight's frame turning away from the Ladbrokes pitch and heading down the rails to Francis Habbershawe. It was 3.42 p.m. I saw him talking to Habbershawe and presumably striking a bet but it was impossible to know who the bet was for. Then I saw him move across to the boards to the pitch of 'Captain George' of Harrogate. The Captain leaned forward to accept his commission. Fortunately the punter next to me had a pair of bins around his neck which he wasn't using. Hastily training them on the Captain's board I was in time to see him point enquiringly at one of the horse's names. I saw Kincaid nodding. I saw the Captain taking a handful of cash and returning a ticket. He made no effort to reduce the odds. I looked down at my racecard. The horse, naturally, was a four-year-old sprint-bred filly – let's call her Hyacinth Lady – twice a Redcar course and distance winner who had finished down the field on her previous two runs. She was to be ridden by a Newmarket-based jockey, a second string to a leading yard. And her current price? 7–1. It was 3.43. p.m.

I charged frantically out of the ring through the underpass and around to the on-course cash betting shop at the back of Tatts. This bleak and airless little office was packed with smoking, sweat-shirted punters. Until that point I had never really believed that the coup would come off. I had heard and seen it all too many times before. It seemed plain daft to take any of it seriously. And yet, now that we were actually here with the crucial action only minutes away, it would have been equally foolish not to try to get the maximum excitement out of it all. So why not double up the filly with another horse in another race?

The 3.45 at Ascot was about to start. It, too, was a six-furlong handicap, the £35,000 Wokingham Stakes for three-year-olds and up. There were twenty-eight runners and a plethora of tempting big-priced bets. But never mind the horses for once. Which jockey would you back if your life depended on it? If you had to choose one rider above all others, one jockey with the skill, the strength, the determination and the sheer ruthless will to win? No, you wouldn't pick Willie Carson. He's got the strength but he rides into too many holes. You wouldn't pick Steve Cauthen either. He's an artist not a street fighter. You'd pick Pat Eddery. One hundred per cent dead behind the eyes but the consummate driven professional. He's almost as lost off a racehorse as Lester Piggott.

Eddery's mount in the Wokingham was a former Ascot course-winner, a southern sprinting specialist from a well-known gambling yard. And yet his price was an unbelievable 14–1. With the betting-shop clock showing less that a minute before 3.45 p.m. I scribbled down the names of Pat's horse and the filly in a double, nominating almost the last pound I had in my possession, fought my way up to the windows, pushed the money and the betting slip into the hands of the cashier, received my counterfoil and then pushed and elbowed my way back out of the shop, ran back through the underpass, across the ring, back into Members' and then stumbled half-way up the terracing to join Moynahan and A. J. Kincaid.

'They're under starters' orders. And they're off,' declared the Redcar course commentator.

'It's Hyacinth Lady,' whispered Moynahan, enigmatically.

'I know,' I said.

'How did you know?' asked Kincaid.

'I guessed,' I replied.

A few feet above me and fractionally to my left I could see the Wokingham Stakes on the television set in the bar. Directly ahead of me the runners in the six-furlong Redcar handicap were coming up the straight. This was racing and gambling with both barrels. Left and right. In stereophonic sound and Panavision. And yet there is something about a race in which you, personally, have everything to lose that is the very opposite of a whip-cracking, heroically struggling, death-or-glory Dick Francis finale. When the money is really down, the horses seem to move as if in slow motion. They seem cut off and cocooned from the world as if the whole thing were happening in a dream with the sound turned down – until that sudden awful or jubilant moment when the volume is turned back up again and you hear either the crash of the trapdoor opening or you see the horse, your horse, coming out of the pack on its own.

The Redcar result was decided within the first half furlong. Shack broke slowly and seemed to be hampered just after the start. The incident cost him valuable lengths and although he started to make the ground up rapidly once he was switched to the outside, he always had too much to do. You had to admire the skill and aplomb with which his jockey had managed to lose the race on purpose. Pat Eddery had other ideas. The Ascot handicap was run at a blinding pace and they had scarcely gone three furlongs at Redcar before I picked up out of the corner of my left eye the sight of Eddery bursting free of a wall of horses inside the final furlong. And going clear. Pat the Knife in full flow. In yellow silks on a chestnut gelding. The power and the glory. At Ascot on a midsummer afternoon. And as Eddery left the winning post behind him I swung back round again live, on-course, to the joyous, unbelievable and never-expected sight of Hyacinth Lady and the Newmarket second string taking it up from Glenside Delaware at the distance. And coming up the standside rail on their own. All the way to the wire. To the line. A big winner at Redcar. In the watery sunshine after the rain. 'Go on, you Hyacinth. Go on, you lady. Go on, you beautiful girl.'

So what does it feel like? Winning? Well, it's the moment of fission. The moment when something just explodes in your head and in front of your eyes. When the third bomb of the final plane bounces and bounces and bounces again and then lifts up majestically out of the water and scores a direct hit on the Mohne Dam, scattering the pieces up high into the air and spreading with it a warm and sensual glow from the tip of your toes to your scalp.

We didn't go down to the unsaddling enclosure. We hung on nervously by the line waiting for the official SP to come through. Would Ladbrokes have fallen for all the decoy wagers or would they have backed the filly at the last minute and depressed the odds? After a pale and deathly two or three minutes our fears were allayed. Hyacinth Lady was officially returned at 7–1, the same price at which Captain George had unconcernedly laid her to A. J. Kincaid.

The relief was overwhelming. We all felt suddenly and totally exhausted. The terracing had virtually emptied now but there, standing just in front of us on his own, was the still debonnair figure of the Major. He doffed his hat and smiled.

JAMIE REID, from *A Licence to Print Money*

Peter O'Sullevan's Calling the Horses *is the finest racing autobiography of recent years. In 1941 the author, during his time with the Chelsea Civil Defence Rescue Service, learns from jockey 'Nobby' Sawers that his ride in a seller at Ludlow is expected to win. O'Sullevan decides to go to the Shropshire course to back the horse.*

I'd had a little 'touch' about two months earlier and, tipped off by a fellow worker in the Rescue Service that a friend wanted to sell a 15 hp Flying Standard saloon in immaculate condition for £50, I bought it and leased it to the Council for £2 a week on the basis of withdrawal at twenty-four hours' notice on either side. On the way back to London from Cheltenham on 20 March I stopped at the garage at Barrington (next to the Inn for all Seasons) which had become a regular staging post and asked the patron what he'd give me for a 1937 Standard. He reckoned that, provided it fulfilled all the usual credentials of a second-hand car – show-room condition, low mileage, original tyres, chauffeur-driven for an elderly person who hardly ever went out, etc. – it could be up to £60. I said I would deliver it the day after tomorrow.

I collected the car on the evening of the 21st. It wasn't taxed because the Council ran it on an official permit, so I wrote 'licence applied for' on a circular cut-out the size of a Road Fund disc and stuck it on the windscreen. If I was going to be at Barrington, twenty miles the London side of Cheltenham, sell the car and reach Ludlow by 2 p.m., I'd have to leave Chelsea before my duty ended at nine o'clock.

There was a very nice elderly Scot, a chauffeur in peacetime, who worked on the opposite shift. Would there ever (I was inclined to lapse into stage Irish in times of stress), would there ever be a chance of him covering for me from 6 a.m. the next day? He'd bandaged a nasty cut for me once after I'd been blown off my bike by bomb blast in Belgrave Square. I'd been cycling back to the depot one night after visiting a girlfriend.

'I suppose,' he reacted drily, 'you'll be wanting to make sure no bombs have fallen in Pembroke Close.'

I explained the different nature of this situation.

He would not only be pleased to co-operate, but he produced a 10s note for investment on the 'good thing', who was trained in Shropshire in the small yard of his owner, Percy Arm, an enthusiast who combined skilful preparation of a few generally modest horses with running a garage business.

My 'relief' was right on time the next morning. He helped push the car out of the depot yard so that no one was alerted by the engine, then assisted for a fraught half-hour in overcoming its reluctance to start.

Detours for craters and unexploded bombs slowed my exit from London. A blasted shop front in Shepherd's Bush bore a placard 'NO BUSINESS AS USUAL'. I drove slowly to conserve petrol, anxious that there might not be enough in the tank to complete the necessary eighty miles.

Shortly before Northolt Aerodrome I was thumbed for a lift by an airman. He'd heard that the Cheltenham road was impassable at High Wycombe. There was no shortage of rumour. Three miles after setting him down, a motorcycle police cop waved me into the side. Bored by the pace, or lack of it, I had been giving a little attention to the *Racing Calendar* which was draped across my knees and, after parking his machine very deliberately, he asked whether I always read a paper while driving.

I thought of replying, 'Only the *Racing Calendar*', but it occurred to me that flippancy might be inappropriate to present circumstances.

He didn't look as if he indulged in anything so trivial as playing the horses, but you never know. Mutual interest in the vagaries of the racing horse had been known, like wine, to undermine disharmony in human relations. I said I had been verifying the name of a horse which was expected to win that afternoon.

He noted that the tax disc on the car was home-made, and asked to see my identity card and driving licence. These, at least, were in order.

'I suggest, sir,' he commented, 'that in future you confine study of the horses to such times as you are stationary.'

I assured him of my compliance. He took a couple of paces towards his bike, then turned and inquired. 'Did you mention the name of that horse?'

'Niersteiner,' I told him.

'Good luck,' he said, and was gone.

By the time I reached Barrington the needle on the petrol gauge had long ceased flickering. There wasn't enough left to fill my cigarette lighter. With a pocketful of readies and around ninety miles cross-country travel ahead, I set off towards Northleach. All the indications were that Niersteiner would be a very fair price – especially in view of his rider's relative obscurity. I would probably have £25 on the boards and £20 at Tote odds – keeping £15 in case of the unthinkable.

I hadn't been walking for more than ten minutes when a car responded to my wave. As every motorist knows, up to 80 per cent of hitch-hikers are 'on the tap'. The driver leaned across his lady passenger and said, 'If you just want a lift, get in. If you want to borrow money, don't.'

I leaped in, assuring my benefactor, idiotically, that I'd just sold my car and had plenty of money.

A sales rep and his girlfriend, their destination was Cheltenham where I bought them a drink and, on the advice of the landlord, caught a bus to Gloucester. It was no use trying to get a lift in a town unless you were in forces uniform (half price at race meetings), so I walked for an hour out of Gloucester before getting a short ride with a farmer and six pigs. I was drifting right off any semblance of a main thoroughfare and time was running out. Chances of making Ludlow for the two o'clock were now all of 50/1 and the odds a place. It became a matter of getting to a telephone and ringing William Hill, with whom I'd opened an account on 3 July 1939, and whose terms included an additional 10 per cent on all Tote commissions.

A tractor-borne farmer reckoned that my best bet was to make for the village of Bredwardine, but if I'd like to come with him, he was going back to the farm about two miles away and I could use his phone. I'd brought several packets of cigarettes for acknowledging assistance and he was delighted with one of them.

Unfortunately his phone was out of order and his wife was out with the car. Fortified by a pint of home-made cider with the near-potency of Calvados, I ran a good three miles before finding a cottage which announced: 'Cream teas with strawberry jam 2s 6d'. It was just about post time. The charming lady who answered my knock would be delighted to serve me, but she regretted she was not on the phone. What the hell! Cream was unheard of in London, and jam was severely rationed – so was tea, come to that.

After lovely hot scones I picked up a lift in a lorry just outside Hereford. He was going to a transport café west of Witney where I might well find a truck bound for London. He was right. Further, for the £3 proffered, the driver of a massive Leyland would also buy me the best breakfast to be had in Hammersmith. We steamed into the Broadway at 6 a.m. and while my friend ordered tea, toast and dripping, fried spam and egg (powder), I walked to the Underground to buy a paper. Under the Ludlow results, I read:

2.0 NIERSTEINER (N. Sawers) 20/1
   Portpatrick (T. Isaac) 20/1
   Caravan Girl (C. Mitchell) 10/1

Winner trained P. J. Arm.
Tote dividends £4 11s 6d (2s unit) places £1 4s 3d; 14s, 6s 6d.
Distances: 2 Lengths, 3. No bid for winner. 23 ran.

When I paid out the £10 10s due to my Scottish friend Bernie, who had kindly stood in for me at the depot, he said, 'Well done, but what a pity you didn't have it on the Tote!'

Such is the peculiar magic of betting that a few winners could even make the view from Alexandra Park – the less than scenic London racecourse which closed down in 1970 – a glorious vista for the Irish poet Patrick Kavanagh.

I have always had good luck at English tracks because at most of these I would be quite unknown, and I was therefore able to contemplate the race card and the form book in detachment. Deafness is a great asset.

I suppose that Leopardstown is one of the world's finest settings for a race track. Yet, for me, the most memorable glimpse of landscape I know appeared to me one evening at Alexandra Park.

I had backed four winners in a row and was sipping a drink in the bar when someone cried out, 'The Aga Khan again.' I rushed out and saw the grey chimneys of East London in all their enchanting beauty. It was a moment to live in the imagination. But coming away from Leopardstown of a Saturday evening totally broke, saying to myself, why did I come? and what will I use for money tomorrow? that arboreal scene about Foxrock appeared to me as ugly and mean.

My idea of a good day's racing is inclined towards the elegant. Point-to-points are too close to hard work for my fancy. I want to be able to sit down and drink tea or whiskey or both among charming company, beautiful women. Such, too, is my vanity that I believe that the fashion is coming round to my view. Fairyhouse and Punchestown are excellent but you have to have your health and strength. Let me have the Park of a Saturday evening.

Backing horses is a horse of a different colour altogether. The first time I backed a horse in a bookie's office was the year that Nimbus won the Derby. I was putting on five shillings each way on Nimbus when a man in the shop sneered at me and said in that roundabout way so typical of the know-all know-nothing punter: 'Wherever Nimbus finishes such and such a horse will finish in front of him.'

Looking at this fellow in all my innocence then I began to say to myself would I pay any attention to him if he advised on any other subject? So I doubled my stake. It was the costliest win I ever had, for since then I have lost a good deal, including time.

For all that, I believe it is possible to win money by judicious betting, but human nature being what it is we nearly always go wrong. It is remarkable how true to form such a temperamental animal as the thoroughbred runs. It is the public which runs false.

If one could just win a little and not want to win much, going racing is surely one of the most delightful pastimes. And, although I often prefer the Flat, I have got tremendous pleasure out of the jumping game. At Navan track, which is so easy for spectators, or the big jumping meetings at Sandown. The three American tracks I was at, Hialeah Park, Belmont Park and Jamaica (which is outside New York on Long Island) seemed to me to lack personality. The racing is too much a pillar-to-post business; there are no bookies and the crowds are too large. It is too efficient. Among the information given on the boards in electric signs is the kind of shoe the nags are wearing – steel, aluminium or a mixture. As if it mattered to the backer, who can lose his money under all circumstances.

from 'Going Racing', in *Irish Farmers' Journal*, 9 August 1958

HARK! HARK! THE PARI-MUTUELS BARK!

I

Willow waley and woe and sorrow,
The horses are coming to town tomorrow.
Chestnut and bay and black and grey
Sport and cavort and snort and neigh.
The horses, the horses are on the way!
The horses are coming to town tomorrow,
And some must beg and others borrow.
The horses are coming, enter the horses,
Exit the remnant of my resources,
Here goes me, and never a doubt of it,
And the horses don't even get anything out of it.
They don't get money or love or fun,
Why in the world must the horses run?
Or if they must, through a fate unholy,
Why must some of them run so slowly?
Brothers, the country's crying need
Is horses that run at an equal speed
And a stone-dead heat on every track
And every-one getting their money back.
Willow waley and woe and sorrow,

The horses are coming to town tomorrow.
Every horse with a personal grudge
Against this modestly hopeful judge,
Holding its life as cheap as a song
If its death in the stretch should prove me wrong.
Well listen, horses, I know you hate me,
But do not think to intimidate me,
Or drive from the track, by deed or threat,
The man who has never cashed a bet.
One day I shall hold a winning ticket,
And swagger up to the teller's wicket,
And take my money and catch a boat
To the land of the horsemeat table d'hôte.
Oh, I'll sit in Paris till Doomsday breaks
Chewing over my old mistakes.

II

O, racing is a ruinous sport,
The race track is an ill resort,
My waxing poverty I owe to it,
I often wonder why I go to it;
I hate the horses I have bet on,
I hate the horses my heart is set on;
Some are outsiders, some are sure things,
But if mine own, are ever poor things.
I hate the hunches, I hate the dope,
I hate the fear, I hate the hope,
I hate the blinkers, I hate the wrappers,
I hate the trainers and handicappers,
I hate the dust, I hate the mud,
I hate the pulsation of sporting blood,
I hate the jumps, I hate the flat,
And the red-hot tips from the stable cat,
The silly saddles, the foolish stirrups,
And the hang-arounders' cheerful chirrups,

The inhuman machines and human bookies,
And the plungers with faces like man-eating cookies,
The rattle and drum of the pounding hoof,
The triumphant shout that rocks the roof.
I hate my horse to be out in front
Lest he should wilt beneath the brunt;
I hate to see my horse behind,
Lest he be trapped in a pocket blind,
And when my horse is in the centre,
The hooks I hang upon are tenter,
And oh, the microphones that retch
And tell you who's leading in the stretch!
Into your helpless ear they quack
Who's moving up, who's falling back,
Your fingers would find their gullets, if
From tearing up tickets they weren't so stiff.
I mean it when I feelingly state
That racing is my bitterest hate.
But of all emotions within the breast,
Hate is by far the ugli-est.
To ugly hate I will not yield,
But bet five dollars on the field.

OGDEN NASH

If you maintain a love-hate relationship with racing and betting, take heed of Ogden Nash's account of the experience of Mr Judd.

MR JUDD AND HIS SNAIL, A SORRY TALE

or, Never Underestimate the Wisdom of a Sage of the Ages

I offer one small bit of advice that Billy Graham could write a
   whole column on:
Never ignore any bit of advice offered by King Solomon.
I call your attention to the case of Philander Judd.
His veins were distended with optimism and sporting blood.
His interest in racing was enormous,
But he was by nature nonconformous.

He was not one of those who set their horses or greyhounds
   whirling around the track to their heart's content, or à gogo,
He said he knew that something fast could go fast, he was
   interested in how fast could something slow go.
He considered conventional races pallid and stale,
So his entire stable consisted of one thoroughbred gastropod, or
   snail.
The snail, of course, is a mollusk akin to the whelk and the slug,
   and, as is known to every gastropodist,
It moves complacently on one ventral muscular foot, to the
   bewilderment of every biped chiropodist.
Mr Judd entered his snail in every kind of race but one, for
   which he refused to name it,
And that one was a claiming race, because he was afraid that
   somebody, perhaps a Gallic gourmet, might claim it.
His snail was beaten in December by a tortoise, so he dropped
   it down a couple of classes,
And in January it lost by eight lengths to a jug of molasses.
By now Mr Judd was deeply indebted to his bookie,
But being an honorable man, he couldn't get out of town or
   stoop to any other form of welsher's hookey.
At last he thought he saw a way to settle with his creditors;
He found the perfect spot for his snail, a race in which an amoeba
   and a glacier were the other two competitors.
The amoeba posed a real threat, but from the glacier he did not
   flinch;
He had clocked it for a full month, during which it had moved
   only three-quarters of an inch.
Therefore, although he could not be certain to win the race,
He knew he had a sure thing to place.
Yes, that was what he happily reckoned,
And he bet his remaining roll on the snail for second.
Well, the amoeba outdistanced the snail and the snail
   outdistanced the glacier, and then just at the finish line
   something out of the ordinary occurred;
The amoeba split apart and finished one two, and the snail ran
   third.

Mr Judd had forgotten what Solomon once told the Queen of
   Sheba:
Never trust an Egyptian or an amoeba.

OGDEN NASH

---

*It seems appropriate to end this book with a piece which opens with
matters of betting but expands from there to an eloquent expression of
what makes horse racing such a captivating activity – 'the lure of the
Turf' with which we began. Les Carlyon is probably the finest racing
writer in Australia, and although some of his local references may escape
readers in the Northern Hemisphere, the love of the Turf which he
describes is universal.*

The turf is a passion. The lore of the turf is a delight. Take Whistling
Bob Smith, the famous American trainer. He won a Kentucky
Derby, and each week churned out winners like Tommy Smith.
Yet he was mostly close to broke – because he backed every single
horse he saddled up. 'I just can't let them run naked,' he once
ventured in one of the turf's more memorable explanations.

   Late in life a heart seizure dropped him at a New York track.
Friends panicked over him. Whistling Bob calmly instructed them
to take three twenties from his right pocket. 'Bet them across the
board for me on Max Hirsch's horse if he likes him. He's a price!'

   A year later, in 1942, an ambulance took him to hospital with
a worse seizure. A friend asked the doctor about Whistling Bob's
chances. 'Only one chance in 10,' said the doctor. The old trainer,
thought to be unconscious, opened his eyes and took 100 to 10.
Moments later he died. But what a death for a punter: he died
'set', akin to absolution. The story, incidentally, is not apocryphal.

   Another American trainer of the same era was unbendingly
rigid in his training regime. The horse worked fast one day, walked
the next, galloped the next two. There could be no deviation; the
trainer even wrote up his work book a month in advance.

   One dawn he was studying the book on his way into the stables
when the foreman rushed up and blurted that the grey colt had
just pulled back on his tie chain and broken his neck. The trainer
never raised his eyes from the tyrannical scrawl. Then he
exploded: 'But, Jeez, this was his fast morning!'

308

Banjo Paterson tells of training two horses for a bush meeting. Some days they didn't have time to work the horses. So next day they worked them twice as far. At these meetings, Paterson explains, the betting was 'double-event'. First you had to win the money; then you had to fight the man for it afterwards.

Damon Runyon, who made slang an art form, tells of the punter who, skint midway through the Saratoga meeting, decides to kill himself. He goes to another punter known to have a gun. The trouble is there is only one shell for the aforementioned shooter and the personality who owns it also does badly at the ponies and wishes badly to kill himself. Then comes the solution. Both citizens hock the shooter, and with the proceeds go back to the punt.

Not only does racing produce its characters, but gentlemen too. Take George Alexander Baird, the celebrated amateur rider of Victorian England, a roistering ratbag, dead from boozing and whoring at 31. He regularly bashed his mistress, Lillie Langtry, but unfailingly gave her £5,000 afterwards. Once he put her in hospital for two weeks: in addition to the usual left-right combinations to the head he did some Frankenstein-like biting as well. A true gentleman, he gave her £50,000 and a yacht.

Why does the turf have so much lore, such a depth of high quality literature going back centuries? I guess because racing ultimately revolves around two eminently fallible creatures. Man with all his vanity, his commonplace greed and occasional nobility. And an animal who can be exquisitely beautiful – but who is born with a congenital tendency to self-destruct.

If you insist two and two must always be four, if you think what should be will be, if you cannot dream a little, forget about the turf. Put on a white coat with a beeper in the pocket and find a laboratory somewhere. To enjoy the turf, you have to accept that two and two is often five, or nine – or, more commonly, nought.

Just as flawed people are often more interesting than saints, so that the saturnine and outrageous Randolph Churchill seems a richer character than his canonised father, so the turf fascinates because it is quirky and fickle, high-brow and low brow, because it combines the romantic and the tawdry, the glory of Kingston Town winning his third Cox Plate, the sadness of a jumps jockey with legs so smashed he makes the effort to walk normally only when he knows you are watching.

It is about dreams rather than probabilities. It involves risks: physical, financial and moral. And here we have perhaps touched on part of its greatness, one of the reasons for all the lore and literature. All great sport involves putting something on the line. All great sport involves some pain, the element of mortal chance, ritualised codes of conduct. That is why racing, boxing and cricket have spawned such great writing. That is why jogging has not, and remains forever a middle-class fad.

The turf is an ongoing pageant of people, and the outrageous fortunes which attend them. The straight and the shifty. Horsemen with artistry in their hands – and camel drivers. Sensational bores who regale you with how they nearly got the quinella, the in-house cavalcade of toffs and nobs and germs and fleas. Jockeys with those lived-in, used-up faces somehow transplanted on young bodies.

Intensely practical men like Phar Lap's owner David J. Davis who, on being told of the great horse's death, said: 'Whatever will Telford [the trainer and racing partner] say when he hears I haven't insured the horse!' Kindly men like Tommy Woodcock, Phar Lap's strapper, giving kids rides on Reckless. Sour men who walk into an early morning stable and begin a litany which goes: 'Get over you mongrel. *Get over you bloody mongrel*! Stupid bloody horse, *J-E-E-Z*!'

Who was the American who said that if a man hung around race stables long enough, cadging off everyone, eventually held in contempt by everyone, he inevitably acquired the kindly nickname 'Doc'?

The turf is timeless rituals. The trainer squatting in straw to sew on the raceday bandages surrounded by towels and brushes. The mounting yard foursome: the trainer, owners and jockey of a well-beaten horse, and the jockey making elaborate shapes with his hands, so that from the grandstand you can read the story of how I got blocked on the rails, and then I've gone to the outside, and this thing's rolled in on me and I've copped a beauty – did you see his head go up? – and I had to stop riding him, and . . .

The yearling sales twosome: the trainer hurrying on urgently, glancing from scuffed catalogue to box and back again, the would-be owner a few paces behind, and a look on the trainer's face which says: don't stop me when I've got one on the hook.

The turf is about hopes and ego. If these things were not occasionally satisfied – and they are – it would be no more than the sport of kings ... and corporate raiders. A rich man buys Paint the Stars for $825,000 and he fails to win; Kingston Town, on his way to his second million, was offered as a yearling for $10,000. A New Zealand breeder becomes so exasperated with a wind-sucking weanling who scars himself on a fence, he considers doing away with him. As a compromise, he gelds him and sells him privately to Australia for $7,000 ... and as Gurner's Lane that pest of a foal wins both cups this year.

Sometimes the perceptions are better than the reality. A friend won a race at Donald last year and, doing a little arithmetic as the car floated him home, he realised he had paid out nearly as much in slings, gratuities and effervescent note-shoving as he had collected in stakes. It bothered him not at all. He is a racing man. Damn the arithmetic: he had won. A syndicate of 30 recently sent their horse to the bush; it won a $600 race and they immediately spent $700 on framed photographs of the finish.

It is a modern argument that the dedicated battlers will be squeezed out by the Sangsters. It's nonsense. Battlers will always buy horses: not because they can afford them, but because they must have them.

Above all, the turf fascinates because of the cavalcade of horses. There are about 32,000 racing in Australia; no two are the same. It is perhaps the greatest tease, the largest ego trip, a matter of the highest aesthetics, to look at the mounting yard parade and discover the one that's 'right'. If you wander along the fence listening to all the opinions, you will end up backing eight 'certainties'.

The process moves on a dimension in the paddock. We look at month-old foals and proclaim them 'racy', 'correct', 'stretchy', and also 'coarse' and 'wrong-legged' and 'weak' – and, God knows, we are assuming a lot. Certainly we are assuming that things will turn out the way they look – and one of the beguiling things about the turf is that they don't.

To be any good, horses are supposed to be correct in the legs, turned neither in nor out, neither back nor over at the knee, truly balanced, possessed of presence – all sorts of things. The trouble is horses with bad legs, no presence, and all sorts of faults keep winning races. So the exercise may seem wasted – except that you always see something you haven't seen before, and it's irresistible, anyway.

And sometimes you see a horse who moves so well – this year's Derby winner Grosvenor, whether he is walking, trotting or galloping, has a liquid-like quality – that you just look and look and let it settle on your brain.

The turf enthrals because of its special places. For me, the walking ring at Moonee Valley is the most evocative of places. It is shaded by a grandfather of a peppercorn tree and three great elms. Runners are walked here before being led to the mounting yard. You stand there; you hear the distant but urgent taps of a farrier's hammer; and the light through the trees is fractured and filtered, reducing a hot sun to a warm glow. Here is a delicate cameo of racing. It could be anywhere in the civilised world. And if it were not for the plastic bridles and the odd strapper in sneakers, it could be any time in the past 40 years.

Dalgety's old saleyards at Flemington, now gone but once home to the likes of Tulloch and Star Kingdom, were something too. There was a huge rotunda, boxes with great hinges which looked as though they had been made by a blacksmith rather than a machine, a sand ring so decrepit it threatened to collapse with the soft groan of an old man.

But the place had mood. After a yearling sale, when the roar of the bar and the chant of the auctioneer had gone, the cats came out. They stretched languorously, changed their positions only to follow the last of the sun. You heard the rustle of straw, the sighs of a yearling lying down, a whinny from one who had seen his paddock mate of the spring sold and taken away. Again, a sense of peace and timelessness, a foil to the bustle and bluster, the frantic one-upmanship, of a sale.

Once, in this tender and cat-ridden atmosphere, a breeder explained to me, in original and slanderous terms, why another doctor had just bought one of his horses.

'There'll be some doctor joker sittin' in the front with the catalogue on his lap and peerin' at the horses through these horn-rimmed glasses and wearin' a dark suit. And there'll be some old boiler of a wife next to him. Doctors' wives are even queerer than doctors. Real types, they are. An' she'll say: "O-o-o-h I L-O-V-E that one". That's 'cos it's all shiny, you see. And it can be as bad-legged as hell, but the old bugger'll buy it. Then they come back here to the box. They won't go in. They might open the top and sort of poke at the horse.'

Flemington is a wondrous place – for its sheer spaciousness alone. When the field comes to the turn, one sees this small group of horses seemingly lost in acres of green. Flemington will never have a rival: no 'modern' course could be built with such disregard for inner suburban property values. Flemington is beautiful, too, on a winter dawn, horses blowing misty balloons into the cold air, fast workers belting along, slow workers snorting at the restraint, necks arched, heads nearly vertical.

There are so many evocative places: Lou Robertson's old stables at Epsom, from a distance looking like a small church; the stone buildings behind the Flemington hill; steeplechasers streaming down the hill at Warrnambool in the weak May sun – a sight some strange people, who will never be poets, want banned.

Talking about poets, the most interesting piece I've read about Adam Lindsay Gordon, who rode down that hill, was written by the delightful columnist Max Harris. Gordon, he said, was 'locked in to the moronism of the horse racing world'. He shot himself in the scrub behind Brighton beach 'because of the dreariness and vacuity of this tedious sporting culture'. And elsewhere: 'It was not an intelligent or socially enriching sporting culture.'

Oh dear! But surely, Max, you'd have to admit to just a touch of 'intelligent culture'. Xenophon, the historian, essayist and disciple of Socrates, was writing about stable management ('Washing down the legs is a thing I absolutely forbid') in 360 BC. Shakespeare knocked out a piece on conformation amid *Venus and Adonis*. Tolstoy wrote a long but pedestrian tract about steeplechasing in *Anna Karenina*, and Hemingway wrote more stylishly about the same subject in 'My Old Man'.

Melbourne indeed has a large bookshop which does a heady trade in nothing but horse books. Dr Aylett, the Victorian Football League president, is so jealous he's thinking of opening a shop selling all the books ever written about footy, but the rental of the telephone booth is still to be arranged.

Lacking culture? The newspaper proprietors Frank Packer and Ezra Norton picked the members' enclosure at Randwick for their celebrated punch-up. It's really hard to think of two more cultured figures. And only in Australia, on one night of the year, does a midnight TV commentator gravely say: 'And on the Victorian TAB, the Epsom Derby winner will pay $16.50 when coupled with No. 6, Plodding Paul, in the last trot at Warragul.'

But who cares? Who cares whether racing is seen to be 'socially desirable' or 'cultured'? It's also supposed to be an industry, and it is – a big one, too.

But ultimately it's an affair of the heart: living on hope, lovely irrepressible hope, open to rich and not-so-rich, for the former are often hours away from disaster and the latter are sure their next $1,000 horse will be Kingston Town.

If there's a sense to the turf, it's more than economic sense.

But, really, it's a passion. And I simply remind you that there are all these beasts in at Flemington on Saturday . . . and that no one with the slightest pretensions to the Higher Things could allow them to run around naked.

Index of Authors